Population Change in the United States

Steve H. Murdock • Michael E. Cline
Mary Zey • Deborah Perez • P. Wilner Jeanty

Population Change in the United States

Socioeconomic Challenges and Opportunities in the Twenty-First Century

Springer

Steve H. Murdock
Hobby Center & Department of Sociology
Rice University
Houston, Texas, USA

Michael E. Cline
Hobby Ctr. for the Study of Texas
Rice University
Houston, Texas, USA

Mary Zey
University of Texas at San Antonio
San Antonio, Texas, USA

Deborah Perez
Alexandria, Virginia, USA

P. Wilner Jeanty
Verizon Wireless
Hilliard, Ohio, USA

ISBN 978-94-017-7287-7 ISBN 978-94-017-7288-4 (eBook)
DOI 10.1007/978-94-017-7288-4

Library of Congress Control Number: 2015944824

Springer Dordrecht Heidelberg New York London

Printed on acid-free paper

Springer Science+Business Media B.V. Dordrecht is part of Springer Science+Business Media (www.springer.com)

We dedicate this book to our children and grandchildren and to the nation that they will inherit.

Acknowledgments

We express our appreciation to the Meadows and Greater Texas Foundations for their support which enabled us to complete the work included in this volume. We also thank William P. Hobby Jr. for his past and continued support of the Hobby Center for the Study of Texas. We express our sincere appreciation to our technical editor, Karen White, for her skillful editing of the volume. We also thank Evelien Bakker and Bernadette Deelen-Mans from Springer for their support, encouragement, and technical guidance during the preparation of this volume.

Contents

List of Figures

List of Tables

Chapter 1
Introduction

1.1 The Rationale for the Work

The current and projected demographic characteristics of a population are often taken for granted by decision makers and members of the public. They are seen as background factors that are important but not necessarily causative. They are viewed as factors with implications that simply exist and either cannot be altered or do not merit concerted actions by decision makers or the public to alter their potential long term effects. In this document we provide a detailed description of the current and projected future size and characteristics of the United States population (as projected by the United States Bureau of the Census 2012a, b). More important we demonstrate how the size and characteristics of the future population of the United States, both now and in the future, may lead to changes in housing, the labor force, the economy, education, health care, transportation, and numerous forms of human services. We use simple rate based techniques to demonstrate how the demographic changes are likely to impact the demand for and characteristics of the future of each of the above noted substantive areas.

From our analysis we conclude that many of the characteristics of our future society and services in the United States may be substantially changed by these demographic and related factors and delineate how they may change the socioeconomic resources of the nation, the characteristics of each of the substantive population-impacted areas noted above and how the projected change could be altered by the creation of socioeconomic closure through increased education and other factors.

The work is largely based on simulations of potential alternative effects of demographic and socioeconomic change on population-related factors to provide an overview of the future characteristics of the United States if the projected population patterns occur and if their relationships to, and their effects on, the major dimen-

S.H. Murdock et al., *Population Change in the United States*,
DOI 10.1007/978-94-017-7288-4_1

sions noted above do not change. We also provide sets of simulations of alternative outcomes based on change in the historical relationships between the subject matter area and population change.

We are aware that, to many scholars, what we have done may seem simplistic. However we believe they will find it useful but we hope that they will also realize that its intended audience includes decision makers and other members of the public who, we believe, must come to understand that they must help to shape the effects that the growth and changing characteristics of their population will have on their society or it may change in ways that increasingly impoverish and eliminate required levels of service for large numbers of their citizens.

1.2 Conceptual Basis for the Work

To some, to suggest even sufficient causality between population structure and change and socioeconomic conditions and economic change to merit a detailed analysis of these interrelationships, such as those presented in this volume, is to promote a false paradigm. Some would declare it an error in scientific logic because how such factors affect populations is also markedly impacted by how individual population members perceive and react and adapt to such factors and how a variety of difficult-to-predict socioeconomic, political, and other factors interact with population dimensions. Although we do not deny the potential value of such insights, we believe that it is important to examine these aggregate organizational interrelationships because many of the demographic dimensions impacting current and future patterns of socioeconomic change are sufficiently well delineated and pervasive as to have substantial implications in the near term and distant future given wide variation in other factors (e.g., general levels of the economy, etc.).

In addition, there is a substantial body of literature suggesting the legitimacy of such levels of analyses. The theoretical basis for the work lies in a body of literature that traces socioeconomic change to demographic compositions and other factors. For example, Wolfgang Lutz (2012), drawing on work and terms used by Ryder (1965), proposed a theory of "demographic metabolism" that postulates "how societies change as a consequence of the changing composition of their members" (2012: 283).

Lutz's perspective is based on four theoretical propositions:

> Proposition 1: People – individual humans – are the primary building blocks of every society and the primary agents in any economy. Hence, they form the basic elements of any theory of social and economic change…
>
> Proposition 2: For any population, members can be sub-divided into disjoint groups (states) according to clearly specified and measurable individual characteristics (in addition to age and sex) for any given point in time…
>
> Proposition 3: At any point in time, members of a sub-population (state) defined by certain characteristics can move to another state (associated with different characteristics) and these individual transitions can be mathematically described by a set of age- and sex-specific transition rates…

> Proposition 4: If any given population consists of sub-groups that are significantly different from each other with respect to relevant characteristics, then a change over time in the relative size of these sub-groups will result in a change in the overall distribution of these characteristics in the population and hence in socioeconomic change (Lutz 2012: 287–288).

This theoretical stance, that demographic structure and population change can change socioeconomic states in a society, is not new but has a long history in subfields of sociology (see Mannheim 1952; Ryder 1965) and areas of theory and analyses employing demographic factors as key determinants of change such as human ecology as delineated by Park (1936), Hawley (1950), Gibbs and Martin (1959), Duncan and Schnore (1959), Duncan (1964), Murdock and Sutton (1974), Murdock and Albrecht (1998), Micklin and Poston (1998), and many others. As in Lutz's delineation the "new" human ecological approach maintains that population (aggregate) level effects are as real as individual effects in changing the conditions in a social unit (e.g., a population) and area [including neighborhoods, places, states, and nations (Berry and Horton 1970)]. What Lutz and these perspectives have in common is that they all assert that change in the characteristics of a population such as its size, age structure, sex ratios, racial/ethnic composition, and other demographic factors can lead to other types of change such as change in the socioeconomic characteristics of a population: that is to population-related socioeconomic change.

Such a perspective is subject to the same criticisms historically leveled against other aggregate, macro-level perspectives. These include criticisms that such perspectives are too inclusive in scope and do not sufficiently specify the mechanisms by which individual and familial socioeconomic decisions are made and thus inappropriately limit the role of the individual in determining his/her socioeconomic conditions (see Murdock and Albrecht 1998 for a discussion addressing these criticisms). Similarly, it is maintained that to the extent that such a perspective depends on patterns of fertility and mortality to partially determine the extent of its impacts it is overly biological in its emphases and fails to properly account for the social role of the individual in society. Human ecologists do not believe that one must focus exclusively on the individual or individual level of explanation but assert the importance of collective properties and processes. Rather, with Hawley (1950), Duncan (1964), Namboodiri (1988), Murdock and Albrecht (1998), and others, we maintain that such aggregate perspectives do recognize the unique creative nature of humans but maintain that to recognize humans as organisms living within a context of environmental, cultural, social, and demographic factors is essential to understanding their behavior and useful to understanding future demographic and socioeconomic events.

Yet another example explicating the reciprocal relationships between demographic and socioeconomic dimensions is evident in the literature denoting the "demographic dividend" for societies' socioeconomic conditions that may arise from specific demographic structures (see Gribble and Bremner 2012). Such examples point to clear linkages between demographic and socioeconomic factors that do not assert complete causality for the demographic but that show strong interrelationships that make understanding demographic change essential to understanding societal (group) level socioeconomic change.

The work contained herein takes the perspective suggested by human ecologists and scholars such as Lutz and Gribble and Bremner in asserting that population change in the United States, in the absence of concerted (and currently unforeseen) policy and other changes, will lead to a nation that, in the coming decades, is not only demographically different but also socioeconomically different, with the socioeconomic differences existing, in part, because its demographic characteristics will be different.

1.3 The State of Knowledge: Population, Education and Socioeconomic Change

As noted above the assertions about the interrelationships of demographic and socioeconomic factors are more than simply our assertions but are supported by a wide body of work in the demographic, economic, and sociological literature.[1] In particular, the role of education in bridging the gaps between demographic and socioeconomic change is widely documented. In this section we provide a brief summary of some of this work while acknowledging that the breadth and depth of such work cannot be adequately addressed given our space limitations. Nevertheless, we believe the review below clearly substantiates the existence and importance of such relationships.

The important interrelationships among demographic, education, and socioeconomic dimensions are well established. For example, a November 2005 "Policy Alert" published by the National Center for Public Policy and Higher Education and drawing upon a report by Kelly (2005a: 1) warned that "if current population trends continue and states do not improve the education of all racial/ethnic groups, the skills of the workforce and the incomes of U.S. residents are projected to decline." This warning (also see Kelly 2005b) is based on several demographic and socioeconomic trends and interrelationships that have established the following:

1. The U.S. workforce is becoming more racially and ethnically diverse;
2. The racial and ethnic groups that are less well educated (e.g., Hispanics) are the fastest growing due to higher rates of natural increase and immigration;
3. The increasing rate of retirement of "baby boomers"—the most highly educated generation in United States history—is expected to lead to a drop in the average level of education of the U.S. workforce now and for several decades;
4. If these current population trends continue and states do not improve the education levels and graduation rates from high school and college for all racial and ethnic groups, the knowledge and skill levels of the U.S. workforce will decline;

[1] This section of this chapter was largely derived from our earlier work, see Murdock et al. (2014).

5. If the knowledge and skill levels of the workforce decline, occupational achievement will be lower;
6. If occupational achievement declines, the income of U.S. residents will decline;
7. If the levels of knowledge and skills of the U.S. workforce decline, more jobs will be exported offshore;
8. As jobs are exported offshore and U.S. residents' incomes decline, the taxes paid by U.S. residents will decline; and;
9. As taxes decline, revenue for state and federal support of state and federal services will decline, including support for education.

This chain of interrelationships is dependent on the validity of three key demographic and socioeconomic trends:

1. The rate of increase in minority populations with reduced socioeconomic resource bases;
2. The relationship between the demographic characteristics of populations and the education level of the populations; and
3. The relationships between education and income (both personal and household) and between education and poverty and other types of socioeconomic change.

A summary of the state of knowledge regarding these factors is examined below.

1.3.1 Growth in Minority Populations

The increasing racial and ethnic diversity of the nation will be extensively delineated in Chapters 2 and 3. Such data were provided for earlier time periods in previous works (Murdock 1995; Murdock et al. 1997, 2003). Similarly, clear documentation of national patterns is evident in work by Passel and Cohn (2008a, b), Perez and Hirschman (2009), and Johnson and Lichter (2010: 151). The description of the U.S. Census Bureau projections notes that, "The U.S. is projected to become a majority-minority nation for the first time in 2043" (U.S. Census Bureau 2012a). These projections (U.S. Census Bureau 2012a, b) show the minority population (the population other than the nonHispanic White population) increasing to more than 241 million by 2060. Immigration and high fertility are the major contributors to growing racial and ethnic diversity among American children and youth.

Among minority groups, Hispanic children (especially those 0–4 years of age) are the largest contributors to this growth (Perez and Hirschman 2009; Cohn and Bahrampour 2006; Mather 2009; Murdock et al. 2012), while the absolute number of nonHispanic White children in these ages is declining. Johnson and Lichter (2010) and Murdock et al. (2012) further demonstrate that these trends manifest themselves unevenly over U.S. counties, with major concentrations in the Southwest. Such groups are leading the trends in these patterns by exhibiting rates of growth in "majority-minority" populations of children considerably larger than those for the United States population overall (Johnson and Lichter 2010: 152; Murdock et al. 2012).

At the same time, although higher levels of minority population growth are more concentrated in some regions of the nation than in others, there is little doubt that patterns of minority population growth are increasingly pervasive across the United States. Thus Murdock et al. (2012) reported that while only four states showed increases in their numbers of nonHispanic White children from 2000 to 2010, all 50 states reported increases in their numbers of Hispanic children.

The growth in minority populations has created a new "generational rift" along racial and ethnic lines—between a slow-growing older nonHispanic White population and a faster growing younger Hispanic population (Mather 2009). These conflicts are not only between ethnic and racial groups, but also between the old and young, and even more importantly between those who are economically mobile and those who are not, due to cultural, educational, and language differences. Mather (2009) argues that increased racial and ethnic diversity among American children has heightened the need for appropriate public policy responses to improve and expand specialized school programs, especially pre-kindergarten programs, English as a Second Language (ESL), Limited English Proficiency (LEP), and community educational services in reading and math, to accelerate learning among such youth.

1.3.2 Race/Ethnicity and Education

Substantial evidence shows that educational attainment varies across racial and ethnic groups in the U.S. According to 2009 census data, 90% of nonHispanic White adults reported that they had at least a high school level of education, while only 61% of Hispanics had a high school diploma or equivalent (Ryan and Siebens 2012). Asians reported the highest percentage with bachelor's, master's and professional, and doctorate degrees. NonHispanic Blacks were more likely to have completed some college than any of the other groups, however they were less likely to have completed a bachelor's, masters, doctorate, or professional degree than those who were nonHispanic White. Similarly, results from the National Assessment of Education Progress (NAEP) have for some time shown that reading and writing skills of Black and Hispanic children are substantially below those of nonHispanic White children at grade levels 3, 7, and 11 (Beaton 1986; Milne et al. 1986; Milne and Gombert 1983; NAEP 1985; Baretz-Snowden et al. 1988).

What lies at the base of educational differences is educational and socioecononomic disadvantage that, due to a variety of historical, discriminatory, and other factors, varies by race/ethnicity (Psacharopoulos and Tilak 1992). Among the demographic factors that are predictive of such educational disadvantage are: (1) having minority racial/ethnic status, (2) living in a poverty household, (3) having a poorly educated mother (or surrogate), (4) living in a single parent family, or (5) having a non-English-language family background. Children who are disadvantaged on several of these indicators are generally at greater risk of educational failure—performing poorly on standardized tests, dropping out of high school, or never attaining a higher education degree. As a result, children who come from poor families, and especially those who have the additional disadvantage of having parents who are not fluent in English, are especially disadvantaged (Ekstrom et al. 1986; Denny et al. 2000; Duncan et al. 2007; Gottschalk 2008; Gordon and Becker 2012).

1.3.3 Education, Income, and Socioeconomic Change

Among the most frequently studied relationships in economics and sociology, across numerous countries (Mincer 1974; Ashenfelter and Rouse 1999; Card 1999; Abdullah et al. 2011) and multiple time periods (Becker 1967; Hanoch 1967; Schultz 1968) to post-2000 periods (U.S. Census Bureau and U. S. Bureau of Labor Statistics 2011), is the relationship between an individual's education and income (Rosen 1987; Romer 1990; Reardon 2011). These studies document that increased education results in increased wages and higher incomes. For example, in 2000, college graduates could expect to earn an average of $2.1 million over their working lives, compared to $1.0 million for high school dropouts (Cheeseman Day and Newburger 2002). A similar analysis based on 2010 data (Julian and Kominski 2011) provided lifetime earning estimates for males and females by both educational attainment and race/ethnicity. This analysis clearly showed that increased levels of education increase lifetime earnings. For example, the authors find that among nonHispanic White males a graduate degree leads to a lifetime income advantage of nearly $1.9 million compared to a nonHispanic White male with less than a high school degree. The differences for the same educational levels were $1.6 million for an Hispanic male, $1.4 million for a nonHispanic Black male, and $2.3 million for a nonHispanic Asian male. Although clear racial/ethnic (and gender, as shown in other parts of this book) differences exist, it is evident that, for all racial/ethnic and gender groups, education pays.

Additionally, educated individuals not only earn more, they also experience less unemployment and work in higher paying occupations than their less well-educated counterparts. Higher levels of education result in the creation of higher levels of skills and human capital that increase productivity, which increases market demand and higher occupational achievement and results in higher incomes (see Cohn and Addison 1998 and Abdullah et al. 2011 for selective reviews describing such effects). Such analyses show that children's future incomes are largely determined by the education they attain. Children from poor families are less likely to achieve in school, and low levels of educational attainment lead to future low occupational attainment and thus low income. The 2010 Current Population Survey data (U.S. Census Bureau and U.S. Bureau of Labor Statistics 2011) demonstrate a strong positive correlation between education and income. They show that, among adults 24–64 years of age, as education increases, median income increases.

Still other analysts have studied macro-level relationships at the state and national levels. These aggregative analyses (Denison 1962; Bowman and Anderson 1963; Schultz 1963) have estimated the contribution of education expenditures to national income and how state educational expenditures affect state income. They have consistently found that increased levels of education contribute (Breton 2010) to higher state and national income (Tolley and Olson 1971; Davern and Fisher 2001). In fact, an analysis by McKinsey and Company (2009) asserts that the persistent achievement gap between Hispanic and nonHispanic Black compared to nonHispanic White students in the United States will over time have the economic effect of a "permanent national recession." The authors argue that if the achievement gap had not existed between Black and Hispanic and nonHispanic Whites so that all earned at the level of nonHispanic Whites, GDP in 2008 would have been \$310–\$525 billion higher (2–4%). If the gap between (all) low-income persons and their peers had been narrowed, GDP in that same year would have been \$400 billion to \$670 billion higher (3–5%).

In a comprehensive quantitative review of the econometrics literature through a meta-regression analysis of 64 empirical studies that collectively reported 868 estimates of the effects of education on income, Abdullah et al. (2011) found that education is, on average, an effective tool for reducing income differences among social and racial/ethnic groups. They conclude that the distribution of education is critically important and that ensuring fair and equitable access to education is an important means of increasing individual, household, and national income levels.

The effects of education on income are pervasive even during periods of economic decline and/or stagnation. Between 2008 and 2010, during the depth of the "Great Recession," people with the highest educational attainment were the least likely to be unemployed (Ryan and Siebens 2012:15). These authors also found that for any given month, those without a high school diploma were the most likely to be unemployed, while high school graduates were more likely to be unemployed than those with bachelor's degrees. In August 2010, the unemployment rate for people with less than a high school education was 13.1%, while the unemployment rate for people with an advanced degree was 4.1%. The rates for these two groups in March 2008, before the recession, were 9.5% and 1.5%, respectively. In August of 2012 the national unemployment rate was 8.3% overall, while the unemployment rate for those with a college education was 4.1%.

It is evident that poorly educated persons experience long-term economic impacts (Isaacs 2010, 2011, 2012). Children and youth from families with low family income and low maternal education do poorly. They perform less well on standardized tests compared with advantaged youth and are less likely to graduate from high school and complete college. These lower levels of academic achievement and educational attainment result in lower levels of economic success as adults. For example, children born into families with family incomes in the bottom 20% are twice as likely as middle-class children to be in the bottom income brackets as adults.

Education plays a key role. The likelihood of being school ready is increased 9% by children attending preschool before starting kindergarten (Isaacs 2012). In addition, such analyses suggest that expanding preschool programs to focus on 4-year-olds from poor families has a high potential for increasing school readiness.

Efforts to improve economic prospects of children from low-income families have often focused on the existing formal educational system as it is presently structured, but often with disappointing results (Jacob and Ludwig 2009). Research has demonstrated that disparities in academic skills are apparent well before children begin their formal schooling, suggesting that efforts targeted earlier than kindergarten may well be effective in preventing the disparities that schools and policy makers seek to remediate.

Scholars have recommended that policy makers emphasize early childhood education programs to remediate the intricate economic causes of poor academic achievement that keep children from low-income families at low-income levels as adults (Isaacs and Magnuson 2011). Bartik (2011) in Chapter 8 of *Investing in Kids* suggests that the evidence is strong that early childhood education can significantly increase the future earnings and income of low-income children. They estimate that half-day prekindergarten programs for 4-year-olds, if such programs are high quality, can raise the future income among those from households with earnings in the lowest income quintile by 7%. Their analysis suggests that with even 1 year of a full-time high quality child care and preschool program, from shortly after birth to age 5, children from the lowest income quintile would increase their annual incomes as adults by 35%, a six times greater return than that obtained from a half-day 1 year early childhood education program.

It must be acknowledged, of course, that not only does education affect income but income also affects education. This issue is generally examined as an intergenerational query beginning with individual education achievement and asking the question: What parental background (education, occupation, and income) and demographic/contextual characteristics (region of the county, urban versus rural residence, family structure) lead to various levels of educational attainment? These analyses find that mothers' education and family income are generally the strongest predictors of their children's level of educational attainment. Combining these findings with those above suggests that mother's education and family of origin's income disproportionately determine a child's education and the child's education determines his or her future income. An analysis by Maralani (2013) using sophisticated models has provided evidence that demographic factors work interactively with education and other factors to effect intergenerational change in socioeconomic levels of minority households.

The lack of adequate income as experienced in poverty households has particularly negative impacts on education. Poor children in the United States start school at a disadvantage in terms of their skills. Less than half (48%) of poor children are ready for school at age 5, compared to 75% of children from middle and higher income families (Isaacs 2012). The importance of demographic variables is evident in that this 27% gap is reduced to roughly 7% when key demographic characteristics (such as household composition and racial/ethnic status) are controlled.

That income and education disparities are not historical but current in their effects is evident in several analyses. For example, an analysis by Acs et al. (2013) shows that the socioeconomic characteristics of nonHispanic Black and Hispanic populations in the United States continue to lag behind those of nonHispanic Whites. Published nearly 50 years after Moynihan's famous study of the Black family, this work suggests that there has been a lack of substantial progress in closing socioeconomic differences between nonHispanic Black and nonHispanic White Americans and shows that Hispanics in the United States have similar patterns of continuing disparity. Similarly, an analysis by Turner et al. (2013) indicates that although such disparity has been reduced substantially compared to earlier decades, disparity is still evident, with nonHispanic Black and Hispanic customers receiving disparate treatment in housing relative to nonHispanic Whites.

1.4 The Current Demographic Context

In recent decades the United States has experienced rapid change in the characteristics of its population and growth that is substantially greater than that in most developed nations. The growth in the total size of the population and the increasing racial/ethnic diversity of the population, coupled with increasing proportions of young minority and older nonHispanic White residents and an increasing diversity of household types, are likely to produce a nation in which population change may result in a variety of generally desirable, as well as less desirable, socioeconomic outcomes.

Among the reasons for such impacts are the differences in socioeconomic resources associated with the changing characteristics of the nation's population. For example, the nation's population and households are projected to show dramatic increases in the number of minority (especially Hispanic) populations and households. As shown in Table 1.1, incomes in 2010 varied dramatically among racial/ethnic groups, with nonHispanic Black and Hispanic households having median household incomes of $33,568 and $40,165, while nonHispanic White and nonHispanic Asian households had income levels of $54,168 and $70,644, respectively. The nation is also projected to have increases in the number and proportion of young minority populations and elderly nonHispanic White populations, and both the young and the old have clear income limitations. Table 1.1 also shows that those households with a householder who was less than 25 years of age in 2010 had median incomes of $24,143 and those with householders 65 years of age or older had incomes of $34,381. Households with middle-aged adult householders had incomes varying from $54,024 to $60,683. In addition, the nation is projected to have a larger proportion of married couple and a smaller proportion of nonfamily households in the future than today. As also shown in Table 1.1, married couple households had a median income of $72,596 in 2010. Female householder households had a median income of $30,085, male householder households had a median income of $41,474, and nonfamily households had a median income of $30,440.

Such socioeconomic differences are not inherent in the demographic differences associated with them, but these and other factors that interact with population change make it clear that understanding how the demographic characteristics of the nation may change its economic, service, and social structure is of critical importance. It is essential for decision makers and residents to understand how the change in demographic characteristics may impact the levels of demand for, and utilization of, specific types of private and public sector services and may change the socioeconomic characteristics of the nation. Exploring these changes is the central purpose of this volume.

We have previously argued that change in the size and rate of growth in the racial/ethnic, age, and household composition of the population is forming critical challenges for the United States (Murdock 1995). These challenges are those of providing the social and economic resources that will allow all Americans to obtain the skills and education necessary to become competitive in increasingly socially and culturally diverse, and economically competitive, national and international economies. In the earlier work what could happen to the socioeconomic characteristics of the population depending on what occurs or does not occur to increase the skills and education of the nation's increasingly diverse population was discussed. In this work, we extend that analysis both by describing past and recent patterns of demographic and related socioeconomic change and by delineating the future of the nation's population and related socioeconomic change through 2060. This work provides an explication of the nation's future depending on how its population changes and how the nation adapts to and develops the population and related socioeconomic resources resulting from such change.

Table 1.1 Median household income in the United States by age, household type, and race/ethnicity of householder, 2010

Characteristic	Median household income
Total	$50,046
Age	
<25 years	$24,143
25 to 44 years	$54,024
45–64 years	$60,683
65 or more years	$34,381
Household type	
Family	$60,609
Married couple	$72,596
Male householder	$41,474
Female householder	$30,085
Non-family	$30,440
Race/ethnicity	
NH[a] White	$54,168
NH Black	$33,568
Hispanic	$40,165
NH Asian	$70,644

Source: U.S. Census Bureau, 2010 American Community Survey

[a]NH refers to nonHispanic; values for categories labeled NH are only for nonHispanic persons in each category. Hispanic includes Hispanics of all races

1.5 The Intended Audience for, and Focus of, the Work

The intended audience for this work includes academics interested in tracing the consequences of various levels of socioeconomic disparity among subpopulations in the United States but especially policy and other decision-makers who may wish to investigate the implications of various courses of actions or inactions given such change. To what extent and how quickly are current demographic and related social and economic patterns leading to increased levels of socioeconomic disparity? What are the implications of actions that maintain current levels, or minimize reductions in current levels, of socioeconomic inequality among age groups, racial/ethnic groups, or household types? If current conditions and levels of disparity continue, what will be the implications for total household and societal-level income, poverty levels, annual household expenditures, housing purchases, enrollment in various levels of education, and general consumer expenditures? What will be the effects on the demand for various types of public services, on tax revenues, on levels of national debt, and on the overall financial state of the United States? Although these conditions and states are determined by many factors in addition to demographics, we believe that examining demographic dimensions is critical to understanding the level and types of public and private sector efforts that may be necessary to maintain and expand the overall socioeconomic resources of the population of the United States.

1.6 The Content of the Volume

This volume examines socioeconomic and service implications of future population change in the United States. It discusses what will happen if population patterns projected by the United States Census Bureau (2012) for the United States (through 2060) occur as projected and impact public service usage and private sector factors at historical rates as the population changes in size, age, and level of racial/ethnic diversity. It examines the implications of such patterns for income (median household, per capita, and aggregate), poverty levels, consumer expenditures, household net worth and assets, and government revenues and expenditures. It evaluates the implications for households and for owner and renter housing occupancy levels, values, and rents. The work examines the likely effects of future population change on the labor force including its size, occupational structure, skill levels, and wages and salaries. It delineates the implications of population patterns for health care including the incidence of different diseases/disorders, the likely effect on the number and characteristics of physicians and other health care professionals and on the level of demand on hospitals and health care and related costs. It describes the impacts on services for the elderly including Medicare, Social Security, and long-term care. Human services such as the impacts on Medicaid, TANF, SNAP, CHIP, and similar programs are also examined. It further describes the impacts of demographic change on the number of students enrolled in elementary and secondary and college education programs overall and within specific program areas and examines what current patterns of cost increases in colleges and universities are likely to mean for future students' debt levels. It also examines the role that changing populations will have on highway transportation, accidents and drivers in the coming decades.

We also examine the implications of change in the socioeconomic characteristics of subpopulations within the population of the United States on the overall socioeconomic welfare of the nation. We look specifically at what the implications of alternative levels of socioeconomic closure among diverse populations would mean for the total population's average household incomes, poverty levels, household assets, levels of occupational attainment, education attainment levels and other factors. We thus compare elements of the future as current patterns would suggest it will be with the future that could occur under alternative patterns of socioeconomic change.

1.7 Inherent Limitations of the Methodology Underlying the Work

The projections of populations, population characteristics (such as future age, sex, and race/ethnicity distributions), households and household characteristics, and socioeconomic and service factors presented in this work will be inaccurate to various degrees, as are all projections including those of populations and population-related factors (see for example Murdock and Ellis 1991; Murdock et al. 1991; Ahlburg and Land 1992; Smith et al. 2001; Siegel 2002; Siegel and Swanson 2004; ESRI 2007; Tayman et al. 2011). We have no illusions that the projections in this work will be any different. However, our intent is not to produce point accurate projections but rather to produce projections of the direction of change that will occur if the projections of the population are correct in their forecasts of demographic change and in their assumptions about the continuance of current patterns of interrelationships between demographic and population-related socioeconomic and service dimensions in the United States.

Our intent is to provide projections that will make the reader aware of the implications of projected future population change for socioeconomic and public and private services in the United States in the coming decades. By so doing, we hope to create awareness of the fact that projected patterns of population change will, in the absence of change in socioeconomic differentials, lead to substantial societal levels of socioeconomic change and disparity and that actions to ameliorate such disparity may be beneficial for the future of the United States.

1.8 Summary

The literature reviewed in this chapter provides substantial support for the major underlying premises of the present effort. This literature indicates that there is a substantial nation-wide increase in minority populations and households and that, because of a variety of historical, discriminatory, and other factors, many of these populations' members have low levels of education. These low levels of education lead, in turn, to reduced levels of income and to reduced levels of other socioeconomic factors linked to income. The interrelationships between demographic, educational, and socioeconomic factors have substantial interactive impacts on the social and economic events affecting society. Thus, levels of change in education among segments of the state's population may have substantial and significant effects on the socioeconomic characteristics of individuals, households, communities, and the United States as a whole.

In sum, this work describes the implications of projected patterns of population change for the socioeconomic future of the United States. It evaluates the implications of such relationships for a wide variety of socioeconomic factors. It examines the implications, if the current relationships between demographic, socioeconomic factors and race/ethnicity specific usage rates continue over the coming decades and the implications if, through educational change and other factors, these historic relationships are altered. It presents one means of assessing the importance of changing such relationships not only for the individuals whose socioeconomic futures are altered but also for the overall socioeconomic development of the nation as a whole. It provides one assessment of the implications of the United States demographic future for its socioeconomic development and competitiveness over the next 50 years.

References

Abdullah, A. J., Doucouliagos, H., Manning, E. (2011). *Education and income inequality: A meta-regression analysis*. Paper presented at MAER-NET colloquium (September 16–18, 2011), Wolfson College. University of Cambridge.

Acs, G., Bracewell, K., Sorenson, E., & Turner, M. (2013). *The Moynihan report revisited*. Washington, DC: The Urban Institute.

Ahlburg, D. A., & Land, K. C. (1992). Population forecasting: Guest editors' introduction. *International Journal of Forecasting, 8*, 289–299.

Ashenfelter, O., & Rouse, C. (1999). *Schooling, intelligence and income in America: Cracks in the bell curve* (Working paper 6902 (January)). Cambridge, MA: National Bureau of Economic Research.

Baretz-Snowden, J., Rock, D., Pollock, J., & Wilder, G. (1988). *Educational progress of language minority children: Findings from the NAEP 1985–86 special study*. Princeton: National Assessment of Educational Progress/Educational Testing Service.

Bartik, T. J. (2011). Who benefits? Distributional effects of early childhood programs and business incentives, and their implications for policy. In T. Bartik (Ed.), *Investing in kids: Early childhood programs and local economic development* (pp. 219–266). Kalamazoo: W.E. Upjohn Institute for Employment Research.

Beaton, A. E. (1986). *National assessment of educational progress 1983–84, technical report*. Princeton: National Assessment of Educational Progress/Educational Testing Service.

Becker, G. S. (1967). *Human capital and the personal distribution of income*. Ann Arbor: University of Michigan Press.

Berry, B. J. L., & Horton, F. E. (1970). *Geographic perspectives on urban systems with integrated readings*. Englewood Cliffs: Prentice-Hall.

Bowman, M. J., & Anderson, C. A. (1963). Concerning the role of education in development. In C. Geetz (Ed.), *Old societies and new states* (pp. 247–279). Glencoe: Free Press.

Breton, T. R. (2010). Schooling and national income: How large are the externalities? *Education Economics, 18*(1), 67–92.

Card, D. (1999). The casual effect of education on earnings. In O. Ashenfelter & D. Card (Eds.), *Handbook of labor economics* (Vol. 3, pp. 1801–1834). Amsterdam: Elsevier Science.

Cheeseman Day, J., & Newburger, E. C. (2002). *The big payoff: Educational attainment and synthetic estimates of work-life earnings* (Current population reports P23-210 (July)). Washington, DC: U.S. Census Bureau.

Cohn, E., & Addison, J. T. (1998). The economic returns to lifelong learning. *Education Economics, 6*(3), 253–308.

Cohn, D., & Bahrampour, T. (2006, May 10). Of U.S. children under 5, nearly half are minorities. *The Washington Post*. http://www.washingtonpost.com/wp-dyn/concent/article/2006/05/09/AR2006050901841.html. Accessed 22 Jan 2011.

Davern, M. E., & Fisher, P. J. (2001). *Household net worth and asset ownership: 1995* (Current population reports P70-71 (February)). Washington, DC: U.S. Census Bureau.

Denison, E. F. (1962). *The sources of economic growth in the United States and alternatives before us* (Supplementary paper no. 13). New York: Committee on Economic Development.

Denny, K., Harmon, C., & Redmond, S. (2000). *Functional literacy, educational attainment and earnings-evidence from the international adult literacy survey* (April). London, UK: The Institute for Fiscal Studies, WP 00/09.

Duncan, O. D. (1964). Social organization and the ecosystem. In R. Farris (Ed.), *Handbook of modern sociology* (pp. 36–82). Chicago: Rand McNally and Co.

Duncan, O. D., & Schnore, L. F. (1959). Cultural, behavioral, and ecological perspectives in the study of social organization. *American Journal of Sociology, 65*(2), 132–153.

Duncan, G., Ludwig, J., & Magnuson, K. (2007). Reducing poverty through pre-school intervention. *The Future of Children, 17*, 143–160.

Ekstrom, R. B., Goertz, M. E., Pollack, J. M., & Rock, D. A. (1986). Who drops out of high school and why? Findings from a national study. *Teachers College Record, 87*, 356–373.

ESRI. (2007). Evaluating population projections – The importance of accurate forecasting. White paper. http://www.esri.com/library/whitepapers/pdfs/evaluating-population.pdf. Accessed 12 Mar 2014.

Gibbs, J. P., & Martin, W. T. (1959). Toward a theoretical system of human ecology. *The Pacific Sociological Review, 2*(1), 29–36.

Gordon, R. J., & Becker, I. D. (2012). *Controversies about the rise of American inequality: A survey* (Working paper no. 13982). New York: NBER.

Gottschalk, A. O. (2008). *Net worth and the assets of households: 2002* (Current population reports P70-115 (April)). Washington, DC: U.S. Census Bureau.

Gribble, J. N., & Bremner, J. (2012). *Achieving a demographic dividend*. Washington, DC: Population Reference Bureau. http://www.prb.org/pdf12/achieving-demographic-dividend.pdf. Accessed 12 Oct 2014.

Hanoch, G. (1967). An economic analysis of earning and schooling. *Journal of Human Resources, 2*(Summer), 310–329.

Hawley, A. H. (1950). *Human ecology: A theory of community structure*. New York: Ronald.

Isaacs, J. B. (2010). *Child poverty during the great recession: Predicting state child poverty rates for 2010* (Executive summary (December)). Washington, DC: The Brookings Institution.

Isaacs, J. B. (2011). *The recession's ongoing impact on America's children: Indicators of children's economic well-being through 2011*. Washington, DC: The Brookings Institution.

Isaacs, J. B. (2012). *Starting school at a disadvantage: The school readiness of poor children* (Executive summary (March)). Washington, DC: The Brookings Institution.
Isaacs, J. B., & Magnuson, K. (2011). *Income and education as predictors of children's school readiness*. Washington DC: Brookings Institution.
Jacob, B. A., & Ludwig, J. (2009). Improving educational outcomes for poor children. In M. Cancian & S. Danziger (Eds.), *Changing poverty, changing politics*. New York, NY: Russell Sage Foundation.
Johnson, K. M., & Lichter, D. T. (2010). Growing diversity among America's children and youth: Spatial and temporal dimensions. *Population and Development Review, 36*(1), 151–176.
Julian, T. A., & Kominski, R. A. (2011). *Education and synthetic work – Life earnings estimates* (American community survey reports. ACS-14). Washington, DC: U.S. Census Bureau.
Kelly, P. J. (2005a). *Income of U.S. workforce projected to decline if education doesn't improve. Policy alert*. San Jose: National Center for Public Policy and Higher Education.
Kelly, P. J. (2005b). *As America becomes more diverse: The impact of State higher education inequality* (Report). Boulder: National Center for Higher Education Management Systems (NCHEMS).
Lutz, W. (2012). Demographic metabolism: A predictive theory of socioeconomic change. *Population and Development Review, 38*, 283–301.
Mannheim, K. (1952 [1928]). The problem of generations. In P. Kecskemeti (Ed.), *Essays on the sociology of knowledge*. New York: Routledge & Kegan Paul. Originally published as Das problem der generationen. *Kölner Vierteljahreshefte für Soziologie 7 (1928)*, pp. 157–185.
Maralani, V. (2013). The demography of social mobility: Black-white differences in the process of educational reproduction. *American Journal of Sociology, 118*(6), 1509–1558.
Mather, M. (2009). *Children in immigrant families chart new path* (Reports on America). Washington, DC: Population Reference Bureau.
McKinsey & Company. (2009). *The economic impact of the achievement gap in America's schools, summary of findings*. New York: Social Sector Office.
Micklin, M., & Poston, D. L., Jr. (Eds.). (1998). *Continuities in sociological human ecology*. New York: Plenum Press.
Milne, A., & Gombert, J. (1983). Students with a primary language other than English: Distribution and service rates. In K. Baker & A. DeKanter (Eds.), *Bilingual education* (pp. 133–138). Lexington: Heath.
Milne, A., Myers, D. E., Rosenthal, A. S., & Ginsberg, A. (1986). Single parents, working mothers, and the educational achievement of school children. *Sociology of Education, 59*, 125–139.
Mincer, J. (1974). *Schooling, experience and earnings*. New York: Columbia University Press.
Murdock, S. H. (1995). *An America challenged: Population change and the future of the United States*. Boulder: Westview Press.
Murdock, S. H., & Albrecht, D. E. (1998). An ecological investigation of agricultural patterns in the United States. In M. Micklin & D. L. Poston Jr. (Eds.), *Continuities in sociological human ecology* (pp. 299–316). New York: Plenum Press.
Murdock, S. H., & Ellis, D. (1991). *Applied demography: An introduction to basic concepts, methods, and data*. Boulder: Westview Press.
Murdock, S. H., & Sutton, W. A., Jr. (1974). The new ecology and community theory: Similarities, differences, and convergences. *Rural Sociology, 39*, 319–333.
Murdock, S. H., Backman, K., Hoque, M. N., & Ellis, D. (1991). The implications of change in population size and composition on future participation in outdoor recreational activities. *Journal of Leisure Research, 23*, 238–259.
Murdock, S. H., Hoque, N., Michael, M., White, S., & Pecotte, B. (1997). *The Texas challenge: Population change and the future of Texas*. College Station: Texas A&M University Press.
Murdock, S. H., White, S., Hoque, M. N., Pecotte, B., You, X., & Balkan, J. (2003). *The new Texas challenge: Population change and the future of Texas*. College Station: Texas A&M University Press.

Murdock, S. H., Cline, M. E., & Zey, M. (2012). *The children of the Southwest*. Washington, DC: First Focus.

Murdock, S. H., Cline, M. E., Zey, M., Jeanty, P. W., & Perez, D. (2014). *Changing Texas: Implications of addressing or ignoring the Texas challenge*. College Station: Texas A&M University Press.

Namboodiri, K. (1988). Ecological demography: Its place in sociology. *American Sociological Review, 53*(4), 619–633.

National Assessment of Educational Progress. (1985). *The reading report card*. Princeton: Educational Testing Service.

National Center for Public Policy and Higher Education. (2005). *Income of U.S. workforce projected to decline if education doesn't improve*. San Jose: National Center for Public Policy and Higher Education.

Park, R. E. (1936). Human ecology. *American Journal of Sociology, 42*, 1–15.

Passel, J., & Cohn, D. (2008a). *Trends in unauthorized immigration: Undocumented inflow now trails legal inflow* (October). Washington, DC: Pew Hispanic Center.

Passel, J., & Cohn, D. (2008b). *U.S. population projections: 2005–2050* (11 February). Washington DC: Pew Hispanic Center.

Perez, A. D., & Hirschman, C. (2009). The changing racial and ethnic composition of the U.S. population: Emerging American identities. *Population and Development Review, 35*, 1–51.

Psacharopoulos, G., & Tilak, J. B. G. (1992). Education and wage earnings. In M. C. Alkin (Ed.), *The encyclopedia of educational research* (pp. 419–423). New York: American Educational Research Association. Macmillan.

Reardon, S. F. (2011). The widening academic achievement gap between the rich and poor: New evidence and possible explanations. In R. Murname & G. Duncan (Eds.), *Social inequality and economic disadvantage* (pp. 91–116).

Romer, P. M. (1990). Human capital and growth: Theory and evidence. *Carnegie-Rochester Series on Public Policy, 32*, 251–286.

Rosen, S. (1987). Human capital. In J. Eatwell, M. Milgrate, & P. Newman (Eds.), *The new Palgrave dictionary of economics* (Vol. 2, pp. 681–690). London: Macmillan.

Ryan, C., & Siebens, J. (2012). *Educational attainment in the United States: 2009* (Current population reports P20-566 (February)). Washington, DC: U.S. Census Bureau.

Ryder, N. (1965). The cohort as a concept in the study of social change. *American Sociological Review, 30*(6), 843–861.

Schultz, T. W. (1963). *The economic values of education*. New York: Columbia University Press.

Schultz, T. W. (1968). Resources for higher education: An economist's view. *Journal of Political Economy, 76*, 327–347.

Siegel, J. S. (2002). *Applied demography: Applications to business, government, law, and public policy*. Salt Lake City: Academic.

Siegel, J. S., & Swanson, D. (Eds.). (2004). *The methods and materials of demography*. San Diego: Elsevier Academic Press.

Smith, S. K., Tayman, J., & Swanson, D. A. (2001). *State and local population projections: Methodology and analysis*. New York: Kluwer Academic/Plenum Publishers.

Tayman, J., Smith, S. K., & Rayer, S. (2011). Evaluating population forecast accuracy: A regression approach using county data. *Population Research and Policy Review, 30*(2), 235–262.

Tolley, G. S., & Olson, E. (1971). The interdependence between income and education. *Journal of Political Economy, 79*, 460–480.

Turner, M., Santos, R., Levy, D., Wissoker, D., Aranda, C., & Pitingolo, R. (2013). *Housing discrimination against racial and ethnic minorities 2012*. Washington, DC: U.S. Department of Housing and Urban Development.

U.S. Census Bureau. (2011). *2010 American community survey*. Washington, DC: U.S. Census Bureau.

U.S. Census Bureau. (2012a). *Population projections press release December 12, 2012*. Press release. U.S. Census Bureau. http://www.census.gov/newsroom/releases/archives/population/cb12-243.html. Accessed 12 Dec 2012.

U.S. Census Bureau. (2012b). *2012 National population projections*. Washington, DC: U.S. Census Bureau.

U.S. Census Bureau, & U.S. Bureau of Labor Statistics. (2011). *Educational attainment-people 25 years old and over, by total money earnings in 2010, work experience in 2010, age, race, Hispanic origin, and sex* (Current population survey, annual social and economic supplement). Washington, DC: U.S. Census Bureau.

Chapter 2
Historic and Projected Patterns of Population and Household Change in the United States

Given the demographic emphasis of this work, and the premises noted in the previous chapter that understanding demographic, and related household, and other patterns of change are critical to understanding the socioeconomic characteristics and related public service use for the future of the United States, it is important to examine recent demographic history and the historical change in households in the United States. In this chapter, we first examine population change, the demographic processes responsible for such change (i.e., fertility, mortality and migration), and the status and recent and projected change in key demographic characteristics. We then examine the characteristics and composition of households and of the change in households that has occurred in recent decades.

Because of the numerous demographic and household characteristics that may affect socioeconomic factors, no comprehensive analysis of all such characteristics is possible and thus the examination is selective of those that we believe have the largest impact on aggregate patterns of change in socioeconomic factors and public and private sector service use. Finally, we utilize United States Census Bureau projections of the U.S. population and our derived projections of households based on demographic change through 2060. This analysis provides the basis for delineating the nature of future, demographically impacted, socioeconomic and public service related demand for the United States. The chapter thus provides an examination of critical demographic and household components used in the remainder of the analysis presented in this work.

2.1 Historic Patterns of Population Change

The United States has shown rapid population growth throughout its history. As is evident in the data in Table 2.1, in only three decades, the 1930s (the period of the Great Depression), the 1980s, and the period from 2000 to 2010, has population growth been less than 10%. The major source of growth has been natural increase

S.H. Murdock et al., *Population Change in the United States*,
DOI 10.1007/978-94-017-7288-4_2

Table 2.1 Population change in the United States by components of change, 1790–2010

Year	Total population	Population change	Total immigrants	Total natural increase	Percent population change	Percent of population change due to	
						Immigration	Natural increase
1790	3,929,214	–	–	–	–	–	–
1800	5,308,483	1,379,269	–	–	35.1	–	–
1810	7,239,881	1,931,398	–	–	36.4	–	–
1820	9,638,453	2,398,572	–	–	33.1	–	–
1830	12,866,020	3,227,567	132,237	3,095,330	33.5	4.1	95.9
1840	17,069,453	4,203,433	553,567	3,649,866	32.7	13.2	86.8
1850	23,191,876	6,122,423	1,498,815	4,623,608	35.9	24.5	75.5
1860	31,443,321	8,251,445	2,760,469	5,490,976	35.6	33.5	66.5
1870	39,818,449	8,375,128	2,139,652	6,235,566	26.6	25.5	74.5
1880	50,155,783	10,337,334	2,759,650	7,577,684	26.0	26.7	73.3
1890	62,947,714	12,791,931	5,248,079	7,543,852	25.5	41.0	59.0
1900	75,994,575	13,046,861	3,692,612	9,354,249	20.7	28.3	71.7
1910	91,972,266	15,977,691	8,350,637	7,627,054	21.0	52.3	47.7
1920	105,710,620	13,738,354	6,194,488	7,543,866	14.9	45.1	54.9
1930	122,775,046	17,064,426	4,248,435	12,815,991	16.1	24.9	75.1
1940	131,669,275	8,894,229	656,639	8,237,590	7.2	7.4	92.6
1950	151,325,790	19,656,515	901,216	18,755,299	14.9	4.6	95.4
1960	179,323,175	27,997,385	2,503,320	25,494,065	18.5	8.9	91.1
1970	203,302,031	23,978,856	3,240,731	20,738,125	13.4	13.5	86.5
1980	226,545,805	23,243,774	4,375,330	18,868,444	11.4	18.8	81.2
1990	248,709,873	22,164,068	6,583,679	15,580,389	9.8	29.7	70.3
2000	281,421,906	32,712,033	11,876,667	20,835,366	13.2	36.3	63.7
2010	308,745,538	27,323,632	10,356,331	16,967,301	9.7	37.9	62.1

Source: Murdock 1995; Martin et al. 2012; Murphy et al. 2013; U.S. Census Bureau, 2011; and U.S. Department of Homeland Security 2012, Yearbook of immigration statistics

Note: Immigration statistics were not systematically collected prior to 1820, thus components of population change were not computed until the 1820–1830 period

(the excess of births relative to deaths). In fact, in only one decade, the decade from 1900 to 1910, did the percentage of growth from immigration exceed that from natural increase. Despite this, immigration has been an important source of growth in virtually all decades and is expected to be an important source of growth in the future (U.S. Census Bureau 2012a). Only in the two decades when the United States first began to count immigrants separately, in the decade of the 1930s when the Great Depression impacted the country, and the 1940s when the nation was involved in World War II, has immigration been less than one million persons per decade. Immigration was numerically largest in the decades preceding and directly following 1900 and exceeded 10 million in each of the last two decades (from 1990 to 2000 and from 2000 to 2010). In sum, the United States population history has been one of continuous and rapid growth from both natural increase and net migration.

Latin America and Asia have dominated the immigration streams to the United States (see Table 2.2). In every decade since data on migration origins were first identified, beginning in 1820 through 1959, Europe accounted for more than 50% of all immigrants. Beginning in the 1960s, Latin America, and by the 1970s Asia also became a larger source of immigrants than Europe (Martin 2013:6). Beginning in the 1970s, Asia and Latin America together accounted for more than 70% of all immigrants to the United States. Although many people from the United States tend

Table 2.2 Immigration into the United States by period and area of origin of immigrants, 1820–2012

Time period	Number of immigrants	Percent by area of origin					
		Europe	Canada	Asia	Latin America	Africa	Other
1820–1829	128,502	77.5	1.8	0.0	5.7	0.0	15.0
1830–1839	538,381	78.5	2.2	0.0	3.7	0.0	15.6
1840–1849	1,427,337	95.9	2.4	0.0	1.1	0.0	0.6
1850–1859	2,814,554	93.2	2.3	1.3	0.7	0.0	2.5
1860–1869	2,081,261	90.3	5.7	2.6	0.6	0.0	0.8
1870–1879	2,742,137	82.1	11.8	4.9	0.8	0.0	0.4
1880–1889	5,248,568	88.4	9.4	1.4	0.7	0.0	0.1
1890–1899	3,694,294	96.8	0.1	1.7	1.0	0.0	0.4
1900–1909	8,202,388	92.3	1.5	3.7	1.9	0.1	0.5
1910–1919	6,347,380	78.5	11.2	4.2	5.7	0.1	0.3
1920–1929	4,295,510	59.6	22.1	3.0	14.9	0.1	0.3
1930–1939	699,375	63.5	23.3	2.8	9.7	0.3	0.4
1940–1949	856,608	55.2	18.8	4.0	19.6	0.8	1.6
1950–1959	2,499,268	56.2	14.1	5.4	22.7	0.5	1.1
1960–1969	3,213,749	35.3	13.5	11.2	38.6	0.7	0.7
1970–1979	4,248,203	19.5	4.2	33.1	40.6	1.7	0.9
1980–1989	6,244,379	10.7	2.5	38.3	40.6	2.3	5.6
1990–1999	9,775,398	13.8	2.0	29.3	50.6	3.5	0.8
2000–2009	10,299,430	13.1	2.3	33.7	40.8	7.4	2.7
2010–2012	3,136,296	8.7	1.9	40.3	38.3	9.5	1.3

Source: U.S. Department of Homeland Security, Yearbook of immigration statistics, 2012

to see Asian and Latin American immigration as a recent phenomenon, these sources have dominated immigration to the United States for more than 40 years.

Table 2.3 shows key characteristics of the three demographic processes that lead to demographic change. The top panel of this table shows data on patterns of fertility since 1940. The total fertility rate (TFR) is often used as a summary measure of fertility relative to population replacement. A total fertility rate of 2.1 births per female is the average number of births necessary for a replacement level of fertility

Table 2.3 Birth, death, and net migration measures for the United States, 1940–2010

Fertility measures			
Year	Crude birth rate	General fertility rate	Total fertility rate
1940	19.4	79.9	2.3
1950	24.1	106.2	3.1
1960	23.7	118.8	3.7
1970	18.4	87.9	2.5
1980	15.9	68.4	1.8
1990	16.7	71.1	2.1
2000	14.4	65.9	2.1
2010	13.0	64.1	1.9
Mortality measures			
Year	Crude death rate	Infant mortality rate	Life expectancy at birth
1940	10.8	54.9	62.9
1950	9.6	33.0	68.2
1960	9.5	27.0	69.7
1970	9.5	21.4	70.8
1980	8.7	12.9	73.7
1990	8.6	9.2	75.4
2000	8.5	6.9	76.8
2010	8.0	6.2	78.7
Migration measures			
Year ending	Annual number of immigrants	Period	Percent of the population involved in internal migration
1940	70,756	–	–
1950	249,187	1950–1951	5.6
1960	265,798	1960–1961	6.3
1970	438,000	1970–1971	6.5
1980	530,639	1980–1981	6.2
1990	656,111	1990–1991	6.1
2000	849,807	2000–2001	5.6
2010	1,042,625	2010–2011	3.6

Source: Martin et al. 2012; Murphy et al. 2013; U.S. Department of Homeland Security, Yearbook of immigration statistics 2012; and U.S. Census Bureau, 2012b

Table 2.5 United States population in 1990, 2000, and 2010, percent change in population for 1990–2000 and 2000–2010, and proportion of the population by race/ethnicity for 1990, 2000, and 2010

	Number			Percent change		Population proportion		
Race/ethnicity	1990	2000	2010	1990–2000	2000–2010	1990	2000	2010
NH[a] White	188,128,296	194,552,774	196,817,552	3.4	1.2	75.6	69.1	63.7
NH Black	29,216,293	33,947,837	37,685,848	16.2	11.0	11.7	12.1	12.2
Hispanic	22,354,059	35,305,818	50,477,594	57.9	43.0	9.0	12.5	16.4
NH Asian	9,011,225	17,615,477	23,764,544	95.5	34.9	3.6	6.3	7.7
Total	248,709,873	281,421,906	308,745,538	13.2	9.7	100.0	100.0	100.0

Source: U.S. Census Bureau, 1991, 2001, 2011

[a]NH refers to nonHispanic; values for categories labeled NH are only for nonHispanic persons in each category. Hispanic includes Hispanics of all races

Table 2.6 Number and percentage of households by persons in the household and average household size for the United States, 1960–2010 (numbers in thousands)

Household size	1960		1970		1980		1990		2000		2010	
	Number	%	Number	%	Number	%	Number	%	Number	%	Number	%
One person	6,871	13.1	10,692	17.0	18,300	22.6	22,580	24.6	27,230	25.8	31,205	26.7
Two persons	14,616	27.8	18,129	28.8	25,300	31.3	29,454	32.0	34,418	32.6	38,243	32.8
Three persons	9,941	18.9	10,903	17.3	14,100	17.5	15,970	17.4	17,439	16.5	18,758	16.1
Four persons	9,277	17.6	9,935	15.8	12,700	15.7	13,860	15.1	14,973	14.2	15,625	13.4
Five or more	11,905	22.6	13,215	21.0	10,400	12.9	10,083	11.0	11,420	10.8	12,886	11.0
All households	52,610	100.0	62,874	100.0	80,800	100.0	91,947	100.0	105,480	100.0	116,716	100.0
Average persons per household	3.35	–	3.17	–	2.75	–	2.63	–	2.59	–	2.58	–

Source: Murdock 1995; U.S. Census Bureau, 1991, 2001, 2011

Table 2.7 Population in the United States by race/ethnicity in 2000 and 2010 and projected to 2060 under alternative projection scenarios

Year	NH[a] White	NH Black	Hispanic	NH Asian & Other	Total
Census					
2000	194,552,774	33,947,837	35,305,818	17,615,477	281,421,906
2010	196,817,552	37,685,848	50,477,594	23,764,544	308,745,538
Low scenario					
2020	199,118,409	41,648,248	63,310,300	28,730,878	332,807,835
2030	197,966,553	44,884,450	76,505,495	34,227,395	353,583,893
2040	192,169,027	47,548,405	90,358,651	39,745,063	369,821,146
2050	183,741,983	49,979,255	104,638,585	45,532,584	383,892,407
2060	175,473,820	52,349,393	118,879,806	51,457,476	398,160,495
Middle scenario					
2020	199,312,742	41,775,711	63,784,157	29,022,943	333,895,553
2030	198,817,220	45,451,967	78,654,856	35,547,099	358,471,142
2040	193,887,051	48,768,830	94,875,732	42,484,070	380,015,683
2050	186,334,175	51,987,965	111,731,705	49,749,524	399,803,369
2060	178,950,774	55,302,410	128,780,232	57,234,317	420,267,733
High scenario					
2020	199,507,071	41,903,150	64,257,970	29,314,877	334,983,068
2030	199,668,083	46,019,492	80,803,956	36,866,680	363,358,211
2040	195,606,135	49,989,284	99,391,381	45,223,080	390,209,880
2050	188,928,980	53,996,660	118,821,184	53,967,048	415,713,872
2060	182,432,253	58,255,367	138,674,230	63,012,523	442,374,373

Source: U.S. Census Bureau, 2001, 2011, 2012a

[a]NH refers to nonHispanic; values for categories labeled NH are only for the nonHispanic persons in each race category. Hispanic includes Hispanics of all races

to 2010 (due in large part to the recession), a rate of just 9.7%. The only decade of slower growth was the period from 1930 to 1940 (the period of the Great Depression when the rate of growth was 7.2%). Even under the scenario of high growth (see Table 2.8), no decade would have growth exceeding 8.5% for any decade, and in the middle (preferred) scenario, growth would not exceed 8.1%, the rate of growth from 2010 to 2020. The remaining decades under the middle projection scenario would have rates of growth of 7.4% (2020–2030), 6.0% (2030–2040), 5.2% (2040–2050), and 5.1% (2050–2060). The United States will be a nation that is growing more slowly in the future than it was in the past.

What is also evident (see Table 2.8) is that growth would be nearly entirely due to increases in minority populations. The nonHispanic White population shows a decrease in every decade, except 2010–2020, in every projection scenario except the highest growth scenario, and even in this scenario the nonHispanic White population declines in all decennial periods starting in 2030. For the total projection period for all of the scenarios shown, the nonHispanic White population would decrease

Table 2.8 Percent change in the population in the United States by race/ethnicity from 2000 to 2010 and projected to 2060 under alternative projection scenarios

Time period	NH[a] White	NH Black	Hispanic	NH Asian & Other	Total
2000–2010					
2000–2010	1.2	11.0	43.0	34.9	9.7
Low scenario					
2010–2020	1.2	10.5	25.4	20.9	7.8
2020–2030	−0.6	7.8	20.8	19.1	6.2
2030–2040	−2.9	5.9	18.1	16.1	4.6
2040–2050	−4.4	5.1	15.8	14.6	3.8
2050–2060	−4.5	4.7	13.6	13.0	3.7
2010–2060	−10.8	38.9	135.5	116.5	29.0
Middle scenario					
2010–2020	1.3	10.9	26.4	22.1	8.1
2020–2030	−0.2	8.8	23.3	22.5	7.4
2030–2040	−2.5	7.3	20.6	19.5	6.0
2040–2050	−3.9	6.6	17.8	17.1	5.2
2050–2060	−4.0	6.4	15.3	15.0	5.1
2010–2060	−9.1	46.8	155.1	140.8	36.1
High scenario					
2010–2020	1.4	11.2	27.3	23.4	8.5
2020–2030	0.1	9.8	25.7	25.8	8.5
2030–2040	−2.0	8.6	23.0	22.7	7.4
2040–2050	−3.4	8.0	19.5	19.3	6.5
2050–2060	−3.4	7.9	16.7	16.8	6.4
2010–2060	−7.3	54.6	248.3	165.2	43.3

Source: U.S. Census Bureau, 2001, 2011, 2012a
[a]NH refers to nonHispanic; values for categories labeled NH are only for the nonHispanic persons in each race category. Hispanic includes Hispanics of all races

between 7.3 and 10.8% under the high, medium, and low growth scenarios, while growth in the nonHispanic Black population would be between 38.9 and 54.6%, growth in the Hispanic population is projected to be between 135.5 and 248.3%, and growth for the NonHispanic Asian population would be between 116.5 and 165.2%.

As a result of such changes, the 63.8% of the total population that was nonHispanic White in 2010 would be less than 50% in all scenarios by 2060 (see Table 2.9). The nonHispanic Black population would increase by between 0.9 and 1.0% from 2010 levels by 2060, making up between 13.1 and 13.2% of the total population; the Asian and Other population would increase between 5.2 and 6.5% to become between 12.9 and 14.2% of the population; and Hispanics that represented 16.3% of the population in 2010 would increase their percentage of the total population by between 13.6 and 15.0% and account for between 29.9 and 31.3% of the total population of the United States by 2060. Finally, the data in Table 2.10 indicate that nonHispanic White populations shows declines under all scenarios, and all of the

Table 2.9 Percentage of the population by race/ethnicity in the United States for 2000 and 2010 and projected to 2060 under alternative projection scenarios

Year	NH[a] White	NH Black	Hispanic	NH Asian & Other	Total
Census					
2000	69.1	12.1	12.5	6.3	100.0
2010	63.8	12.2	16.3	7.7	100.0
Low scenario					
2020	59.9	12.5	19.0	8.6	100.0
2030	56.0	12.7	21.6	9.7	100.0
2040	52.0	12.9	24.4	10.7	100.0
2050	47.8	13.0	27.3	11.9	100.0
2060	44.1	13.1	29.9	12.9	100.0
Middle scenario					
2020	59.7	12.5	19.1	8.7	100.0
2030	55.5	12.7	21.9	9.9	100.0
2040	51.0	12.8	25.0	11.2	100.0
2050	46.7	13.0	27.9	12.4	100.0
2060	42.6	13.2	30.6	13.6	100.0
High scenario					
2020	59.5	12.5	19.2	8.8	100.0
2030	55.0	12.7	22.2	10.1	100.0
2040	50.1	12.8	25.5	11.6	100.0
2050	45.4	13.0	28.6	13.0	100.0
2060	41.3	13.2	31.3	14.2	100.0

Source: U.S. Census Bureau, 2001, 2011, 2012a

[a]NH refers to nonHispanic; values for categories labeled NH are only for the nonHispanic persons in each race category. Hispanic includes Hispanics of all races

growth in the population from 2010 to 2060 would be due to minority populations; the nonHispanic Black population would account for between 15.4 and 16.4% of the total population increase, Hispanic populations for between 66 and 76.5%, and nonHispanic Asians and others for between 29.4 and 31.0% of all population growth.

Due to the changes noted above, the age structure of the racial/ethnic group population would change substantially (see Table 2.11). Overall the total population would become older, with the percentage of all persons 65 years of age or older increasing over the projection period in all scenarios for all racial/ethnic groups, from between 5.5 and 15.8% for the Hispanic population from 16.4 to 29.0 for the nonHispanic White population, to between 9.1 and 21.4% of the total population for the nonHispanic Black population, and from 8.0 to 17.5% for nonHispanic Asians and Other population. Overall, the population of the United States would become older, with the percentage of the total population 65 years of age or older increasing from 13.0% in 2010 to between 21.3 and 22.6% in 2060.

Table 2.10 Number and percent of net change in the United States population due to each race/ethnicity group under alternative projection scenarios, 2010–2060

Race/ethnicity	Number	Percent
Low scenario		
NH[a] White	−21,343,732	−23.9
NH Black	14,663,545	16.4
Hispanic	68,402,212	76.5
NH Asian & Other	27,692,932	31.0
Total	89,414,957	100.0
Middle scenario		
NH[a] White	−17,866,778	−16.0
NH Black	17,616,562	15.8
Hispanic	78,302,638	70.2
NH Asian & Other	33,469,773	30.0
Total	111,522,195	100.0
High scenario		
NH[a] White	−14,385,299	−10.8
NH Black	20,569,519	15.4
Hispanic	88,196,636	66.0
NH Asian & Other	39,247,979	29.4
Total	133,628,835	100.0

Source: U.S. Census Bureau, 2011, 2012a

[a]NH refers to nonHispanic; values for categories labeled NH are only for the nonHispanic persons in each race category. Hispanic includes Hispanics of all races

The data in this chapter demonstrate that the population of the United States has shown reduced growth in recent decades and is likely to continue to do so in the future but in 2060 the United States would still have one of the largest populations of any nation in the world. The United States has also become older, with the proportion of its population that is 65 years of age or older likely to increase by roughly 9% from 2010 to 2060. The population would also become more diverse. The U. S. population would become a majority minority nation due in large part to an increase in the Hispanic population. These changes are likely to have significant impacts on the socioeconomic characteristics of the population and affect public and private service related demands in the coming years.

2.4 Historic and Projected Patterns of Household Change

In the last several decades, households in the United States have increased substantially and changed markedly (Jacobsen et al. 2012). As shown in Table 2.12, the total number of households increased by nearly 24.8 million from 1990 to 2010, a total increase of 26.9%. As with population change, this increase was disproportionately due to growth in the minority population. The total number of households with

Table 2.11 U.S. Census Bureau projections of the percentage of the population in the United States by age and race/ethnicity for 2010 and projected to 2060 under alternative projection scenarios

Year	Age group	NH[a] White	NH Black	Hispanic	NH Asian & Other	Total
2010 census						
2010	<18	20.2	27.4	33.9	29.3	24.0
2010	18–24	8.9	11.6	12.2	10.9	9.9
2010	25–44	24.9	27.4	31.2	30.0	26.7
2010	45–64	29.6	24.5	17.2	21.8	26.4
2010	65+	16.4	9.1	5.5	8.0	13.0
Low scenario						
2060	<18	16.4	21.0	26.3	25.0	21.1
2060	18–24	7.0	8.4	9.8	9.2	8.3
2060	25–44	23.0	25.6	26.9	26.4	24.9
2060	45–64	24.6	23.6	21.2	21.9	23.1
2060	65+	29.0	21.4	15.8	17.5	22.6
Middle scenario						
2060	<18	16.4	21.2	26.3	24.9	21.2
2060	18–24	7.0	8.4	9.9	9.2	8.4
2060	25–44	23.1	26.1	27.3	26.9	25.3
2060	45–64	24.7	23.6	21.3	22.2	23.2
2060	65+	28.8	20.7	15.2	16.8	21.9
High scenario						
2060	<18	16.4	21.4	26.4	24.9	21.4
2060	18–24	7.1	8.5	9.9	9.2	8.5
2060	25–44	23.3	26.2	27.7	27.2	25.6
2060	45–64	24.7	23.7	21.4	22.5	23.2
2060	65+	28.5	20.2	14.6	16.2	21.3

Source: U.S. Census Bureau, 2011, 2012a

[a]NH refers to nonHispanic; values for categories labeled NH are only for the nonHispanic persons in each race category. Hispanic includes Hispanics of all races

a nonHispanic White householder (the person in whose name the housing unit is owned or rented) increased by 11.8% from 1990 to 2010, nonHispanic Black households increased by 38.3%, Hispanic households increased by 124.3%, and nonHispanic Asian and Other households increased by 205.1%. As a result of such changes, the percentage of all households with a nonHispanic White householder decreased from 80.2 in 1990 to 70.6% in 2010, while the percentage of all households that were nonHispanic Black increased from 10.8 to 11.8, the percentage of Hispanic households increased from 6.5 to 11.5, and the percentage of nonHispanic Asian and Other households increased from 2.5 to 6.1.

The data in Table 2.13 show that household size and forms have changed. For example, in 1980, 28.5% of all households were households with four or more persons, compared to 24.4% in 2010. On the other hand, the number of one-person

Table 2.12 Number and percentage of households and percent change in households in the United States by race/ethnicity of the householder, 1990–2010

Race/ethnicity	Number			Percent			Percent change		
	1990	2000	2010	1990	2000	2010	1990	2000	2010
NH[a] White	73,633,749	79,093,136	82,333,080	80.2	75.1	70.6	7.4	4.1	11.8
NH Black	9,976,161	11,862,087	13,795,544	10.8	11.2	11.8	18.9	16.3	38.3
Hispanic	6,001,719	9,222,402	13,461,366	6.5	8.7	11.5	53.7	46.0	124.3
NH Asian & Other	2,335,782	5,302,476	7,126,302	2.5	5.0	6.1	127.0	34.4	205.1
Total	91,947,411	105,480,101	116,716,292	100.0	100.0	100.0	14.7	10.7	26.9

Source: U.S. Census Bureau, 1991, 2001, 2011

[a]NH refers to nonHispanic; values for categories labeled NH are only for the nonHispanic persons in each race category. Hispanic includes Hispanics of all races.

households increased from 22.7 in 1980 to 26.7% of all households in 2010 and the number of two-person households from 31.3 to 32.8% of all households. In fact, the percentage of households in all household size categories of three or more decreased while the proportion of one- or two-person households increased. Households have become smaller.

The relative composition of all households has also changed. As shown in Table 2.13, the number of family households (households consisting of two or more people related by kinship, marriage, or adoption) decreased from 73.7 in 1980 to 66.4% of all households in 2010 while married-couple households decreased from 60.8 to 48.3% of all households. Female-householder households increased from 10.8% to 13.1% and male-householder households from 2.1% in 1980 to 5.0% in 2010. Nonfamily households (consisting of a single person or two or more unrelated persons living in the same housing unit) increased from 26.3% of all households in 1980 to 33.6% of all households in 2010.

The data in Table 2.13 verify the often-noted fact that American households are changing both in size and in form. The data in Table 2.14 provide projections of the number of households obtained by multiplying householder rates by race/ethnicity

Table 2.13 Number, percentage of, and percent change in households by size and type, 1980–2010

	Households				Percent change in number of households		
Size/type of household	1980	1990	2000	2010	1980–1990	1990–2000	2000–2010
Total households (in thousands)	80,776	91,947	105,480	116,716	13.8	14.7	10.7
Households by size							
One-person	22.7	24.6	25.8	26.7	23.4	20.6	14.6
Two-person	31.3	32.0	32.6	32.8	16.3	16.9	11.1
Three-person	17.5	17.4	16.5	16.1	13.0	9.2	7.6
Four-person	15.7	15.1	14.2	13.4	9.4	8.0	4.4
Five-person	7.5	6.7	6.6	6.5	2.1	12.1	8.7
Six-person	3.1	2.5	2.5	2.6	−8.7	14.6	16.7
Seven or more person	2.2	1.7	1.8	1.9	−10.3	15.9	23.0
Households by type							
Family	73.7	71.0	68.1	66.4	9.7	9.9	8.0
Married couple family	60.8	56.1	51.7	48.3	5.1	5.6	3.7
Female householder	10.8	11.6	12.2	13.1	22.2	21.2	18.2
Male householder	2.1	3.3	4.2	5.0	76.6	43.6	31.5
Nonfamily	26.3	29.0	31.9	33.6	25.5	26.5	16.3

Source: U.S. Census Bureau, 1981, 1991, 2001, 2011

Table 2.14 Number of households in the United States by race/ethnicity of the householder and projected to 2060 under alternative projection scenarios

Year	NH[a] White	NH Black	Hispanic	NH Asian & Other	Total
Low scenario					
2010	82,333,080	13,795,544	13,461,366	7,126,302	116,716,292
2020	86,400,183	16,217,526	18,042,508	8,920,336	129,580,553
2030	88,138,518	18,160,183	22,760,952	10,844,252	139,903,905
2040	86,939,619	19,738,132	27,752,527	12,819,996	147,250,274
2050	83,856,280	21,150,107	32,941,851	14,881,897	152,830,135
2060	80,831,785	22,529,219	38,254,850	17,017,725	158,633,579
Middle scenario					
2010	82,333,080	13,795,544	13,461,366	7,126,302	116,716,292
2020	86,468,741	16,262,093	18,168,502	9,009,401	129,908,737
2030	88,452,999	18,364,603	23,362,849	11,253,292	141,433,743
2040	87,603,182	20,188,859	29,063,515	13,682,913	150,538,469
2050	84,901,654	21,912,269	35,068,394	16,244,019	158,126,336
2060	82,290,325	23,680,466	41,317,810	18,933,911	166,222,512
High scenario					
2010	82,333,080	13,795,544	13,461,366	7,126,302	116,716,292
2020	86,537,296	16,306,643	18,294,429	9,098,379	130,236,747
2030	88,767,519	18,569,011	23,964,766	11,662,149	142,963,445
2040	88,266,744	20,639,595	30,374,618	14,545,635	153,826,592
2050	85,947,075	22,674,411	37,194,943	17,606,033	163,422,462
2060	83,749,225	24,831,700	44,380,547	20,850,098	173,811,570

Source: Projections by the authors derived from U.S. Census Bureau, 2011, 2012a
[a]NH refers to nonHispanic; values for categories labeled NH are only for the nonHispanic persons in each race category. Hispanic includes Hispanics of all races

to the projected population 15 years of age or older. The data in this table point to an increase (under the middle projection scenario) from 116,716,292 households in 2010 to 166,222,512 in 2060, an increase of 49,506,220 or 42.4% from 2010 to 2060 (see Table 2.15). As with population, this increase in the number of households represents a significant decline in the rate of growth in households. If the rate of growth in households from 1990 to 2010 prevailed from 2010 to 2060, the overall increase would be more than 67%. The household growth rate would decline. However, since these projections were completed using household formation rates from 2010, the decline is largely due to the underlying decrease in the projected rate of growth of the population.

The data in Table 2.15 also show that just as with population the increase in the number of households would be largely dependent on the growth in minority households. Thus, only in 2010–2020 and 2020–2030 are there any increases in the number of nonHispanic White households, and these increases are substantially smaller (in percentage terms) than those for households from all other racial and ethnic

Table 2.15 Percent change in households in the United States by race/ethnicity of the householder and projected to 2060 under alternative projection scenarios

Period	NH[a] White	NH Black	Hispanic	NH Asian & Other	Total
Low scenario					
2010–2020	4.9	17.6	34.0	25.2	11.0
2020–2030	2.0	12.0	26.2	21.6	8.0
2030–2040	−1.4	8.7	21.9	18.2	5.3
2040–2050	−3.5	7.2	18.7	16.1	3.8
2050–2060	−3.6	6.5	16.1	14.4	3.8
2010–2060	−1.8	63.3	184.2	138.8	35.9
Middle scenario					
2010–2020	5.0	17.9	35.0	26.4	11.3
2020–2030	2.3	12.9	28.6	24.9	8.9
2030–2040	−1.0	9.9	24.4	21.6	6.4
2040–2050	−3.1	8.5	20.7	18.7	5.0
2050–2060	−3.1	8.1	17.8	16.6	5.1
2010–2060	−0.1	71.7	206.9	165.7	42.4
High scenario					
2010–2020	5.1	18.2	35.9	27.7	11.6
2020–2030	2.6	13.9	31.0	28.2	9.8
2030–2040	−0.6	11.2	26.7	24.7	7.6
2040–2050	−2.6	9.9	22.5	21.0	6.2
2050–2060	−2.6	9.5	19.3	18.4	6.4
2010–2060	1.7	80.0	229.7	192.6	48.9

Source: Projections by the authors derived from U.S. Census Bureau, 2011, 2012a
[a]NH refers to nonHispanic; values for categories labeled NH are only for the nonHispanic persons in each race category. Hispanic includes Hispanics of all races

groups. Only under the highest growth scenario is there an increase in the number of nonHispanic White households from 2010 to 2060. As shown in Table 2.15, under the middle projection scenario the number of nonHispanic White households decreases by 0.1% from 2010 to 2060 while the number of nonHispanic Black households increases by 71.7%, the number of Hispanic households increases by 206.9%, and the number of nonHispanic Asian and Other households increases by 165.7% from 2010 to 2060.

As a result of these changes, the proportion of all households that are minority households would increase substantially from 2010 to 2060 (see Table 2.16). The percentage of all households with a nonHispanic White householder would decrease (under the middle projection scenario) from 70.6% in 2010 to 49.5% in 2060 while increased proportions are evident for all minority populations. The percentage of nonHispanic Black households would increase from 11.8 to 14.2, the percentage of all households that are Hispanic would increase from 11.5 to 24.9, and the percentage of all households that are nonHispanic Asian and Other would increase from 6.1 to 11.4%.

Table 2.16 Percent of total households in the United States by race/ethnicity from 2010 to 2060 under alternative scenarios

Period	NH[a] White	NH Black	Hispanic	NH Asian & Other	Total
Low scenario					
2010	70.6	11.8	11.5	6.1	100.0
2020	66.7	12.5	13.9	6.9	100.0
2030	62.9	13.0	16.3	7.8	100.0
2040	59.1	13.4	18.8	8.7	100.0
2050	54.9	13.8	21.6	9.7	100.0
2060	51.0	14.2	24.1	10.7	100.0
Middle scenario					
2010	70.6	11.8	11.5	6.1	100.0
2020	66.6	12.5	14.0	6.9	100.0
2030	62.5	13.0	16.5	8.0	100.0
2040	58.2	13.4	19.3	9.1	100.0
2050	53.6	13.9	22.2	10.3	100.0
2060	49.5	14.2	24.9	11.4	100.0
High scenario					
2010	70.6	11.8	11.5	6.1	100.0
2020	66.5	12.5	14.0	7.0	100.0
2030	62.0	13.0	16.8	8.2	100.0
2040	57.4	13.4	19.7	9.5	100.0
2050	52.5	13.9	22.8	10.8	100.0
2060	48.2	14.3	25.5	12.0	100.0

Source: Projections by the authors derived from U.S. Census Bureau, 2011, 2012a

[a]NH refers to nonHispanic; values for categories labeled NH are only for the nonHispanic persons in each race category. Hispanic includes Hispanics of all races

When examined in terms of net change from 2010 to 2060 (see Table 2.17), the proportion of change in households due to nonHispanic White households would decline by −0.1% while 20% of the increase would be due to growth in the number of nonHispanic Black households, 56.2% would be due to growth in the number of Hispanic households, and 23.9% to an increase in the number of nonHispanic Asian and Other households.

The data in Table 2.18 show that households would also come to have older householders. For example, in 2010, 22.2% of all householders were 65 years of age or older, by 2040, 33.4% of all householders, and by 2060, 34.2% of all householders would be 65 years of age or older. There would remain substantial differences in the age structures of minority households compared to nonHispanic White households. In 2010, 25.6% of nonHispanic White, 16.7% of nonHispanic Black, 11.1% of Hispanic, and 13.5% of nonHispanic Asian and Other households had a householder who was 65 years of age or older, but in 2060, 41.1% of nonHispanic White, 32.7% of nonHispanic Black, 25.4% of Hispanic, and 25.6% of nonHispanic Asian and Other households would have a householder who is 65 years of age or older. Members of all racial and ethnic populations are expected to age but minority

Table 2.17 Number and percent of net change in United States households due to each race/ethnicity group under alternative projection scenarios, 2010–2060

Race/ethnicity	Number	Percent
Low scenario		
NH[a] White	−1,501,295	−3.6
NH Black	8,733,675	20.8
Hispanic	24,793,484	59.2
NH Asian & Other	9,891,423	23.6
Total	41,917,287	100.0
Middle scenario		
NH[a] White	−42,755	−0.1
NH Black	9,884,922	20.0
Hispanic	27,856,444	56.2
NH Asian & Other	11,807,609	23.9
Total	49,506,220	100.0

Source: Projections by the authors derived from U.S. Census Bureau, 2011, 2012a

[a]NH refers to nonHispanic; values for categories labeled NH are only for the nonHispanic persons in each race category Hispanic includes Hispanics of all races

households are expected to continue to be younger than nonHispanic White households.

The data in Table 2.19 show that the overall distribution of households by type is not expected to change substantially in terms of the total distribution of households between 2010 and 2060. However, there would continue to be substantial differences among racial and ethnic groups. For example, in 2010, 78.4% of Hispanics were in family households, as would be true for 76.2% of Hispanic households in 2060. These values would be 64.3 and 61.9% for nonHispanic Whites, 64.8 and 62.6% for nonHispanic Blacks, and 71.1 and 70.4% for nonHispanic Asians and Others. On the other hand, the percentages in nonfamily households were 21.6 in 2010 and 23.8 in 2060 for Hispanics, 35.7 and 38.1 for nonHispanic Whites, 35.2 and 37.4 for nonHispanic Blacks, and 28.9 and 29.6 for nonHispanic Asians and Others.

2.5 Summary

In this chapter we have examined the recent patterns of change in the number and characteristics of the population and households and presented and described projections of the number and characteristics of the projected future population and households of the United States. The analysis in this chapter indicates the following:

1. The population of the United States has shown continued growth and only during the depression of the 1930s, the 1980s, and the 2000 to 2010 decade was the decade rate of growth less than 10%.

Table 2.18 Percent of total households in the United States by age and race/ethnicity using the middle projection scenario

Year/age of householder	NH[a] White	NH Black	Hispanic	NH Asian & Other	Total
2010					
15–24	4.0	5.6	6.6	5.7	4.6
25–34	13.4	17.3	23.2	20.3	15.4
35–44	16.2	20.4	25.6	23.3	18.2
45–54	21.2	22.6	20.9	21.6	21.3
55–64	19.6	17.4	12.6	15.6	18.3
65–74	13.0	9.8	6.6	8.1	11.6
75–84	8.8	5.2	3.5	4.1	7.5
85+	3.8	1.7	1.0	1.3	3.1
2020					
15–24	3.5	4.4	5.6	5.0	4.0
25–34	13.5	18.5	20.6	19.4	15.5
35–44	14.7	18.0	23.3	21.8	16.8
45–54	15.9	17.9	20.8	19.8	17.1
55–64	20.2	19.4	15.5	16.3	19.2
65–74	17.9	13.8	8.8	11.1	15.7
75–84	10.1	6.0	4.0	5.0	8.4
85+	4.2	2.0	1.4	1.6	3.3
2040					
15–24	3.2	3.9	4.8	4.7	3.7
25–34	11.4	14.5	18.0	17.4	13.6
35–44	14.0	17.4	20.7	20.3	16.3
45–54	16.0	19.2	19.2	19.4	17.5
55–64	15.4	15.8	15.7	15.5	15.5
65–74	15.6	14.1	12.0	11.8	14.3
75–84	16.2	11.1	7.3	7.8	13.1
85+	8.2	4.0	2.3	3.1	6.0
2060					
15–24	2.9	3.4	4.4	4.4	3.4
25–34	11.1	13.6	16.2	16.1	13.3
35–44	14.0	17.0	19.4	19.5	16.5
45–54	14.8	16.6	18.7	18.6	16.5
55–64	16.1	16.7	15.9	15.8	16.1
65–74	17.5	17.0	12.8	12.8	15.7
75–84	14.3	10.5	8.7	8.6	11.7
85+	9.3	5.2	3.9	4.2	6.8

Source: Projections by the authors derived from U.S. Census Bureau, 2011, 2012a
[a]NH refers to nonHispanic; values for categories labeled NH are only for the nonHispanic persons in each race category. Hispanic includes Hispanics of all races

Table 2.19 Number and percentage of households in the United States by type of household and race/ethnicity of the householder in 2010 and projected for 2060 under the middle projection scenario

	NH[a] White		NH Black		Hispanic		NH Other		Total	
Household type	Number	%	Number	%	Number	%	Number	%	Number	%
2010										
Family households	52,977,468	64.3	8,934,833	64.8	10,557,925	78.4	5,068,070	71.1	77,538,296	66.4
Married-couple family:	42,087,655	51.1	3,917,181	28.4	6,742,765	50.1	3,762,776	52.8	56,510,377	48.4
With own children	15,669,198	19.0	1,742,097	12.6	4,206,967	31.3	1,970,006	27.6	23,588,268	20.2
Without own children	26,418,457	32.1	2,175,084	15.8	2,535,798	18.8	1,792,770	25.2	32,922,109	28.2
Other family	10,889,813	13.2	5,017,652	36.4	3,815,160	28.3	1,305,294	18.3	21,027,919	18.0
Male householder, spouse absent	3,292,569	4.0	866,122	6.3	1,226,466	9.1	392,413	5.5	5,777,570	5.0
With own children	1,605,555	2.0	399,523	2.9	627,517	4.7	156,829	2.2	2,789,424	2.4
Without own children	1,687,014	2.0	466,599	3.4	598,949	4.4	235,584	3.3	2,988,146	2.6
Female householder, spouse absent	7,597,244	9.2	4,151,530	30.1	2,588,694	19.2	912,881	12.8	15,250,349	13.1
With own children	3,875,646	4.7	2,387,394	17.3	1,629,845	12.1	473,027	6.6	8,365,912	7.2
Without own children	3,721,598	4.5	1,764,136	12.8	958,849	7.1	439,854	6.2	6,884,437	5.9
Nonfamily households	29,355,612	35.7	4,860,711	35.2	2,903,441	21.6	2,058,232	28.9	39,177,996	33.6
1 person	23,523,993	28.6	4,127,147	29.9	2,043,012	15.2	1,510,757	21.2	31,204,909	26.7
2 or more person	5,831,619	7.1	733,564	5.3	860,429	6.4	547,475	7.7	7,973,087	6.8
Total households	82,333,080	100.0	13,795,544	100.0	13,461,366	100.0	7,126,302	100.0	116,716,292	100.0
2060										
Family households	50,961,433	61.9	14,820,364	62.6	31,482,958	76.2	13,330,908	70.4	110,595,663	66.5
Married-couple family:	40,848,287	49.6	6,713,381	28.3	20,428,653	49.4	9,964,898	52.6	77,955,219	46.9
With own children	15,207,782	18.5	2,985,658	12.6	12,745,909	30.8	5,217,135	27.6	36,156,484	21.8
Without own children	25,640,505	31.2	3,727,723	15.7	7,682,744	18.6	4,747,763	25.1	41,798,735	25.1

(continued)

Table 2.19 (continued)

Household type	NH[a] White Number	%	NH Black Number	%	Hispanic Number	%	NH Other Number	%	Total Number	%
Other family	10,113,146	12.3	8,106,983	34.2	11,054,305	26.8	3,366,010	17.8	32,640,444	19.6
Male householder, spouse absent	2,938,550	3.6	1,398,827	5.9	3,381,637	8.2	978,645	5.2	8,697,659	5.2
With own children	1,432,925	1.7	645,248	2.7	1,730,203	4.2	391,118	2.1	4,199,494	2.5
Without own children	1,505,625	1.8	753,579	3.2	1,651,434	4.0	587,527	3.1	4,498,165	2.7
Female householder, spouse absent	7,174,596	8.7	6,708,156	28.3	7,672,668	18.6	2,387,365	12.6	23,942,785	14.4
With own children	3,660,037	4.4	3,857,617	16.3	4,830,721	11.7	1,237,059	6.5	13,585,434	8.2
Without own children	3,514,559	4.3	2,850,539	12.0	2,841,947	6.9	1,150,306	6.1	10,357,351	6.2
Nonfamily households	31,328,892	38.1	8,860,102	37.4	9,834,852	23.8	5,603,003	29.6	55,626,849	33.5
1 person	26,230,770	31.9	7,734,271	32.7	7,511,014	18.2	4,331,182	22.9	45,807,237	27.6
2 or more person	5,098,122	6.2	1,125,831	4.8	2,323,838	5.6	1,271,821	6.7	9,819,612	5.9
Total households	82,290,325	100.0	23,680,466	100.0	41,317,810	100.0	18,933,911	100.0	166,222,512	100.0

Source: Projections by the authors derived from U.S. Census Bureau, 2011, 2012a

[a]NH refers to nonHispanic; values for categories labeled NH are only for the nonHispanic persons in each race category. Hispanic includes Hispanics of all races

2. Growth has been primarily from natural increase. In only one decade, 1900–1910, did growth through immigration exceed growth through natural increase.
3. Population growth has been characterized by increased aging of the population (from a median age of 22.9 years in 1900 to 37.2 years of age in 2010) and racial/ethnic diversification. In 1990, 75.6% of the population was nonHispanic White, 11.7% nonHispanic Black, 12.5% Hispanic and 3.6% nonHispanic Asian and Other. By 2010 these percentages were 63.7, 12.2, 16.3 and 7.7% for nonHispanic Whites, nonHispanic Blacks, Hispanics and nonHispanic Asians and Others respectively. In 2010 13.0% of the population was 65 years of age or older.
4. The number and diversity of both households and populations would increase in the future. According to the Census Bureau's middle projection scenario projections, the population of the United States would increase from the 308.7 million that it was in 2010 to 420.3 million by 2060 and its population that was 63.8% nonHispanic White, 12.2% nonHispanic Black, 16.3% Hispanic and 7.7% nonHispanic Asian and Other in 2010 would become 42.6% nonHispanic White, 13.2% nonHispanic Black, 30.6% Hispanic, and 13.6% nonHispanic Asian and Other by 2060. Similarly, the number of households would increase from the 116.7 million that it was in 2010 to 166.2 million in 2060 (under the middle projection scenario) with the racial/ethnic composition of householders changing from 70.6% nonHispanic White, 11.8% nonHispanic Black, 11.5% Hispanic and 6.1% nonHispanic Asian and Other in 2010 to 49.5%, 14.2%, 24.9% and 11.4% of households in these racial/ethnic categories in 2060 (under the middle projection scenario).

The data in this chapter clearly indicate that both households and the population of the United States will continue to grow and diversify. The population will become larger, older and more racially and ethnically diverse.

References

Coale, A. J. (1986). Demographic effects of below-replacement fertility and their social implications. *Population and Development Review, 12*, 203–216.

Jacobsen, L. A., Mather, M., & Dupuis, G. (2012). Household change in the United States. *Population Bulletin, 67*(1), 2–12.

Martin, P. (2013). *The global challenge of managing migration*. Washington, DC: Population Reference Bureau. http://www.prb.org/pdf13/global-migration.pdf. Accessed 12 Jan 2014.

Martin, J. A., Hamilton, B. E., Ventura, S. J., Osterman, M. J. K., Wilson, E. D., & Mathews, T. J. (2012). *Births: Final data for 2010* (National vital statistics reports, Vol. 61(1)). Hyattsville: National Center for Health Statistics.

Mather, M. (2012). *Fact sheet: The decline in U.S. fertility*. Washington, DC: Population Reference Bureau.

Murdock, S. H. (1995). *An America challenged: Population change and the future of the United States*. Bolder: Westview Press.

Murphy, S. L., Xu, J., & Kochanek, K. D. (2013). *Deaths: Final data for 2010* (National vital statistics reports, Vol. 61(4)). Hyattsville: National Center for Health Statistics.

Smallwood, S., & Chamberlain, J. (2005). Replacement fertility, what has it been and what does it mean? *Population Trends, 119*, 16–27.

U.S. Census Bureau. (1981). *1980 census of population and housing, summary tape file 1*. Washington, DC: U.S. Census Bureau.

U.S. Census Bureau. (1991). *1990 census of population and housing, summary tape file 1*. Washington, DC: U.S. Census Bureau.

U.S. Census Bureau. (2001). *2000 census summary file 1*. Washington, DC: U.S. Census Bureau.

U.S. Census Bureau. (2002). *2000 census special report CENSR-4*. Washington, DC: U.S. Census Bureau.

U.S. Census Bureau. (2011). *2010 census summary file 1*. Washington, DC: U.S. Census Bureau.

U.S. Census Bureau. (2012a). *2012 National population projections*. Washington, DC: U.S. Census Bureau.

U.S. Census Bureau. (2012b). *CPS historical geographical mobility/migration tables*. Washington, DC: U.S. Census Bureau. http://www.census.gov/hhes/migration/data/cps/historical.html. Accessed 13 Sept 2012.

U.S. Census Bureau. (2012c). The 2012 statistical abstract: Pdf version. Washington, DC: U.S. Census Bureau. http://www.census.gov/compendia/statab/2012edition.html. Accessed 13 Sept 2014.

U.S. Department of Homeland Security. (2012). *2012 yearbook of immigration statistics*. Washington, DC: U.S. Department of Homeland Security.

Chapter 3
Effects of Population Change on the Size and Characteristics of the Labor Force of the United States

Among the most critical factors impacted by population change are the size and characteristics of the labor force (United States Bureau of Labor Statistics 2012; Toossi 2012). The size, age, sex, race/ethnicity, and other characteristics of workers affect the competitiveness of the labor force and the overall economic competitiveness of the nation (Altonji et al. 2012; Crespo Cuaresma et al. 2014). In this chapter we examine recent trends in the size and characteristics of the labor force of the United States and describe the implications of these changes for the occupations, educational characteristics, and wage and salary characteristics of the labor force given expected future change. We examine both the challenges and opportunities inherent in the changing characteristics of future labor forces and delineate how changes in specific demographic characteristics of the labor force may impact both members of the labor force and the overall economic conditions of households and individuals in the United States in the coming decades.

3.1 Current Characteristics and Recent Trends in the Labor Force of the United States

The data in Tables 3.1, 3.2, and 3.3 show key characteristics and recent patterns of change in the labor force of the United States. As shown in Table 3.1, from a labor force of nearly 28.4 million in 1900, the labor force of the United States increased to nearly 142.6 million by 2000 and to nearly 153.9 million by 2010. Reflecting the underlying patterns of demographic change, the largest numerical and percentage increases occurred in the 1960s, 1970s, and 1980s as the children of the baby boom period (born between 1946 and 1964) reached working ages and participated in the labor force. These periods showed increases of roughly 13.1, 24.2, and 18.9 million workers, representing increases of 18.8, 29.3, and 17.7%, respectively. These data also show the effects of the baby bust generations with the decline in growth to only 7.9% from 2000 to 2010.

S.H. Murdock et al., *Population Change in the United States*,
DOI 10.1007/978-94-017-7288-4_3

Table 3.1 Civilian labor force in the United States, 1900–2020 (annual averages in thousands)

Year	Labor force	Change from preceding period	Percent change from preceding period
1900	28,376	–	–
1910	36,709	8,333	29.4
1920	41,340	4,631	12.6
1930	48,523	7,188	17.4
1940	55,640	7,112	14.7
1950	62,208	6,568	11.8
1960	69,628	7,420	11.9
1970	82,771	13,087	18.8
1980	106,940	24,225	29.3
1990	125,840	18,900	17.7
2000	142,583	16,743	13.3
2010	153,889	11,306	7.9

Source: Carter et al. 2006, Historical Statistics of the United States: Earliest Times to the Present, Table Ba478-486 and Ba487-506; and U.S. Census Bureau, Statistical Abstract of the United States, 2012; U.S. Census Bureau and U.S. Bureau of Labor Statistics, 1981, 1991, 2001, 2011

Table 3.2 Characteristics of the civilian labor force in the United States, 1990–2010 (decennial census and annual averages in thousands)

				Percent change	
Characteristics[a]	1990	2000	2010	1990–2000	2000–2010
Total civilian labor force	123,473	137,669	155,717	11.5	13.1
Male labor force	66,986	73,285	81,750	9.4	11.6
Female labor force	56,487	64,383	73,967	14.0	14.9
Percent of population	64.9	63.4	64.0	–	–
Percent of male population	74.0	69.8	69.1	–	–
Percent of female population	56.7	57.4	59.2	–	–
NH[b] White labor force	101,526	100,178	102,939	−1.3	2.8
NH Black labor force	13,095	14,454	17,689	10.4	22.4
Hispanic labor force	10,022	14,720	23,694	46.9	61.0
NH Asian & Other races labor force	8,853	8,318	11,448	−6.0	37.6
Percent of NH White population	66.8	64.4	63.6	–	–
Percent of NH Black population	63.3	59.4	61.7	–	–
Percent of Hispanic population	67.0	60.9	67.4	–	–
Percent of NH Asian & Other population	64.9	63.1	65.1	–	–

Source: U.S. Census Bureau, 1992, 2002, 2003, 2011a, b, c

[a]For population and labor force age 16 and older

[b]NH refers to nonHispanic; values for categories labeled NH are only for the nonHispanic persons in each category. Hispanic includes Hispanics of all races

Other recent changes in the labor force from 1990 through 2010 are shown in Table 3.2. Of particular importance are the more rapid growth in the female labor force (a 14.9% increase from 2000 to 2010) and the rapid growth of minority

Table 3.3 Civilian labor force participation rates in the United States by sex, age, and race/ethnicity, civilian labor force, 2000 and 2010, and percent change in labor force, 2000–2010

	Participation rate (percent)		Civilian labor force		% change in labor force
Group	2000	2010	2000	2010	2000–2010
Total, 16+ years	63.4	64.0	137,668,798	155,716,908	13.1
Male, 16+	69.8	69.1	73,285,305	81,749,755	11.5
16–19	49.5	36.2	4,059,115	3,305,067	−18.6
20–24	74.6	72.6	7,243,298	7,999,006	10.4
25–34	83.8	85.9	16,675,419	17,731,562	6.3
35–44	85.3	88.0	19,457,194	17,989,878	−7.5
45–54	84.7	85.4	15,609,549	18,905,238	21.1
55–59	74.7	77.6	4,822,693	7,385,681	53.1
60–64	54.2	59.7	2,773,103	4,823,786	73.9
65+	18.4	20.8	2,644,934	3,609,537	36.5
Female, 16+	57.4	59.2	64,383,493	73,967,153	14.9
16–19	50.1	38.4	3,871,206	3,329,521	−14.0
20–24	71.4	71.5	6,657,887	7,561,764	13.6
25–34	72.5	76.8	14,264,948	15,691,256	10.0
35–44	73.8	76.6	17,057,131	15,810,532	−7.3
45–54	73.8	76.3	14,136,982	17,438,762	23.4
55–59	59.8	67.6	4,145,226	6,859,000	65.5
60–64	39.8	50.6	2,256,302	4,424,343	96.1
65+	9.7	12.5	1,993,811	2,851,975	43.0
NH[a] White, 16+	64.4	63.6	100,177,990	102,939,056	2.8
Male	71.6	68.9	53,734,245	54,317,080	1.1
Female	57.7	58.5	46,443,745	48,621,976	4.7
NH Black, 16+	59.4	61.7	14,453,507	17,688,799	22.4
Male	59.5	60.7	6,663,955	8,116,324	21.8
Female	59.4	62.6	7,789,552	9,572,475	22.9
NH Asian & Other, 16+	63.1	65.1	8,317,584	11,395,026	37.0
Male	69.5	70.6	4,396,844	5,847,772	33.0
Female	57.7	58.5	46,443,745	48,621,976	4.7
Hispanic, 16+	60.9	67.4	14,719,717	23,694,027	61.0
Male	68.6	75.7	8,490,261	13,468,579	58.6
Female	52.9	58.9	6,229,456	10,225,448	64.1

Source: U.S. Census Bureau, 1992, 2002, 2011a, 2011b

[a]NH refers to nonHispanic; values for categories labeled NH are only for the nonHispanic persons in each category. Hispanic includes Hispanics of all races

workforces compared to that of nonHispanic Whites. Whereas the number of nonHispanic White workforce members showed an increase of only 2.8% from 2000 to 2010, the size of the Hispanic labor force increased by 61%, the Asian and Other racial/ethnic group workforce increased by 37.6%, and the nonHispanic Black labor force increased by 22.4%. As a result of such patterns, the percentages of the Hispanic and Asian and Other populations in the workforce increased throughout the period from 1990 to 2010, while the percentages in the nonHispanic White labor force and nonHispanic Black groups decreased. This largely reflects the younger age structure of the nonHispanic Asian and Other and Hispanic populations.

Also apparent is the growth in the number of women in the labor force compared to the growth in the number of males in the labor force. Although the total number of males in the labor force remained larger, the number of women in the United States labor force increased by nearly 17.5 million from 1990 to 2010 compared to an increase of 14.8 million for males. The growth in both the number of women and the number of minorities in the labor force is clearly evident in these data.

Table 3.3 provides detailed information on the labor force participation rate and the size and percent change in the labor force from 2000 to 2010. The data in this table further indicate that the percentage of women in the labor force has increased among all racial/ethnic groups but that there have been declines in participation rates for White males (from 71.6 to 68.9%). Similarly, the data in this table indicate that whereas the nonHispanic White labor force increased by only 2.8% from 2000 to 2010, the nonHispanic Black labor force increased by 22.4%, the nonHispanic Asian and Other labor force increased by 37.0%, and the Hispanic labor force increased by 61.0%. These data reinforce the patterns shown in Chapter 2 that indicate that minority populations would be increasingly responsible for the change that occurs not only in populations but in the labor force and labor force productivity in the coming decades.

3.2 Future Characteristics of the Labor Force of the United States

The data in Tables 3.4, 3.5, 3.6, 3.7, 3.8, and 3.9 show projections of the size and characteristics of the United States labor force from 2010 to 2060. Three scenarios reflecting low, moderate, and high rates of population growth are shown. These data show a range of total workforce size from 155,716,908 in 2010 to between 184,809,278 (under the low growth scenario) and 207,651,964 by 2060 (under the high growth scenario) (see Table 3.4).

What is apparent under all of the projected scenarios (see Table 3.4) is that the absolute size of the nonHispanic White labor force and its proportion (see also Table 3.5) of the total labor force would decline. From 102.9 million in 2010, the nonHispanic White labor force would decline to between 83.2 and 87.1 million by 2060. At the same time, its proportion of the labor force would decline from 66.1% to between 42 and 45% (depending on the scenario).

The growth in minority labor forces would show very different patterns. As shown in Table 3.4, the nonHispanic Black labor force would increase from the 17.7 million it was in 2010 to between 23.2 (under the low growth scenario) and 26.1 million (under the high growth scenario) by 2060. The Hispanic labor force is

Table 3.4 Projections of the civilian labor force in the United States from 2010 to 2060 by race/ethnicity under alternative scenarios

Year	NH[a] White	NH Black	Hispanic	NH Asian & Other	Total
Low scenario					
2010	102,939,056	17,688,799	23,694,027	11,395,026	155,716,908
2020	99,494,751	19,322,356	29,917,502	13,537,867	162,272,476
2030	94,303,820	20,230,981	35,766,795	15,864,930	166,166,526
2040	91,762,724	21,512,694	41,954,677	18,389,949	173,620,044
2050	88,079,361	22,527,327	48,376,156	20,957,278	179,940,122
2060	83,193,406	23,166,380	54,897,134	23,552,358	184,809,278
Middle scenario					
2010	102,939,056	17,688,799	23,694,027	11,395,026	155,716,908
2020	99,610,787	19,390,991	30,187,710	13,700,092	162,889,580
2030	94,806,097	20,527,482	36,953,630	16,569,545	168,856,754
2040	92,772,446	22,137,201	44,380,558	19,812,502	179,102,707
2050	89,590,132	23,539,014	52,122,896	23,124,432	188,376,474
2060	85,162,226	24,618,302	59,993,621	26,456,470	196,230,619
High scenario					
2010	102,939,056	17,688,799	23,694,027	11,395,026	155,716,908
2020	99,726,808	19,459,614	30,457,866	13,862,204	163,506,492
2030	95,308,357	20,823,968	38,140,450	17,273,943	171,546,718
2040	93,782,156	22,761,708	46,806,522	21,234,941	184,585,327
2050	91,101,063	24,550,696	55,869,412	25,291,674	196,812,845
2060	87,132,032	26,070,250	65,088,871	29,360,811	207,651,964

Source: Projections by the authors derived from U.S. Census Bureau, 2011a, 2011b, 2011c, 2012
[a]NH refers to nonHispanic; values for categories labeled NH are only for the nonHispanic persons in each category. Hispanic includes Hispanics of all races

projected to increase from 23.7 million in 2010 to between 54.9 and 65.1 million under the low and high growth immigration scenarios, respectively, by 2060, and the nonHispanic Asian and Other racial/ethnic group is projected to increase from 11.4 million in 2010 to between 23.6 million (under the low growth scenario) and 29.4 million (under the high growth scenario).

Overall (see Table 3.5) whereas nonHispanic Whites accounted for 66.1% of the total labor force in 2010, by 2060 they would account for between about 42 to 45%. Under all of the scenarios their proportion of the total labor force would drop below 50% sometime between 2040 and 2050.

Among minority populations, the nonHispanic Black labor force accounts for a relatively stable percentage of the labor force, that is between 12.5 and 12.6% of the labor force (up from 11.4 in 2010) by 2060. It is projected to continue to account for about one of every eight workers. The Hispanic and nonHispanic Asian and Other populations would, as with the population, account for a large percentage of all growth in the labor force and for increasing proportions of the total labor force. As shown in Table 3.6, Hispanics would increase the size of their labor force

Table 3.5 Percent of the civilian labor force in the United States by race/ethnicity in 2010 and projected through 2060 under alternative scenarios (percentage within year)

Year	NH[a] White	NH Black	Hispanic	NH Asian & Other	Total
Low scenario					
2010	66.1	11.4	15.2	7.3	100.0
2020	61.3	11.9	18.4	8.4	100.0
2030	56.8	12.2	21.5	9.5	100.0
2040	52.9	12.4	24.2	10.5	100.0
2050	48.9	12.5	26.9	11.7	100.0
2060	45.0	12.5	29.7	12.8	100.0
Middle scenario					
2010	66.1	11.4	15.2	7.3	100.0
2020	61.2	11.9	18.5	8.4	100.0
2030	56.1	12.2	21.9	9.8	100.0
2040	51.8	12.4	24.8	11.0	100.0
2050	47.6	12.5	27.7	12.2	100.0
2060	43.4	12.5	30.6	13.5	100.0
High scenario					
2010	66.1	11.4	15.2	7.3	100.0
2020	61.0	11.9	18.6	8.5	100.0
2030	55.6	12.1	22.2	10.1	100.0
2040	50.8	12.3	25.4	11.5	100.0
2050	46.3	12.5	28.4	12.8	100.0
2060	42.0	12.6	31.3	14.1	100.0

Source: Projections by the authors derived from U.S. Census Bureau, 2011a, 2011b, 2011c, 2012
[a]NH refers to nonHispanic; values for categories labeled NH are only for the nonHispanic persons in each category. Hispanic includes Hispanics of all races

between 131.7 and 174.7% (depending on the scenario) between 2010 and 2060, and nonHispanic Asians and Others would show increases of between 106.7 and 157.7% between 2010 and 2060, while the number of nonHispanic White workers would show absolute declines over all time periods and the increases in the NonHispanic Black labor force would be between 31.0 and 47.4% between 2010 and 2060. For the total labor force the percentage increase for the 2010–2060 period would range from 18.7 to 33.4%, but because of the dramatic decline in the nonHispanic White labor force, in none of the individual decades from 2010 through 2060 would the rate of growth be as large as the 13.1% increase from 2000 to 2010. In fact, the percentage increases per decade from 2010 to 2060 would be smaller than any period in the last century.

The data in Table 3.7 further show that the increase in the size of the U.S. labor force would be due to growth in the minority labor force. Under all scenarios, the nonHispanic White labor force declines and, of the total growth in the work force (from 29 to nearly 52 million workers under the alternative scenarios), Hispanic workers would account for the largest proportion of the growth followed by nonHispanic Asian and Other workers and then nonHispanic Black workers.

Table 3.6 Percent change in the civilian labor force in the United States from 2010 to 2060 by race/ethnicity under alternative scenarios

Period	NH[a] White	NH Black	Hispanic	NH Asian & Other	Total
Low scenario					
2010–2020	−3.3	9.2	26.3	18.8	4.2
2020–2030	−5.2	4.7	19.6	17.2	2.4
2030–2040	−2.7	6.3	17.3	15.9	4.5
2040–2050	−4.0	4.7	15.3	14.0	3.6
2050–2060	−5.5	2.8	13.5	12.4	2.7
2010–2060	−19.2	31.0	131.7	106.7	18.7
Middle scenario					
2010–2020	−3.2	9.6	27.4	20.2	4.6
2020–2030	−4.8	5.9	22.4	20.9	3.7
2030–2040	−2.1	7.8	20.1	19.6	6.1
2040–2050	−3.4	6.3	17.4	16.7	5.2
2050–2060	−4.9	4.6	15.1	14.4	4.2
2010–2060	−17.3	39.2	153.2	132.2	26.0
High scenario					
2010–2020	−3.1	10.0	28.5	21.7	5.0
2020–2030	−4.4	7.0	25.2	24.6	4.9
2030–2040	−1.6	9.3	22.7	22.9	7.6
2040–2050	−2.9	7.9	19.4	19.1	6.6
2050–2060	−4.4	6.2	16.5	16.1	5.5
2010–2060	−15.4	47.4	174.7	157.7	33.4

Source: Projections by the authors derived from U.S. Census Bureau, 2011a, 2011b, 2011c, 2012
[a]NH refers to nonHispanic; values for categories labeled NH are only for the nonHispanic persons in each category. Hispanic includes Hispanics of all races

3.2.1 *A Diverse Labor Force Also Differentiated by Age and Gender*

As noted above the labor force of the United States would increase substantially and become older but this age differentiation would occur within the diversity of the labor force. As shown in Table 3.8, in 2010, only 10% of the total labor force was 60 years of age or older, but that included 12.1% of the nonHispanic White labor force, 7.3% of the nonHispanic Black labor force, 4.8% of the Hispanic labor force, and 7.6% of the nonHispanic Asian and Other labor force. By 2060, 14.0% of the labor force would be 60 years of age or older, including 17.4% of the nonHispanic White, 13.0% of the nonHispanic Black, 10.4% of the Hispanic, and 12.0% of the nonHispanic Asian and Other labor force. The labor force in all racial/ethnic groups would get older, but the nonHispanic White labor force would continue to be the oldest and the Hispanic labor force the youngest. Thus, those issues related to age differentials in the labor force would continue to be differentiated by race/ethnicity.

Table 3.7 Number and percentage of net change in the civilian labor force in the United States due to each race/ethnicity under alternative scenarios, 2010–2060

Race/ethnicity	Number	Percent
Low scenario		
NH[a] White	−19,745,650	−67.9
NH Black	5,477,581	18.8
Hispanic	31,203,108	107.3
NH Asian & Other	12,157,332	41.8
Total	29,092,370	100.0
Middle scenario		
NH White	−17,776,830	−43.9
NH Black	6,929,503	17.1
Hispanic	36,299,592	89.6
NH Asian & Other	15,061,444	37.2
Total	40,513,712	100.0
High scenario		
NH White	−15,807,024	−30.4
NH Black	8,381,451	16.1
Hispanic	41,394,844	79.7
NH Asian & Other	17,965,784	34.6
Total	51,935,056	100.0

Source: Projections by the authors derived from U.S. Census Bureau, 2011a, 2011b, 2011c, 2012
[a]NH refers to nonHispanic; values for categories labeled NH are only for the nonHispanic persons in each category. Hispanic includes Hispanics of all races.

The data in Table 3.9 assume no change in male and female participation rates by age during the projection period. They clearly show that unless there are increases in female participation rates women would continue to represent a smaller part of the labor force than males. The data in this table indicate that both the number of nonHispanic White males and females in the labor force would decline but while the number of males would decline by 15.4% the number of females would decline by 19.4%. For all other populations the number of both males and females would increase but the number of males would increase more rapidly than the number of females. The number of nonHispanic Black males would increase by 47.0% but the number of nonHispanic Black females by 32.6%. The number of Hispanic males would increase by 161.2% compared to 142.7% for females, and the values for nonHispanic Asians and Others would be 140.0% for males and 123.9% for females. In fact, due to lower participation rates for older females in all race/ethnicity groups, unless labor force participation rates for older women increase, sex ratios in the labor force increase for all racial/ethnic groups from 2010 to 2060. In the absence of increases in participation rates for older women, the sex ratios for nonHispanic Whites would increase from 111.7 males per 100 females in the labor force in 2010

Table 3.8 Percentage of civilian labor force in the United States by year, age, and race/ethnicity from 2010–2060 using the middle projection scenario

Year/age group	Percentage of labor force by age and race/ethnicity				Total
	NH[a] White	NH Black	Hispanic	NH Asian & Other	
2010					
16–19	3.9	4.9	5.4	3.9	4.3
20–24	9.0	11.4	13.4	10.1	10.0
25–34	19.3	22.8	28.1	25.2	21.5
35–44	20.5	23.0	24.8	24.5	21.7
45–54	24.9	22.9	18.2	21.1	23.3
55–59	10.4	7.9	5.3	7.6	9.1
60–64	7.0	4.5	3.0	4.8	5.9
65+	5.1	2.8	1.8	2.8	4.1
2020					
16–19	3.6	3.7	4.7	3.5	3.8
20–24	8.6	10.4	12.3	9.3	9.6
25–34	21.1	26.1	26.5	25.4	23.1
35–44	20.1	21.8	23.9	24.0	21.3
45–54	20.3	19.4	19.2	20.4	20.0
55–59	10.9	8.6	6.8	8.0	9.6
60–64	8.4	5.9	4.1	5.6	7.1
65+	7.0	4.0	2.5	3.9	5.6
2040					
16–19	3.6	3.6	4.4	3.5	3.8
20–24	8.5	9.8	11.7	9.3	9.5
25–34	19.4	22.3	25.2	24.0	21.7
35–44	20.9	22.9	23.2	23.5	22.0
45–54	22.2	22.7	19.4	21.0	21.4
55–59	9.5	7.8	7.1	8.1	8.6
60–64	6.6	5.1	4.8	5.4	5.8
65+	9.4	5.8	4.2	5.2	7.2
2060					
16–19	3.3	3.4	4.2	3.4	3.6
20–24	7.9	9.1	11.1	8.9	9.2
25–34	19.4	22.0	23.9	23.0	21.6
35–44	21.3	23.5	22.9	23.5	22.4
45–54	20.9	20.7	19.9	20.8	20.6
55–59	9.7	8.2	7.6	8.4	8.7
60–64	7.5	6.0	5.2	5.9	6.4
65+	9.9	7.0	5.2	6.1	7.6

Source: Projections by the authors derived from U.S. Census Bureau, 2011a, 2011b, 2011c, 2012
[a]NH refers to nonHispanic; values for categories labeled NH are only for the nonHispanic persons in each category. Hispanic includes Hispanics of all races

Table 3.9 Projections of the civilian labor force in the United States by sex and race/ethnicity from 2010 to 2060 using the middle projection scenario

	Labor force by race/ethnicity and sex				
Year	NH[a] White	NH Black	Hispanic	NH Asian & Other	Total labor force
Males by race/ethnicity					
2010	54,317,080	8,116,324	13,468,579	5,847,772	81,749,755
2020	52,987,681	9,045,749	17,381,375	7,081,542	86,496,347
2030	50,788,193	9,722,497	21,491,156	8,613,177	90,615,023
2040	49,801,986	10,608,761	25,982,292	10,371,610	96,764,649
2050	48,214,914	11,361,614	30,570,261	12,199,216	102,346,005
2060	45,950,367	11,927,189	35,175,529	14,036,910	107,089,995
Females by race/ethnicity					
2010	48,621,976	9,572,475	10,225,448	5,547,254	73,967,153
2020	46,623,106	10,345,242	12,806,335	6,618,550	76,393,233
2030	44,017,904	10,804,985	15,462,474	7,956,368	78,241,731
2040	42,970,460	11,528,440	18,398,266	9,440,892	82,338,058
2050	41,375,218	12,177,400	21,552,635	10,925,216	86,030,469
2060	39,211,859	12,691,113	24,818,092	12,419,560	89,140,624

Source: Projections by the authors derived from U.S. Census Bureau, 2011a, 2011b, 2011c, 2012
[a]NH refers to nonHispanic; values for categories labeled NH are only for the nonHispanic persons in each category. Hispanic includes Hispanics of all races

to 117.2 in 2060, that for the nonHispanic Black population would increase from 84.8 to 94.0, that for Hispanics from 131.7 to 141.7, and that for nonHispanic Asians and Others from 105.4 to 113.0.

3.2.2 *Socioeconomic Characteristics of the Workforce*

The data in Tables 3.10, 3.11, 3.12, 3.13, and 3.14 show current and expected future characteristics of the labor force in the United States assuming the demographic trends noted above and the continuation of racial/ethnic-specific characteristics of the population and labor force from 2010. The data in Table 3.10 show the distribution of the projected labor force (see Table 3.4 for the projections of the total labor force in the United States) by education level. The data in this table indicate the substantial disparity in educational levels among racial/ethnic groups in 2010 and the effects of these differentials if continued to 2060. The data in Table 3.10 indicate that the overall effect of these projected values, in the absence of improvement in minority levels of education, would be to increase the percentage of the labor force with less than a high school level of education from 10.0 to 14.0%, while the percentage with a bachelor's degree would decline from 19.2 to 17.4% and the percentage with a graduate or professional degree would decrease from 10.5 to 10.1%.

Table 3.10 Civilian labor force in the United States by level of education and race/ethnicity in 2010 and projected for 2060 using the middle projection scenario (percentages computed within race/ethnicity group)

Level of attainment	NH[a] White		NH Black		Hispanic		NH Asian & Other		Total	
	Number	%	Number	%	Number	%	Number	%	Number	%
2010										
Less than 9th grade	1,017,278	1.0	319,310	1.8	3,860,200	16.3	428,826	3.8	5,625,614	3.6
9th to 12th grade, no diploma	4,841,335	4.7	1,445,955	8.2	3,063,658	12.9	542,560	4.8	9,893,508	6.4
High school graduate	35,368,029	34.4	6,997,004	39.6	8,598,946	36.3	2,880,196	25.3	53,844,175	34.6
Some college	17,626,530	17.1	3,982,040	22.5	3,697,135	15.6	1,777,971	15.6	27,083,676	17.4
Associate degree	9,275,693	9.0	1,412,801	8.0	1,354,628	5.7	818,374	7.2	12,861,496	8.3
Bachelor's degree	22,334,055	21.7	2,364,010	13.4	2,176,119	9.2	2,974,193	26.1	29,848,377	19.2
Graduate/professional	12,476,136	12.1	1,167,678	6.5	943,342	4.0	1,972,906	17.2	16,560,062	10.5
Total	102,939,056	100.0	17,688,798	100.0	23,694,028	100.0	11,395,026	100.0	155,716,908	100.0
2060										
Less than 9th grade	922,011	1.1	531,547	2.2	10,611,051	17.7	1,071,746	4.1	13,136,355	6.7
9th to 12th grade, no diploma	3,865,673	4.5	1,939,510	7.9	7,365,887	12.3	1,235,342	4.7	14,406,412	7.3
High school graduate	29,221,944	34.3	9,718,429	39.5	21,399,371	35.7	6,688,750	25.3	67,028,494	34.2
Some college	14,414,711	16.9	5,409,143	22.0	9,009,776	15.0	4,028,254	15.2	32,861,884	16.7
Associate degree	7,534,548	8.8	1,973,695	8.0	3,419,167	5.7	1,897,501	7.2	14,824,911	7.6
Bachelor's degree	18,470,280	21.7	3,314,432	13.5	5,551,244	9.3	6,874,488	26.0	34,210,444	17.4
Graduate/professional	10,733,058	12.5	1,731,546	6.9	2,637,124	4.3	4,660,389	17.5	19,762,117	10.1
Total	85,162,225	100.0	24,618,302	100.0	59,993,620	100.0	26,456,470	100.0	196,230,617	100.0

Source: Projections by the authors derived from U.S. Census Bureau, 2011a, 2011b, 2011c, 2012; Ruggles et al. 2010

[a]NH refers to nonHispanic; values for categories labeled NH are only for the nonHispanic persons in each category. Hispanic includes Hispanics of all races

Given the fact that workers in the coming years of this century would need to have higher levels of education to be competitive, this finding suggests that, in the absence of improved educational attainment among minority populations, the overall effect of population growth in the absence of improvements in the educational levels of the minority work force would be to make the total labor force in the United States less well educated and thus less competitive in the future in international markets.

By 2060 (see Table 3.11), because of rapid growth in the Hispanic labor force, in the absence of improvements in Hispanic levels of education, 80.8% of the members of the labor force with less than a 9th grade and 51.1% of those with 9–12 years of education would be Hispanic, compared to only 16.2% of those with a bachelor's degree and 13.3% of those with a graduate degree who would be Hispanic. On the other hand, more than 54% in each of these two latter categories would be nonHispanic White and more than 20% with a bachelor's or graduate degree would be members of nonHispanic Asian and Other racial/ethnic groups. Such data suggest that in the absence of improvements in the educational attainment of the fastest growing segments of the population of the United States, the nation as a whole could experience reduced levels of education.

Table 3.12 presents data arranged similarly to that in Table 3.11. The data in this table indicate that although (as shown above) minority populations, particularly Hispanic populations, are projected to dominate future U.S. population growth, in the absence of improvements in the occupational opportunities for the fastest growing minority populations, they would continue to show smaller occupational improvements than their percentage of the labor force would suggest. Hispanics would represent 30.6% of the total labor force in 2060, but less than 20% of those employed in management, business and finance; computer, engineering and science; and healthcare occupations, but nearly 75% of those employed in farming, fishing and forestry, nearly 48% of those employed in construction and maintenance, and nearly 46% of those employed in general (other) service occupations. Similarly, nonHispanic Black workers, who would make up 12.5% of the workforce in 2060, would be underrepresented in higher paying occupations such as management and engineering. On the other hand nonHispanic Whites, although representing 43.4% of the total labor force in 2060, would occupy 53.6% of the positions in management, 48.8% of those in computer, engineering and science occupations, 54% of those in education, legal, and arts and media, and 51.6% of those in healthcare practitioner occupations. In the absence of change in educational and other factors that impact competitiveness, Hispanic populations and African American populations would continue to be underrepresented in those occupations that lead to larger socioeconomic returns.

Tables 3.13 and 3.14 show the income distribution of the workforce within racial/ethnic groups (Table 3.13) and within income categories (Table 3.14) in both 2010 and 2060. The data in Table 3.13 show that in the absence of change in the relative distribution of wages and salaries among racial/ethnic groups in the labor force, the absolute number of minority workers at the lowest income levels would change substantially. Whereas about 11.7 million Hispanics earned less than $25,000 in 2010 by 2060 this number would be more than 29.7 million, while the number of

Table 3.11 Civilian labor force in the United States by level of education and race/ethnicity in 2010 and projected for 2060 using the middle projection scenario (percentages computed within level of educational attainment)

	NH[a] White		NH Black		Hispanic		NH Asian & Other		Total
Level of attainment	Number	%	Number	%	Number	%	Number	%	Number
2010									
Less than 9th grade	1,017,278	18.1	319,310	5.7	3,860,200	68.6	428,826	7.6	5,625,614
9th to 12th grade, no diploma	4,841,335	48.9	1,445,955	14.6	3,063,658	31.0	542,560	5.5	9,893,508
High school graduate	35,368,029	65.7	6,997,004	13.0	8,598,946	16.0	2,880,196	5.3	53,844,175
Some college	17,626,530	65.1	3,982,040	14.7	3,697,135	13.7	1,777,971	6.6	27,083,676
Associate degree	9,275,693	72.1	1,412,801	11.0	1,354,628	10.5	818,374	6.4	12,861,496
Bachelor's degree	22,334,055	74.8	2,364,010	7.9	2,176,119	7.3	2,974,193	10.0	29,848,377
Graduate/professional	12,476,136	75.3	1,167,678	7.1	943,342	5.7	1,972,906	11.9	16,560,062
2060									
Less than 9th grade	922,011	7.0	531,547	4.0	10,611,051	80.8	1,071,746	8.2	13,136,355
9th to 12th grade, no diploma	3,865,673	26.8	1,939,510	13.5	7,365,887	51.1	1,235,342	8.6	14,406,412
High school graduate	29,221,944	43.6	9,718,429	14.5	21,399,371	31.9	6,688,750	10.0	67,028,494
Some college	14,414,711	43.9	5,409,143	16.5	9,009,776	27.4	4,028,254	12.3	32,861,884
Associate degree	7,534,548	50.8	1,973,695	13.3	3,419,167	23.1	1,897,501	12.8	14,824,911
Bachelor's degree	18,470,280	54.0	3,314,432	9.7	5,551,244	16.2	6,874,488	20.1	34,210,444
Graduate/professional	10,733,058	54.3	1,731,546	8.8	2,637,124	13.3	4,660,389	23.6	19,762,117

Source: Projections by the authors derived from U.S. Census Bureau, 2011a, 2011b, 2011c, 2012; Ruggles et al. 2010

[a]NH refers to nonHispanic; values for categories labeled NH are only for the nonHispanic persons in each category. Hispanic includes Hispanics of all races

Table 3.12 Civilian labor force in the United States by occupation and race/ethnicity in 2010 and projections for 2060 using the middle projection scenario (percentages computed within occupations)

Occupation	NH[a] White		NH Black		Hispanic		NH Asian & Other		Total
	Number	%	Number	%	Number	%	Number	%	Number
2010									
Management, business, & financial	29,809,065	74.4	3,409,176	8.5	3,428,309	8.6	3,414,911	8.5	40,061,461
Computer, engineering, & science	4,259,878	71.6	367,988	6.2	412,138	6.9	912,393	15.3	5,952,397
Education, legal, community, service, arts, & media	8,906,883	74.2	1,201,929	10.0	1,159,268	9.7	728,159	6.1	11,996,239
Healthcare practitioners & technical	4,252,683	72.3	600,062	10.2	421,879	7.2	604,920	10.3	5,879,544
Healthcare support	1,353,159	52.1	650,007	25.0	410,469	15.8	185,495	7.1	2,599,130
Protective service	1,633,304	63.7	469,684	18.3	341,403	13.3	118,266	4.6	2,562,657
Other services	7,834,497	53.3	1,891,090	12.9	3,887,488	26.4	1,093,539	7.4	14,706,614
Sales & related	9,001,644	70.1	1,197,195	9.3	1,771,683	13.8	873,021	6.8	12,843,543
Office & administrative support	10,732,851	66.6	2,042,409	12.7	2,339,335	14.5	992,778	6.2	16,107,373
Farming, fishing, & forestry	338,132	39.8	40,357	4.8	450,316	53.0	20,542	2.4	849,347
Construction & maintenance	6,972,761	64.3	712,028	6.6	2,755,173	25.4	398,696	3.7	10,838,658
Production occupations	4,349,244	58.9	836,027	11.3	1,696,296	23.0	499,647	6.8	7,381,214
Transportation & material moving	4,195,865	58.5	1,117,123	15.6	1,538,938	21.4	324,314	4.5	7,176,240
Unemployed	9,299,090	55.5	3,153,724	18.8	3,081,332	18.4	1,228,345	7.3	16,762,491
Total	102,939,056	66.1	17,688,799	11.4	23,694,027	15.2	11,395,026	7.3	155,716,908

2060									
Management, business, & financial	24,679,169	53.6	4,766,741	10.3	8,658,838	18.8	7,949,102	17.3	46,053,850
Computer, engineering, & science	3,572,486	48.8	530,549	7.2	1,061,413	14.5	2,153,880	29.4	7,318,328
Education, legal, community, service, arts, & media	7,324,317	54.0	1,670,920	12.3	2,899,313	21.4	1,681,170	12.4	13,575,720
Healthcare practitioners & technical	3,479,197	51.6	822,031	12.2	1,052,944	15.6	1,389,410	20.6	6,743,582
Healthcare support	1,098,459	32.2	882,816	25.9	1,010,064	29.6	422,107	12.4	3,413,446
Protective service	1,372,354	42.7	678,975	21.1	882,381	27.5	280,604	8.7	3,214,314
Other services	6,458,510	30.0	2,663,204	12.4	9,843,622	45.8	2,529,761	11.8	21,495,097
Sales & related	7,466,434	47.7	1,677,819	10.7	4,473,002	28.6	2,028,229	13.0	15,645,484
Office & administrative support	8,774,681	44.5	2,831,252	14.3	5,845,073	29.6	2,279,102	11.6	19,730,108
Farming, fishing, & forestry	284,926	18.3	59,145	3.8	1,163,156	74.8	48,627	3.1	1,555,854
Construction & maintenance	5,903,936	39.0	1,059,571	7.0	7,214,217	47.7	956,413	6.3	15,134,137
Production occupations	3,644,637	35.2	1,203,248	11.6	4,344,948	41.9	1,169,336	11.3	10,362,169
Transportation & material moving	3,532,735	35.6	1,641,857	16.5	3,988,960	40.2	770,874	7.8	9,934,426
Unemployed	7,570,385	34.3	4,130,174	18.7	7,555,690	34.3	2,797,855	12.7	22,054,104
Total	85,162,226	43.4	24,618,302	12.5	59,993,621	30.6	26,456,470	13.5	196,230,619

Source: Projections by the authors derived from U.S. Census Bureau, 2011a, 2011b, 2011c, 2012; Ruggles et al. 2010

[a]NH refers to nonHispanic; values for categories labeled NH are only for the nonHispanic persons in each category. Hispanic includes Hispanics of all races

Table 3.13 Wage and salary income of the civilian labor force in the United States by race/ethnicity in 2010 and projections for 2060 (in 2010 constant dollars) using the middle projection scenario (percentages computed by race/ethnicity group)

Wage & salary	NH[a] White		NH Black		Hispanic		NH Asian & Other		Total	
earnings	Number	%	Number	%	Number	%	Number	%	Number	%
2010										
<10,000	17,718,885	17.2	2,747,658	15.5	4,362,932	18.4	1,871,203	16.4	26,700,678	17.1
10,000–24,999	18,239,051	17.7	3,892,712	22.0	7,365,944	31.1	2,276,330	20.0	31,774,037	20.4
25,000–34,999	12,145,456	11.8	2,460,109	13.9	3,165,380	13.4	1,233,557	10.8	19,004,502	12.2
35,000–49,999	15,249,911	14.8	2,402,076	13.6	2,705,728	11.4	1,417,848	12.4	21,775,563	14.0
50,000–74,999	15,596,031	15.2	1,930,473	10.9	1,892,913	8.0	1,532,061	13.4	20,951,478	13.5
75,000–99,999	6,687,972	6.5	641,362	3.6	624,042	2.6	821,085	7.2	8,774,461	5.6
100,000 or more	7,998,240	7.8	457,227	2.6	497,285	2.1	1,014,037	8.9	9,966,789	6.4
Unemployed	9,303,510	9.0	3,157,182	17.9	3,079,803	13.0	1,228,905	10.9	16,769,400	10.8
Total	102,939,056	100.0	17,688,799	100.0	23,694,027	100.0	11,395,026	100.0	155,716,908	100.0
2060										
<10,000	14,649,908	17.2	3,868,013	15.7	11,041,903	18.4	4,337,402	16.4	33,897,226	17.3
10,000–24,999	15,020,146	17.6	5,453,782	22.2	18,710,067	31.2	5,274,348	19.9	44,458,343	22.7
25,000–34,999	10,030,712	11.8	3,460,419	14.1	8,066,456	13.4	2,864,348	10.8	24,421,935	12.4
35,000–49,999	12,630,662	14.8	3,393,902	13.8	6,906,347	11.5	3,298,190	12.5	26,229,101	13.4
50,000–74,999	12,967,796	15.2	2,738,750	11.1	4,839,501	8.1	3,573,106	13.5	24,119,153	12.3
75,000–99,999	5,580,715	6.6	913,125	3.7	1,597,692	2.7	1,921,101	7.3	10,012,633	5.1
100,000 or more	6,708,213	7.9	655,265	2.7	1,279,847	2.1	2,388,799	9.0	11,032,124	5.6
Unemployed	7,574,074	8.9	4,135,046	16.7	7,551,808	12.6	2,799,176	10.6	22,060,104	11.2
Total	85,162,226	100.0	24,618,302	100.0	59,993,621	100.0	26,456,470	100.0	196,230,619	100.0

Source: Projections by the authors derived from U.S. Census Bureau, 2011a, 2011b, 2012; Ruggles et al. 2010

[a]NH refers to nonHispanic; values for categories labeled NH are only for the nonHispanic persons in each category. Hispanic includes Hispanics of all races

Table 3.14 Wage and salary income of civilian labor force in the United States by race/ethnicity in 2010 and projections for 2060 (in constant dollars) using the middle projection scenario (percentages computed within income group)

Wage & salary	NH[a] White		NH Black		Hispanic		NH Asian & Other		
earnings	Number	%	Number	%	Number	%	Number	%	Total number
2010									
<10,000	17,718,885	66.4	2,747,658	10.3	4,362,932	16.3	1,871,203	7.0	26,700,678
10,000–24,999	18,239,051	57.4	3,892,712	12.3	7,365,944	23.2	2,276,330	7.2	31,774,037
25,000–34,999	12,145,456	63.9	2,460,109	12.9	3,165,380	16.7	1,233,557	6.5	19,004,502
35,000–49,999	15,249,911	70.0	2,402,076	11.0	2,705,728	12.4	1,417,848	6.5	21,775,563
50,000–74,999	15,596,031	74.4	1,930,473	9.2	1,892,913	9.0	1,532,061	7.3	20,951,478
75,000–99,999	6,687,972	76.2	641,362	7.3	624,042	7.1	821,085	9.4	8,774,461
100,000 or more	7,998,240	80.2	457,227	4.6	497,285	5.0	1,014,037	10.2	9,966,789
Unemployed	9,303,510	55.5	3,157,182	18.8	3,079,803	18.4	1,228,905	7.3	16,769,400
Total	102,939,056	66.1	17,688,799	11.4	23,694,027	15.2	11,395,026	7.3	155,716,908
2060									
<10,000	14,649,908	43.2	3,868,013	11.4	11,041,903	32.6	4,337,402	12.8	33,897,226
10,000–24,999	15,020,146	33.8	5,453,782	12.3	18,710,067	42.1	5,274,348	11.9	44,458,343
25,000–34,999	10,030,712	41.1	3,460,419	14.2	8,066,456	33.0	2,864,348	11.7	24,421,935
35,000–49,999	12,630,662	48.2	3,393,902	12.9	6,906,347	26.3	3,298,190	12.6	26,229,101
50,000–74,999	12,967,796	53.8	2,738,750	11.4	4,839,501	20.1	3,573,106	14.8	24,119,153
75,000–99,999	5,580,715	55.7	913,125	9.1	1,597,692	16.0	1,921,101	19.2	10,012,633
100,000 or more	6,708,213	60.8	655,265	5.9	1,279,847	11.6	2,388,799	21.7	11,032,124
Unemployed	7,574,074	34.3	4,135,046	18.7	7,551,808	34.2	2,799,176	12.7	22,060,104
Total	85,162,226	43.4	24,618,302	12.5	59,993,621	30.6	26,456,470	13.5	196,230,619

Source: Projections by the authors derived from U.S. Census Bureau, 2011a, 2011b, 2012; Ruggles et al. 2010

[a]NH refers to nonHispanic; values for categories labeled NH are only for the nonHispanic persons in each category. Hispanic includes Hispanics of all races

persons in these income groups who are nonHispanic White would decline from 35.9 to 29.6 million persons. Similarly the data in Table 3.14 show that the more rapid growth of Hispanic and other minority populations would result in larger percentages of such populations in all salary groups, but the increases would be less at upper income levels and larger at lower income levels. For example, the proportion of labor force members making less than $10,000 would decrease from 66.4 to 43.2% among nonHispanic Whites but increase from 16.3% of all Hispanic workers making this salary level in 2010 to 32.6% of all Hispanic workers in 2060. The percentage of nonHispanic White persons who earn less than $10,000 would **decrease** by 34.9%, while the percentage of Hispanics earning less than $10,000 would **increase** by 100%.

3.3 Summary

The data in this chapter have been used to examine recent and projected patterns of change in the workforce of the United States. The results reported indicate the following:

1. The labor force of the United States has increased dramatically from 28.4 million in 1900 to 153.9 million in 2010. Reflecting the entrance of the baby boom generation into the workforce, rates of growth in the labor force were most rapid during the period from the 1960s through the 1990s and have slowed in the recent decade.
2. Among the important trends in the labor force has been the increased participation of women. In just the 20-year period from 1990 to 2010, the number of women in the labor force has increased by 30.9%, compared to 22.0% for men, but participation rates for 2010 indicate that 59.2% of women in the working ages in the United States were in the labor force in 2010, compared to 69.1% of men.
3. The growth in the size of the minority workforce has been extensive. Whereas the nonHispanic White labor force increased by only 2.8% from 2000 to 2010, the nonHispanic Black labor force increased by 22.4%, the nonHispanic Asian and Other labor force by 37%, and the Hispanic labor force by 61%.
4. Projected change in the labor force indicates that the labor force would increase by 29.1 to 51.9 million from 2010 to 2060. Of this increase, under the middle projection scenario (an increase of 40.5 million), a decline of nearly 17.8 million nonHispanic White workers would be offset by an increase of 6.9 million nonHispanic Black workers, 36.3 million Hispanic workers, and 15.1 million nonHispanic Asian and Other workers. Under this scenario, the percentage of all members of the labor force who would be nonHispanic White declines from 66.1% of all workers in 2010 to 43.4% in 2060. The percentage of the labor force composed of nonHispanic Black workers would increase from 11.4 to 12.5%, the percentage who would be nonHispanic Asian and Other would increase from

7.3 to 13.5, and the percentage who would be Hispanic would increase from 15.2% in 2010 to 30.6% in 2060.

5. The labor force would become older as well. In 2010, 10% of the labor force was 60 years of age or older, but by 2010 (using the middle projection scenario) 14% would be 60 years of age or older. The age of the labor forces varies substantially across racial/ethnic groups with 10.4% of Hispanic workers being 60 years of age or older, 12.0% of nonHispanic Asian and Others, 13.0% of nonHispanic Blacks, and 17.4% of nonHispanic White workers. Median ages of workers in 2010 were 35.3 years for Hispanics, 38.4 years for nonHispanic Asian and Others, 38.7 years for nonHispanic Blacks, and 42.7 years for nonHispanic Whites. In 2060 these median ages would be 38.7 years for Hispanic workers, 40.2 years for nonHispanic Asian and Other workers, 40.6 years for nonHispanic Black workers, and 43.1 years for nonHispanic White workers. The median age of all workers would increase over time.
6. In the absence of improvements in the educational opportunities for the fastest growing segments of the population, particularly the Hispanic population, the nation as a whole would have a less well-educated workforce and its median income would be less. Thus (as shown in Table 3.10) the percentage of the labor force without a high school degree would increase from 10.0% to 14.0% and the percentage with a bachelor's degree or higher would decrease from 29.8% to 27.5%. At the same time, median household income would decrease from $35,045 to $33,065 in 2060 (in 2010 constant dollars).

Overall, then the data in this chapter point to a more diverse and older workforce. At the same time, if educational levels are not improved in the fastest growing segments of the workforce, it will be a less well-educated and poorer population. The future of the labor force of the United States is one that will require concerted attention.

References

Altonji, J. G., Bharadwaj, P., & Lange, F. (2012). Changes in the characteristics of American youth: Implications for adult outcomes. *Journal of Labor Economics, 30*(4), 783–828.

Carter, S. B., Gartner, S. S., Haines, M. R., Olmstead, A. L., & Wright, G. (Eds.). (2006). *Historical statistics of the United States: Earliest times to the present.* New York: Cambridge University Press.

Crespo Cuaresma, J., Lutz, W., & Sanderson, W. (2014). Is the demographic dividend an education dividend? *Demography, 51*(1), 299–315.

Ruggles, S. J., Alexander, T., Genadek, K., Goeken, R., Schroeder, R. B., & Sobek, M. (2010). *Integrated public use microdata series: Version 5.0.* Minneapolis: University of Minnesota.

Toossi, M. (2012). Labor force projections to 2020: A more slowly growing workforce. *Monthly Labor Review, 135*(1), 43–64.

U.S. Bureau of Labor Statistics. (2012). Labor force. *Occupational Outlook Quarterly, 55*(4), 26–32.

U.S. Census Bureau. (1992). *1990 census of population and housing, summary tape file 3.* Washington, DC: U.S. Census Bureau.

U.S. Census Bureau. (2002). *2000 census of population and housing, summary file 3*. Washington, DC: U.S. Census Bureau.

U.S. Census Bureau. (2003). *2000 census of population and housing, summary file 4*. Washington, DC: U.S. Census Bureau.

U.S. Census Bureau. (2011a). *2010 American community survey*. Washington, DC: U.S. Census Bureau.

U.S. Census Bureau. (2011b). *2010 census summary file 1*. Washington, DC: U.S. Census Bureau.

U.S. Census Bureau. (2011c). *2010 census summary file 2*. Washington, DC: U.S. Census Bureau.

U.S. Census Bureau. (2012). *2012 national population projections*. Washington, DC: U.S. Census Bureau.

U.S. Census Bureau and U.S. Bureau of Labor Statistics. (1981). *1980 current population survey: Annual demographic survey*. Washington, DC: U.S. Bureau of Labor Statistics and U.S. Census Bureau.

U.S. Census Bureau and U.S. Bureau of Labor Statistics. (1991). *1990 current population survey: Annual demographic survey*. Washington, DC: U.S. Bureau of Labor Statistics and U.S. Census Bureau.

U.S. Census Bureau and U.S. Bureau of Labor Statistics. (2001). *2000 current population survey: Annual demographic survey*. Washington, DC: U.S. Bureau of Labor Statistics and U.S. Census Bureau.

U.S. Census Bureau and U.S. Bureau of Labor Statistics. (2011). *2010 current population survey: Annual demographic survey*. Washington, DC: U.S. Bureau of Labor Statistics and U.S. Census Bureau.

Chapter 4
Effects of Demographic Change on Selected Economic Factors Impacting the Public and Private Sectors in the United States

The size, characteristics, and distribution of a population impact the private sector. The size and characteristics of populations affect the total level of overall income and other economic resources of populations. For example, populations with a larger proportion of middle-age adults tend to be ones with higher levels of economic productivity because such populations tend to have more experienced labor force members while not yet beginning to experience the effects of aging on their levels of productivity (Feyrer 2008; Lindh 1999; Lindh and Malmberg 1999, 2009). Middle-age adults also tend to have higher incomes and economic purchasing power that affect markets for goods and services (DeNavas-Walt and Proctor 2014: 8). On the other hand, younger workforces tend to have less experienced workforce members and reduced levels of productivity (Feyrer 2008, 2011). Similarly, because of higher levels of discrimination and lower levels of education, minority population members tend to have reduced levels of productivity and lower incomes (King and Knapp 1978; Thomas 1993).

At the same time, the age, gender, race/ethnicity, income, and other characteristics of a population affect its impacts on the markets for many different types of goods and services (Arnott and Chaves 2012; Lee 2014). Similarly, the economic resources available from the taxation of such economic outputs affect the level of resources available to support public-sector programs, infrastructure, and public employment (Felix and Watkins 2013). In a variety of ways, through numerous mechanisms, analyzing demographic change is instrumental to understanding the current and future economy and markets for goods and services. In this chapter we examine some of these effects while acknowledging that no single analysis can consider more than a few of the many implications of the demographic context and its patterns of change on economic factors and the private and public sectors.

S.H. Murdock et al., *Population Change in the United States*,
DOI 10.1007/978-94-017-7288-4_4

4.1 Historical Change in Income and Poverty

Tables 4.1 and 4.2 provide basic income data for the United States in both constant (2010) and current dollars. The data in Table 4.1 show that although there were absolute numerical increases in current dollars over the period from 1989 to 2010, real median household income (shown in constant dollars) was actually less in 2010 than in 1989. Per capita income showed small increases from 1989 to 1999 but declined from 1999 to 2010. Poverty rates also increased over the period shown with declines from 1989 to 1999 being offset by increases in poverty levels from 1999 to 2010.

The data in Table 4.2 show median household, family, and per capita income and poverty rates in 1999 and 2010 and 1999–2010 change in income and poverty levels by the race/ethnicity of the householder. These data show clear income differences, with median 2010 household income for nonHispanic White households ($56,466) being substantially higher than that for nonHispanic Black ($35,189) and Hispanic households ($41,543) and higher than that for nonHispanic Asian and Other households ($54,013). The data in this table for poverty show the largest relative percentage changes from 1999 to 2010 for Hispanics followed by those for nonHispanic Whites, nonHispanic Asians and Others, and nonHispanic Blacks. The largest percentages of families in poverty in 2010 occurred among nonHispanic Black households (21.5%) and Hispanic households (20.0%), followed by nonHispanic Asian and Other (11.0%) and nonHispanic White families (6.3%). However, rates of change (see the bottom panel) generally showed the largest changes for Hispanics and nonHispanics Whites, followed by nonHispanic Asians and Others

Table 4.1 Median household income, per capita income, and percentage of persons in poverty in the United States, 1989–2010

				Percent change		
Income/poverty	1989	1999	2010	1989–1999	1999–2010	1989–2010
Panel A: Constant dollars						
Median household income	52,854	54,964	51,914	4.0	−5.5	−1.8
Per capita income	25,358	28,254	27,334	11.4	−3.3	7.8
Percent of persons in poverty	13.1	12.4	13.8	−5.3	23.4	5.3
Panel B: Current dollars						
Median household income	30,056	41,994	51,914	39.7	23.6	72.7
Per capita income	14,420	21,587	27,334	49.7	26.6	89.6
Percent of persons in poverty	13.1	12.4	13.8	−5.3	23.4	5.3

Source: U.S. Census Bureau, 1992, 1993, 2002, 2003, 2011a

Note: Constant dollars calculated using the U.S. Bureau of Labor Statistics (2011a) Consumer Price Index for all urban consumers, 1982–1984 base. Accessed on August 12, 2014

Table 4.2 Income and poverty characteristics of the population in the United States by race/ethnicity 1999–2010

				Number (in thousands of persons) and percent in poverty							
				Persons		Families		Children		Elderly	
Race/ethnicity	Median household income	Median family income	Per capita income	Number	%	Number	%	Number	%	Number	%
1999											
NH[a] White	45,367	54,698	24,819	15,414.1	8.1	2,889.1	5.5	4,059.6	9.3	2,170.7	7.8
NH Black	29,445	33,332	14,489	7,970.2	24.8	1,742.9	21.6	3,387.1	33.1	619.0	23.5
Hispanic	33,676	34,397	12,111	7,797.9	22.6	1,495.3	20.0	3,339.2	27.8	325.7	19.6
NH Asian & Other[b]	51,967	59,471	21,893	2,717.7	15.5	493.6	12.6	961.0	18.3	172.4	14.3
Total	41,994	50,046	21,587	33,899.8	12.4	6,620.9	9.2	11,746.9	16.6	3,287.8	9.9
2010											
NH White	56,466	70,462	32,136	18,334.8	9.6	3,316.8	6.3	4,535.3	11.3	2,250.1	7.5
NH Black	35,189	41,745	18,342	8,954.8	25.2	1,835.6	21.5	3,648.2	35.4	608.2	19.8
Hispanic	41,543	42,900	15,638	10,471.0	22.4	2,005.8	20.0	4,685.9	29.2	471.4	18.9
NH Asian & Other	54,013	57,937	30,122	3,156.9	14.3	527.2	11.0	1,111.1	17.1	224.5	13.1
Total	51,914	62,982	27,334	40,917.5	13.8	7,685.3	10.1	13,980.5	19.2	3,554.3	9.5
	Percent change 1999–2010			Numeric and percent change 1999–2010							
	%	%	%	Number	%	Number	%	Number	%	Number	%
NH White	24.5	28.8	29.5	2,920.7	18.9	427.7	14.8	475.7	11.7	79.4	3.7
NH Black	19.5	25.2	26.6	984.6	12.4	92.6	5.3	261.1	7.7	–10.7	–1.7
Hispanic	23.4	24.7	29.1	2,673.1	34.3	510.5	34.1	1,346.7	40.3	145.7	44.7
NH Asian & Other	3.9	–2.6	37.6	439.2	16.2	33.6	6.8	150.1	15.6	52.1	30.2
Total	23.6	25.8	26.6	7,017.7	20.7	1,064.4	16.1	2,233.6	19.0	266.5	8.1

Source: U.S. Census Bureau, 2002, 2003, 2011b

[a]NH refers to nonHispanic; values for categories labeled NH are only for the nonHispanic persons in each category. Hispanic includes Hispanics of all races

[b]Median values for NH Asian & Others estimated from income distribution

and nonHispanic Blacks. The reduced economic resources of Hispanic households point to conditions that limit their socioeconomic achievement.

4.1.1 *Fiscal Impacts of Household Income Change*

Table 4.3 shows that the recession of the 2000–2010 period substantially limited government receipts. The data in this table indicate that government receipts tended to lag population growth, meaning that government income per household and person decreased during this period. Although the total population increased by 9.7% and the total number of households by 10.7%, government receipts tended to lag population growth with either declines or smaller than population rates of growth. This meant that government income per household and person decreased during this period.

Similarly, as shown in Table 4.4, except for unemployment and other annual rates of growth in personal benefits, government expenditures also increased less than population. This indicates that the decade of 2000–2010 not only showed reduced income but also reduced government support for American households.

4.2 Projected Effects of Household Change on the Future Economic Characteristics of the United States

Table 4.5 shows projections of income assuming that income levels for 2010 for each demographic group continue through 2060. These data indicate that, in the absence of change in real income, the percentage of households making lower incomes in 2060 than in 2010 (in 2010 constant dollars) would increase for all racial/ethnic groups and the percentage making higher incomes (in constant dollars) would decline. Table 4.6 shows projections of income assuming household poverty rates for 2010 continue to 2060 while the number of households increase as projected above. The data in Panel A of this table show the expected patterns, with aggregate household income growing for nonHispanic Whites through 2030 then declining as their levels of population growth decline and their age increases in later decades. However because of their much higher level of household income, they continue to contribute levels of income that are substantially larger than those for any other group at any age and account for more than 50% of all household income in all time periods despite the fact that nonHispanic Black aggregate income nearly doubles, Hispanic income triples and nonHispanic Asian and Other incomes nearly triple. Panel B demonstrates that closure toward nonHispanic White income levels would lead to higher overall total population incomes with a nearly $9,565 increase in average income with closure.

Tables 4.7 and 4.8 provide additional indication of the change in socioeconomic resources through an examination of the likely change in the percentage of households in poverty between 2010 and 2060, assuming that the household types and poverty

Table 4.3 Federal government receipts in the United States, 2000 and 2010

	Amount in $billions		Percent distribution		Annual rate of change
Category	2000	2010	2000	2010	2000–2010
Current dollars					
Receipts	2,057.1	2,429.6	100.0	100.0	1.7
Tax receipts	1,309.6	1,340.7	63.7	55.2	0.2
Personal taxes	995.5	896.3	48.4	36.9	−1.0
Corporate income taxes	219.4	329.6	10.7	13.6	4.2
Taxes on production and imports	87.3	101.4	4.2	4.2	1.5
Taxes from the rest of the world	7.3	13.3	0.4	0.5	6.2
Contributions for social insurance	698.6	970.9	34.0	40.0	3.3
Income receipts on assets	24.5	36.1	1.2	1.5	3.9
Interest receipts	19.3	29.9	0.9	1.2	4.5
Rents and royalties	5.2	6.2	0.3	0.3	1.8
Transfer receipts	25.7	69.7	1.3	2.9	10.5
From business	15.0	48.8	0.7	2.0	12.5
From persons	10.7	21.0	0.5	0.9	6.9
Surplus of government enterprises	−1.2	−4.8	−0.1	−0.2	14.7
Constant 2010 dollars					
Receipts	2,604.9	2,429.6	100.0	100.0	−0.7
Tax receipts	1,658.3	1,340.7	63.7	55.2	−2.1
Personal taxes	1,260.6	896.3	48.4	36.9	−3.4
Corporate income taxes	277.8	329.6	10.7	13.6	1.7
Taxes on production and imports	110.5	101.4	4.2	4.2	−0.9
Taxes from the rest of the world	9.2	13.3	0.4	0.5	3.8
Contributions for social insurance	884.6	970.9	34.0	40.0	0.9
Income receipts on assets	31.0	36.1	1.2	1.5	1.5
Interest receipts	24.4	29.9	0.9	1.2	2.1
Rents and royalties	6.6	6.2	0.3	0.3	−0.6
Transfer receipts	32.5	69.7	1.2	2.9	7.9
From business	19.0	48.8	0.7	2.0	9.9
From persons	13.5	21.0	0.5	0.9	4.5
Surplus of government enterprises	−1.5	−4.8	−0.1	−0.2	12.3

Source: U.S. Bureau of Economic Analysis, 2013; Byun and Frey 2012; U.S. Bureau of Labor Statistics 2011a

Table 4.4 Federal government expenditures in the United States, 2000 and 2010

	Amount in $billions		Percent distribution		Annual rate of change
Category	2000	2010	2000	2010	2000–2010
Current dollars					
Expenditures	1,871.9	3,703.3	100.0	100.0	7.1
Consumption expenditures	496.0	1,054.0	26.5	28.5	7.8
Transfer payments	1,047.3	2,313.6	55.9	62.5	8.2
Government social benefits	777.8	1,724.9	41.5	46.6	8.3
Social Security benefits	401.4	690.2	21.4	18.6	5.6
Medicare benefits	219.1	518.5	11.7	14.0	9.0
Unemployment benefits	20.8	138.7	1.1	3.7	20.9
Other benefits to persons	127.9	361.0	6.8	9.7	10.9
Benefits to the rest of the world	8.6	16.6	0.5	0.4	6.7
Other transfer payments	269.5	588.8	14.4	15.9	8.1
Grants-in-aid to state & local government	247.3	531.5	13.2	14.4	8.0
To the rest of the world	22.2	57.3	1.2	1.5	9.9
Interest payments	283.2	279.9	15.1	7.6	–0.1
To persons and business	198.7	143.8	10.6	3.9	–3.2
To the rest of the world	84.5	136.1	4.5	3.7	4.9
Subsidies	45.3	55.8	2.4	1.5	2.1
Constant 2010 dollars					
Expenditures	2,370.4	3,703.3	100.0	100.0	4.6
Consumption expenditures	628.1	1,054.0	26.5	28.5	5.3
Transfer payments	1,326.2	2,313.6	55.9	62.5	5.7
Government social benefits	984.9	1,724.9	41.5	46.6	5.8
Social Security benefits	508.3	690.2	21.4	18.6	3.1
Medicare benefits	277.4	518.5	11.7	14.0	6.5
Unemployment benefits	26.3	138.7	1.1	3.7	18.1
Other benefits to persons	162.0	361.0	6.8	9.7	8.3
Benefits to the rest of the world	10.9	16.6	0.5	0.4	4.3
Other transfer payments	341.3	588.8	14.4	15.9	5.6
Grants-in-aid to state & local government	313.2	531.5	13.2	14.4	5.4
To the rest of the world	28.1	57.3	1.2	1.5	7.4
Interest payments	358.6	279.9	15.1	7.6	–2.4
To persons and business	251.6	143.8	10.6	3.9	–5.4
To the rest of the world	107.0	136.1	4.5	3.7	2.4
Subsidies	57.4	55.8	2.4	1.5	–0.3

Source: U.S. Bureau of Economic Analysis 2013; Byun and Frey 2012; U.S. Bureau of Labor Statistics 2011a

Table 4.5 Household income in the United States by income group and race/ethnicity of householder in 2010 and projected for 2060 under the middle projection scenario (percentages computed within race/ethnicity group)

	NH[a] White		NH Black		Hispanic		NH Asian & Other		Total	
Household income	2010	2060	2010	2060	2010	2060	2010	2060	2010	2060
Less than $10,000	5.8	6.0	14.7	15.1	8.6	9.9	8.4	8.8	7.3	8.6
$10,000 to $14,999	5.0	6.0	8.4	9.6	6.5	7.7	4.9	5.9	5.6	6.9
$15,000 to $19,999	4.9	5.8	7.3	7.9	6.9	7.4	4.6	5.2	5.4	6.4
$20,000 to $24,999	5.1	5.8	6.9	7.2	7.1	7.2	4.6	4.9	5.5	6.3
$25,000 to $29,999	4.9	5.5	6.4	6.5	6.7	6.6	4.4	4.6	5.3	5.8
$30,000 to $34,999	5.1	5.4	6.2	6.1	6.5	6.3	4.4	4.5	5.3	5.6
$35,000 to $39,999	4.7	5.0	5.4	5.3	5.9	5.6	4.2	4.2	4.9	5.1
$40,000 to $44,999	4.8	4.9	5.0	4.9	5.6	5.4	4.3	4.3	4.9	4.9
$45,000 to $49,999	4.3	4.4	4.2	4.0	4.8	4.6	3.7	3.7	4.3	4.3
$50,000 to $59,999	8.3	8.2	7.5	7.2	8.7	8.2	7.3	7.1	8.2	8.0
$60,000 to $74,999	10.7	10.2	8.5	8.1	9.9	9.4	9.8	9.4	10.3	9.6
$75,000 to $99,999	13.1	12.1	8.8	8.3	10.3	9.7	12.5	11.9	12.2	10.9
$100,000 to $124,999	8.5	7.6	4.8	4.5	5.6	5.3	9.0	8.5	7.8	6.7
$125,000 to $149,999	4.9	4.4	2.4	2.3	2.9	2.8	5.6	5.3	4.4	3.8
$150,000 to $199,999	4.9	4.3	2.1	1.9	2.4	2.3	6.3	6.0	4.4	3.7
$200,000 or more	5.0	4.4	1.4	1.1	1.6	1.6	6.0	5.7	4.2	3.4
Total households	82,333,080	82,290,325	13,795,544	23,680,467	13,461,366	41,317,810	7,126,302	18,933,909	116,716,292	166,222,511

Source: Projections by the authors derived from U.S. Census Bureau, 2011b, c, d, 2012

[a]NH refers to nonHispanic; values for categories labeled NH are only for the nonHispanic persons in each category. Hispanic includes Hispanics of all races

Table 4.6 Aggregate and mean household income in the United States (in billions of 2010 dollars) by race/ethnicity of the householder in 2010 and projected to 2060 using the middle projection scenario (Panel A) and assuming alternative closure to 2010 nonHispanic White rates by 2060 (Panel B)

Panel A:

	Aggregate household income (in $billions)					
Year	NH[a] White	NH Black	Hispanic	NH Asian & Other	Total	Mean household income ($)
2010	6,302.0	661.4	733.1	566.9	8,263.4	70,799
2020	6,618.6	779.6	989.4	716.7	9,104.3	70,083
2030	6,770.5	880.4	1,272.2	895.3	9,818.4	69,420
2040	6,705.4	967.9	1,582.7	1,088.5	10,344.5	68,717
2050	6,498.6	1,050.5	1,909.7	1,292.3	10,751.1	67,991
2060	6,298.7	1,135.3	2,250.0	1,506.3	11,190.3	67,321

Panel B

	Income differential assumptions					
	Assuming 2010 income differentials		Assuming closure to half of differential between NH White income for minority households		Assuming NH White income for minority households	
Race/ethnicity	Aggregate	Mean ($)	Aggregate	Mean ($)	Aggregate	Mean ($)
NH[a] White	6,298.7	76,543	6,298.7	76,543	6,298.7	76,543
NH Black	1,135.3	47,942	1,473.9	62,243	1,812.6	76,543
Hispanic	2,250.0	54,456	2,706.3	65,500	3,162.6	76,543
NH Asian & Other	1,506.3	79,555	1,506.3	79,555	1,506.3	79,555
Total	11,190.3	67,321	11,985.3	72,104	12,780.2	76,886

Source: Projections by the authors derived from U.S. Census Bureau, 2011b, c, d, 2012
[a]NH refers to nonHispanic; values for categories labeled NH are only for the nonHispanic persons in each category. Hispanic includes Hispanics of all races

rates by race/ethnicity in 2010 prevail in 2060. A comparison of the data in this table indicate that, in the absence of closure toward the lower poverty rates of nonHispanic White populations, current patterns of population change would lead to increased levels of overall poverty. For example, in Table 4.7 from 2010 to 2060 the percentage of households in poverty would increase from 10.3 to 12.1% among family households, from 18.8 to 21.3% for nonfamily households, and from 13.2 to 15.2% overall in the absence of decreased poverty rates for minority populations.

Table 4.8 shows that reductions in minority populations' poverty rates to the rates of nonHispanic Whites would substantially decrease overall poverty rates. In this table, alternative rates of closure are assumed between minorities and nonHispanic Whites. Rather than being the 13.2% poverty rate for the total population that existed in 2010, if poverty rates of minority populations could be reduced to the rates for nonHispanic Whites in 2010 by 2060, the overall rate of poverty for all

Table 4.7 Number and percentage of households in poverty in the United States by household type and race/ethnicity in 2010 and projected for 2060 using the middle projection scenario

	NH[a] White		NH Black		Hispanic		NH Asian & Other		Total	
Family type	Number	%	Number	%	Number	%	Number	%	Number	%
2010										
Family households	3,398,466	6.4	1,928,759	21.6	2,094,891	19.8	564,617	11.1	7,986,733	10.3
Married couple family	1,378,246	3.3	277,963	7.1	894,971	13.3	256,642	6.8	2,807,822	5.0
With related children	675,071	4.3	153,768	8.8	691,867	16.4	153,146	7.8	1,673,852	7.1
Other family[b]	2,020,220	18.6	1,650,796	32.9	1,199,920	31.5	307,975	23.6	5,178,911	24.6
Male, no spouse	371,465	11.3	187,019	21.6	217,244	17.7	60,459	15.4	836,187	14.5
With related children	243,092	15.1	110,926	27.8	149,948	23.9	33,264	21.2	537,230	19.3
Female, no spouse	1,648,755	21.7	1,463,777	35.3	982,676	38.0	247,516	27.1	4,342,724	28.5
With related children	1,188,527	30.7	1,020,875	42.8	745,119	45.7	169,823	35.9	3,124,344	37.3
Nonfamily households	4,759,605	16.2	1,365,719	28.1	753,808	26.0	499,747	24.3	7,378,879	18.8
Total households	8,158,071	9.9	3,294,478	23.9	2,848,699	21.2	1,064,364	14.9	15,365,612	13.2
2060 assuming (current 2010) poverty rates by household type for all race/ethnicity groups										
Family households	3,007,160	5.9	2,974,193	20.1	5,948,328	18.9	1,459,043	10.9	13,388,724	12.1
Married couple family	1,304,854	3.2	474,808	7.1	2,659,394	13.0	705,426	7.1	5,144,482	6.6
With related children	655,192	4.3	263,531	8.8	2,096,161	16.4	405,573	7.8	3,420,457	9.5
Other family[b]	1,702,306	16.8	2,499,385	30.8	3,288,934	29.8	753,617	22.4	8,244,242	25.3
Male, no spouse	313,713	10.7	287,941	20.6	589,812	17.4	147,649	15.1	1,339,115	15.4
With related children	216,955	15.1	179,151	27.8	413,439	23.9	82,959	21.2	892,504	21.3
Female, no spouse	1,388,593	19.4	2,211,444	33.0	2,699,122	35.2	605,968	25.4	6,905,127	28.8
With related children	1,122,407	30.7	1,649,557	42.8	2,208,469	45.7	444,120	35.9	5,424,553	39.9
Nonfamily households	4,957,253	15.8	2,615,503	29.5	2,881,087	29.3	1,417,157	25.3	11,871,000	21.3
Total households	7,964,413	9.7	5,589,696	23.6	8,829,415	21.4	2,876,200	15.2	25,259,724	15.2

Source: Projections by the authors derived from U.S. Census Bureau, 2011b, c, d, 2012

[a]NH refers to nonHispanic; values for categories labeled NH are only for the nonHispanic persons in each category. Hispanic includes Hispanics of all races

[b]By sex of the householder. Households without children not shown

Table 4.8 Number and percentage of households in poverty in the United States by household type and race/ethnicity in 2010 and projected for 2060 using the middle projection scenario

	NH[a] White		NH Black		Hispanic		NH Asian & Other		Total	
Family type	Number	%	Number	%	Number	%	Number	%	Number	%
2060 assuming closure to half of NH White poverty rates by household type for all race/ethnicity groups										
Family households	3,007,160	5.9	2,358,001	15.9	4,309,550	13.7	1,195,373	9.0	10,870,084	9.8
Married couple family	1,304,854	3.2	345,779	5.2	1,664,851	8.1	515,639	5.2	3,831,123	4.9
With related children	655,192	4.3	196,081	6.6	1,322,644	10.4	315,171	6.0	2,489,088	6.9
Other family[b]	1,702,306	16.8	2,012,222	24.8	2,644,699	23.9	679,734	20.2	7,038,961	21.6
Male, no spouse	313,713	10.7	217,514	15.5	483,316	14.3	127,585	13.0	1,142,128	13.1
With related children	216,955	15.1	138,423	21.5	337,702	19.5	71,088	18.2	764,168	18.2
Female, no spouse	1,388,593	19.4	1,794,708	26.8	2,161,383	28.2	552,149	23.1	5,896,833	24.6
With related children	1,122,407	30.7	1,416,278	36.7	1,844,942	38.2	411,742	33.3	4,795,369	35.3
Nonfamily households	4,957,253	15.8	2,021,165	22.8	2,220,777	22.6	1,163,628	20.8	10,362,823	18.6
Total households	7,964,413	9.7	4,379,166	18.5	6,530,327	15.8	2,359,001	12.5	21,232,907	12.8
2060 assuming NH White poverty rates by household type for all race/ethnicity groups										
Family households	3,007,160	5.9	1,741,812	11.8	2,670,774	8.5	931,702	7.0	8,351,448	7.6
Married couple family	1,304,854	3.2	216,751	3.2	670,308	3.3	325,851	3.3	2,517,764	3.2
With related children	655,192	4.3	128,630	4.3	549,128	4.3	224,768	4.3	1,557,718	4.3
Other family[b]	1,702,306	16.8	1,525,061	18.8	2,000,466	18.1	605,851	18.0	5,833,684	17.9
Male, no spouse	313,713	10.7	147,088	10.5	376,820	11.1	107,521	11.0	945,142	10.9
With related children	216,955	15.1	97,695	15.1	261,965	15.1	59,218	15.1	635,833	15.1
Female, no spouse	1,388,593	19.4	1,377,973	20.5	1,623,646	21.2	498,330	20.9	4,888,542	20.4
With related children	1,122,407	30.7	1,182,998	30.7	1,481,415	30.7	379,363	30.7	4,166,183	30.7
Nonfamily households	4,957,253	15.8	1,426,824	16.1	1,560,468	15.9	910,100	16.2	8,854,645	15.9
Total households	7,964,413	9.7	3,168,636	13.4	4,231,242	10.2	1,841,802	9.7	17,206,093	10.4

Source: Projections by the authors derived from U.S. Census Bureau, 2011b, c, d, 2012

[a]NH refers to nonHispanic; values for categories labeled NH are only for the nonHispanic persons in each category. Hispanic includes Hispanics of all races

[b]Percentages computed from unrounded values

Table 4.9 Federal tax revenues by household income in the United States (in millions of 2010 dollars) in 2010 and projected to 2060 using the middle projection scenario

	Number of households		Aggregate revenue		Percent change
Household income (in $2010)	2010	2060	2010	2060	2010–2060
Less than $20,000	21,359,081	36,402,730	4,271.8	7,280.5	70.4
$20,000–$39,999	24,510,421	29,421,384	71,080.2	85,322.0	20.0
$40,000–$59,999	20,308,635	37,067,620	146,222.2	266,886.9	82.5
$60,000–$99,999	26,261,166	34,075,615	372,908.6	483,873.7	29.8
$100,000 or more	24,276,989	29,255,162	1,259,975.7	1,518,342.9	20.5

Source: Projections by the authors derived from U.S. Census Bureau, 2011d, 2012; and Congressional Budget Office 2012

households could be reduced from the 13.2% that it was in 2010 to 10.4% in 2060. The data in this table indicates that reducing minority poverty would lead to less poverty overall as these populations increase as a proportion of all households.

Computations from the data shown in Table 4.9 indicate that the decline in overall income projected above (in the absence of change in race/ethnicity specific income differences) would lead to a relative decline in aggregate federal tax revenue per household. Dividing the aggregate revenue by the total number of households indicates that the average household in the United States paid $15,889 in federal taxes in 2010 but would pay $14,208 in 2060 (assuming no change in tax policy). In the absence of factors that would change the relationship between income and the occupation, industry, and race/ethnicity associated with it, demographic change could decrease the resources necessary to provide federally funded services.

Table 4.10 shows that the decreasing wealth of households would also affect expenditures. Data on the growth in households show an increase from 116.7 million households in 2010 to 166.2 million in 2060, a percentage increase of 42.4% under the middle projection scenario (Table 2.15), while the data in this table show the overall amount and percent change in the amount spent on various goods and services. Theoretically any change in the amount spent on various goods and services should be the same as the change in households, provided these households have the same consumption patterns and resources to purchase the resources as in the past. What is apparent when the data in this table are examined is that future levels of expenditures for all of the expenditure categories shown would be less than total household growth, suggesting that the households making such expenditures would spend less than their size and numbers would suggest. Thus the increase was less than 42.4% for all categories in Table 4.10. This finding supports the data on overall income suggesting that households may be poorer in the future.

Table 4.10 Consumer expenditures by category in the United States in 2010 (in millions of 2010 dollars) and projected to 2060 using the middle projection scenario

	All households		2010–2060 change[a]	
Expenditure category	2010	2060	Numeric	%
Food	745,233.3	1,012,177.9	266,944.7	35.8
Alcohol	50,588.0	59,765.1	9,177.0	18.1
Housing	2,018,817.1	2,730,452.7	711,635.5	35.3
Apparel	207,624.9	287,543.2	79,918.2	38.5
Transportation	923,987.3	1,203,793.4	279,806.1	30.3
Health	394,413.9	541,608.9	147,195.0	37.3
Entertainment	306,655.8	374,857.1	68,201.4	22.2
Personal	71,753.7	97,506.4	25,752.8	35.9
Reading	12,595.6	16,174.0	3,578.3	28.4
Education	129,737.6	158,665.8	28,928.2	22.3
Tobacco	42,136.6	48,269.1	6,132.5	14.6
Miscellaneous	105,484.8	130,831.3	25,346.6	24.0
Cash	208,815.3	282,202.5	73,387.2	35.1
Insurance	674,109.1	818,981.7	144,872.6	21.5
Total	5,891,953.1	7,762,829.2	1,870,876.1	31.8

Source: Projections by the authors derived from U.S. Census Bureau, 2011a, b, 2012; U.S. Census Bureau and U.S. Bureau of Labor Statistics 2011b
[a]Percentages calculated from unrounded values

The data in Table 4.11 clearly demonstrate that expenditures would follow the change in the size of racial/ethnic populations. Although nonHispanic White households are projected to continue to account for a majority of consumer expenditures of all types in 2060 as they did in 2010, the percentages of all expenditures by other than nonHispanic White households increase for all expenditure categories. For those expenditure categories most directly related to per capita needs, the overall percentages of expenditures by a racial/ethnic group closely follow their percentages of the population. For example, by 2060, food, housing, apparel, and entertainment expenditures closely follow the proportions that each group is projected to be of the total population. On the other hand categories of expenditures reflecting more discretionary goods such as alcohol, entertainment, reading, and tobacco are projected to remain more associated with groups (such as nonHispanic Whites) with higher levels of socioeconomic resources.

As shown in Table 4.12, which provides data on net change in consumer expenditures, despite expenditures being greater than their percentage of the total population for those with more socioeconomic resources, the shift of expenditures toward minority populations is also evident. In all categories except health, reading, and cash, the percentage of net change accounted for by nonHispanic Whites declines while increasing for all other racial/ethnic groups. Such data clearly indicate that even in the absence of change in economic differentials among racial/ethnic groups change in the racial/ethnic composition would affect the types and levels of expenditures.

Table 4.11 Percentage of consumer expenditures by category and race/ethnicity of householder in the United States in 2010 and projected for 2060 using the middle projection scenario

2010

Race/ethnicity	Total	Food	Alcohol	Housing	Apparel	Transportation	Health	Entertainment
NH[a] White	74.7	72.2	82.9	72.4	67.3	74.8	82.4	81.0
NH Black	8.6	8.8	5.4	9.8	9.7	8.6	6.4	6.1
Hispanic	9.9	12.1	7.2	10.7	13.1	10.1	6.4	7.6
NH Asian & Other	6.8	6.9	4.5	7.1	9.9	6.5	4.8	5.3

Race/ethnicity	Personal	Reading	Education	Tobacco	Misc.	Cash	Insurance
NH White	73.3	85.6	73.3	82.8	81.3	79.3	76.1
NH Black	10.4	4.6	4.9	7.7	7.4	9.3	7.5
Hispanic	10.9	4.3	9.2	5.3	7.0	7.3	8.8
NH Asian & Other	5.4	5.5	12.6	4.2	4.3	4.1	7.6

2060

Race/ethnicity	Total	Food	Alcohol	Housing	Apparel	Transportation	Health	Entertainment
NH White	54.1	50.7	66.5	51.4	44.9	53.8	64.8	62.7
NH Black	10.8	10.6	7.1	12.1	11.2	10.7	9.1	8.5
Hispanic	22.0	26.1	17.3	23.1	27.0	22.6	16.2	17.9
NH Asian & Other	13.1	12.6	9.1	13.4	16.9	12.9	9.9	10.9

Race/ethnicity	Personal	Reading	Education	Tobacco	Misc.	Cash	Insurance
NH White	52.9	70.9	48.8	66.4	64.0	63.3	54.7
NH Black	12.6	6.7	6.0	10.9	10.1	12.2	9.5
Hispanic	24.4	10.5	20.8	13.6	17.0	16.2	20.5
NH Asian & Other	10.1	11.9	24.4	9.1	8.9	8.3	15.3

Source: Projections by the authors derived from U.S. Census Bureau, 2011b, 2011d, 2012; U.S. Bureau of Labor Statistics 2011b

[a]NH refers to nonHispanic; values for categories labeled NH are only for the nonHispanic persons in each category. Hispanic includes Hispanics of all races

Table 4.12 Percentage of net change in consumer expenditures in the United States by expenditure category and race/ethnicity using the middle projection scenario, 2010–2060

Race/ethnicity	Total	Food	Alcohol	Housing	Apparel	Transportation	Health	Entertainment
NH[a] White	−10.8	−9.4	−23.9	−8.1	−13.3	−15.7	17.6	−19.4
NH Black	17.8	15.7	16.8	18.5	15.2	17.8	16.4	19.1
Hispanic	60.3	65.1	73.3	58.3	63.2	64.0	42.5	64.3
NH Asian & Other	32.7	28.6	33.8	31.3	34.9	33.9	23.5	36.0
Total	100.0	100.0	100.0	100.0	100.0	100.0	100.0	100.0
Race/ethnicity	Personal	Reading	Education	Tobacco	Misc.	Cash	Insurance	
NH White	−4.0	19.2	−61.0	−46.4	−8.3	17.8	−45.2	
NH Black	18.9	14.2	10.5	33.2	21.2	20.6	18.9	
Hispanic	62.0	32.4	72.5	70.8	58.9	41.6	74.7	
NH Asian & Other	23.1	34.2	78.0	42.4	28.2	20.0	51.6	
Total	100.0	100.0	100.0	100.0	100.0	100.0	100.0	

Source: Projections by the authors derived from U.S. Census Bureau, 2011b, 2011c, 2011d, 2012; U.S. Bureau of Labor Statistics 2011b

[a]NH refers to nonHispanic; values for categories labeled NH are only for the nonHispanic persons in each category. Hispanic includes Hispanics of all races

Tables 4.13 and 4.14 provide additional data on consumer expenditures by type of expenditure showing total expenditures by household type (in Table 4.13) and percent change in expenditures from 2010 to 2060 by household type (in Table 4.14). The data in these tables show that the change toward more diverse household types

Table 4.13 Consumer expenditures by household type and expenditure category in the United States in 2010 and projected to 2060 using the middle projection scenario (in millions of 2010 dollars)

Expenditure category	All households	Married couple families	Male householder families	Female householder families	Nonfamily households
2010					
Food	723,892.3	443,451.4	29,400.9	81,858.5	169,181.5
Alcohol	45,872.3	26,802.7	1,880.5	2,113.2	15,075.9
Housing	1,956,871.1	1,151,208.0	89,028.8	218,227.7	498,406.7
Apparel	208,063.4	117,558.9	9,100.9	33,528.9	47,874.7
Transportation	908,170.0	565,100.9	45,144.5	97,777.6	200,146.9
Health	363,005.5	243,459.2	11,549.9	21,784.6	86,211.7
Entertainment	292,700.9	186,507.1	11,729.1	26,262.6	68,202.2
Personal	69,000.3	41,248.0	2,677.6	8,443.3	16,631.4
Reading	11,359.4	7,176.4	331.3	632.4	3,219.3
Education	120,871.4	83,850.4	2,070.0	6,268.5	28,682.5
Tobacco	42,253.1	20,232.9	2,351.1	4,418.7	15,250.4
Miscellaneous	99,932.0	55,843.8	6,455.2	8,095.7	29,537.3
Cash	190,594.1	118,960.8	16,436.6	6,882.9	48,313.7
Insurance	625,946.2	428,827.9	31,082.2	37,262.6	128,773.5
Total	5,658,531.9	3,490,228.3	259,238.4	553,557.3	1,355,507.8
2060					
Food	1,027,476.6	607,145.1	42,961.7	128,551.8	248,818.0
Alcohol	57,913.5	32,587.3	2,531.1	3,179.4	19,615.7
Housing	2,748,740.0	1,572,153.7	135,259.8	333,024.0	708,302.6
Apparel	309,602.0	163,635.5	11,177.3	55,494.7	79,294.5
Transportation	1,245,957.4	751,394.4	73,436.9	141,766.4	279,359.7
Health	453,153.4	297,179.1	14,842.3	30,045.6	111,086.4
Entertainment	373,936.4	232,154.4	15,501.5	35,764.6	90,515.9
Personal	95,831.2	54,891.6	3,966.7	12,990.9	23,981.9
Reading	13,830.7	8,472.1	432.7	933.1	3,992.7
Education	169,057.9	112,965.3	2,492.9	9,499.3	44,100.4
Tobacco	51,048.5	23,829.1	2,561.0	5,163.5	19,495.0
Miscellaneous	126,741.4	69,939.4	8,646.0	10,881.0	37,275.0
Cash	241,713.2	146,829.7	19,196.6	9,950.4	65,736.5
Insurance	841,879.6	564,328.3	42,630.4	54,392.9	180,527.9
Total	7,756,881.8	4,637,505.2	375,637.0	831,637.4	1,912,102.2

Source: Projections by the authors derived from U.S. Census Bureau, 2011b, d, 2012; U.S. Census Bureau and U.S. Bureau of Labor Statistics 2011b

Table 4.14 Percent change in consumer expenditures by household type and expenditure category in the United States using the middle projection scenario, 2010–2060

Expenditure category	All households	Married couple families	Male householder families	Female householder families	Nonfamily households
Food	41.9	36.9	46.1	57.0	47.1
Alcohol	26.2	21.6	34.6	50.4	30.1
Housing	40.5	36.6	51.9	52.6	42.1
Apparel	48.8	39.2	22.8	65.5	65.6
Transportation	37.2	33.0	62.7	45.0	39.6
Health	24.8	22.1	28.5	37.9	28.9
Entertainment	27.8	24.5	32.2	36.2	32.7
Personal	38.9	33.1	48.1	53.9	44.2
Reading	21.8	18.1	30.6	47.5	24.0
Education	39.9	34.7	20.4	51.5	53.8
Tobacco	20.8	17.8	8.9	16.9	27.8
Miscellaneous	26.8	25.2	33.9	34.4	26.2
Cash	26.8	23.4	16.8	44.6	36.1
Insurance	34.5	31.6	37.2	46.0	40.2
Total	37.1	32.9	44.9	50.2	41.1

Source: Projections by the authors derived from U.S. Census Bureau, 2011b, d, 2012; U.S. Census Bureau and U.S. Bureau of Labor Statistics 2011b

would be evident in expenditures. When one examines consumer expenditures by household type one finds that although married-couple households generally show the largest total expenditures both in 2010 and 2060, they also generally show the smallest rates of increase between 2010 and 2060. Married-couple households show the smallest change in all expenditure categories between 2010 and 2060 except for apparel, education, tobacco, and cash, while growth is generally the largest (due to the relative growth in the number of such households) in female householder households. These data indicate that change in household form would have clear economic implications.

Table 4.15 provides projections of the value (in 2010 constant dollars) and percent change in value and total net worth resulting from race/ethnicity and age effects. The data on percent difference in this table indicate that the effects of the aging of the population would be larger than the effects of race/ethnicity on all categories of assets except equity in business and rental property. This is to be expected because older households tend to have more resources, and higher rates of growth are projected for older households. Conversely, because the number of minority households is projected to grow more extensively across time than the number of nonHispanic White households, and minority households tend to have lower levels of assets (given the assumption that current differences in assets remain the same within racial/ethnic groups across time), the projected growth in minority households would be expected to reduce relative levels of growth in assets.

Table 4.15 Race/ethnicity and age of householder effects on estimates of net worth and assets for households in the United States in 2010 and projected to 2060 using the middle projection scenario

Categories of assets[a]	2010	2060	Percent[b] difference
Panel A: Race/ethnicity effects			
Net worth	38,216,034.6	43,602,539.4	14.1
Interest earning assets at financial institutions	2,846,542.9	3,736,959.1	31.3
Regular checking accounts	269,377.9	341,126.3	26.6
Stocks and mutual fund shares	46,154,990.3	65,847,387.2	42.7
Equity in business or profession	18,808,475.7	25,294,897.6	34.5
Equity in motor vehicles	960,060.4	1,289,951.4	34.4
Equity in own home	16,105,553.7	21,941,301.7	36.2
Rental property equity	46,447,143.6	65,139,501.5	40.2
U.S. saving bonds	762,313.9	1,095,958.3	43.8
IRA or KEOGH accounts	12,206,599.3	17,348,545.9	42.1
401 K & thrift savings plan	10,083,970.8	13,422,645.7	33.1
Panel B: Age effects			
Net worth	38,216,034.6	60,760,297.6	59.0
Interest earning assets at financial institutions	2,846,542.9	4,383,998.3	54.0
Regular checking accounts	269,377.9	424,987.3	57.8
Stocks and mutual fund shares	46,154,990.3	73,962,276.6	60.2
Equity in business or profession	18,808,475.7	24,765,418.6	31.7
Equity in motor vehicles	960,060.4	1,361,680.0	41.8
Equity in own home	16,105,553.7	22,739,952.9	41.2
Rental property equity	46,447,143.6	61,297,914.5	32.0
U.S. saving bonds	762,313.9	1,187,389.1	55.8
IRA or KEOGH accounts	12,206,599.3	17,422,822.7	42.7
401 K & thrift savings plan	10,083,970.8	15,663,412.2	55.3

Source: Projections by the authors derived from U.S. Census Bureau, 2011b, d, 2012; U.S. Census Bureau and U.S. Bureau of Labor Statistics 2010
[a]Monetary values in millions of 2010 constant dollars
[b]Percentages computed from unrounded values

The data in Panel A of Table 4.16 indicate that proportions of net worth and of most assets are higher for nonHispanic White households in 2010 and are projected to be so in households in 2060. At the same time, the overall ownership of assets shows shifts toward minority households between 2010 and 2060. The data in Panel B of the table indicate clear and pervasive shifts of net worth and asset ownership for all forms of assets toward older adult households such that by 2060 more than 50% of household net worth for 6 of 10 major categories of assets will be held by elderly households.

The data in Table 4.17 provide validation of the reasons for the patterns as suggested above for the data in Tables 4.15 and 4.16. An examination of the data in

Table 4.16 Proportions of net worth and assets of households in the United States by race/ethnicity (Panel A) and age (Panel B) of householder in 2010 and projected for 2060 using the middle projection scenario

Race/ethnicity and age	Net worth	Interest earning assets	Regular checking	Equity in business/ profession	Equity in motor vehicles	Equity in own home	Equity in rental property	U.S. savings bonds	IRA/ KEOGH	401 K/ thrift	Stocks/ mutual funds
Panel A: Race/ethnicity effects											
2010											
NH[a] White	90.4	80.5	82.0	78.1	77.0	76.0	75.4	74.9	74.5	79.2	77.1
NH Black	3.0	5.3	6.0	6.3	7.7	7.9	6.2	4.4	6.5	5.8	2.9
Hispanic	3.0	4.4	6.6	6.8	8.3	8.0	8.0	9.0	5.0	5.7	1.1
NH Asian/Other	3.6	9.8	5.4	8.8	7.0	8.1	10.4	11.6	14.0	9.3	18.9
2060											
NH[a] White	78.0	60.4	63.8	57.3	56.5	55.0	53.0	51.3	51.7	58.6	53.3
NH Black	4.1	6.4	7.4	7.3	9.0	9.2	7.0	4.9	7.2	6.9	3.2
Hispanic	7.9	9.9	15.4	15.0	18.4	17.3	16.9	18.5	10.5	12.7	2.3
NH Asian/Other	10.0	23.3	13.4	20.4	16.1	18.5	23.1	25.3	30.6	21.8	41.2
Panel B: Age effects											
2010											
15–44	15.2	18.7	29.2	31.6	29.2	16.0	22.3	22.1	19.9	21.8	7.6
45–54	21.7	19.3	18.0	22.5	23.9	22.2	20.2	18.7	20.5	23.6	6.9
55–64	22.1	22.5	17.0	25.7	22.4	23.1	25.8	19.5	22.0	23.2	9.2
65+	41.0	39.5	35.8	20.2	24.5	38.7	31.7	39.7	37.6	31.4	76.3
2060											
15–44	11.7	14.5	23.2	27.8	25.0	12.5	18.2	17.2	15.6	17.9	4.8
45–54	14.9	13.3	12.8	17.6	18.2	15.5	14.7	12.9	14.4	17.2	3.9
55–64	17.2	17.7	13.7	23.0	19.4	18.3	21.3	15.3	17.6	19.2	5.9
65+	56.2	54.5	50.3	31.6	37.4	53.7	45.8	54.6	52.4	45.7	85.4

Source: Projections by the authors derived from U.S. Census Bureau, 2011b, d, 2012; U.S. Census Bureau and U.S. Bureau of Labor Statistics 2010

[a]NH refers to nonHispanic; values for categories labeled NH are only for the nonHispanic persons in each category. Hispanic includes Hispanics of all races

Table 4.17 Race/ethnicity and age of householder effects on estimates of net worth and assets for households in the United States in 2010 and projected to 2060 using the middle projection scenario

Categories of assets[a]	Assuming 2010 distribution in 2060	Assuming the middle scenario	Percent[b] difference
Panel A: Race/ethnicity effects			
Net worth	53,896,967.3	43,602,539.4	−19.1
Interest earning assets at financial institutions	4,053,741.6	3,736,959.1	−7.8
Regular checking accounts	380,104.0	341,126.3	
Stocks and mutual fund shares	67,005,859.9	65,847,387.2	−10.3
Equity in business or profession	26,704,338.4	25,294,897.6	−1.7
Equity in motor vehicles	1,356,473.8	1,289,951.4	−5.3
Equity in own home	22,802,626.0	21,941,301.7	−4.9
Rental property equity	66,125,308.8	65,139,501.5	−3.8
U.S. saving bonds	1,088,920.1	1,095,958.3	−1.5
IRA or KEOGH accounts	17,502,964.0	17,348,545.9	0.6
401 K & thrift savings plan	14,338,883.2	13,422,645.7	−0.9
Panel B: Age effects			
Net worth	53,930,710.4	60,760,297.6	12.7
Interest earning assets at financial institutions	3,918,295.5	4,383,998.3	11.9
Regular checking accounts	388,582.9	424,987.3	
Stocks and mutual fund shares	53,736,555.1	73,962,276.6	9.4
Equity in business or profession	25,101,277.2	24,765,418.6	37.6
Equity in motor vehicles	1,343,135.0	1,361,680.0	−1.3
Equity in own home	20,468,454.7	22,739,952.9	1.4
Rental property equity	57,517,745.2	61,297,914.5	11.1
U.S. saving bonds	1,059,710.8	1,187,389.1	6.6
IRA or KEOGH accounts	15,775,610.6	17,422,822.7	12.0
401 K & thrift savings plan	14,775,231.6	15,663,412.2	10.4

Source: Projections by the authors derived from U.S. Census Bureau, 2011b, d, 2012; U.S. Census Bureau and U.S. Bureau of Labor Statistics 2010

[a]Monetary values in millions of 2010 constant dollars

[b]Percentages computed from unrounded values

Table 4.17, [ascertained by assuming the same race/ethnicity (top panel) and age (bottom panel) distributions in the population in 2060 as in 2010] shows that change in the two key demographic characteristics of age and race/ethnicity would (in the absence of change in current relationships between demographic and socioeconomic factors) substantially affect the overall change shown in earlier tables. An analysis of the data in this table, when compared to Tables 4.15 and 4.16, indicates (by the much smaller percent changes for 2010–2060) that the effects shown are due, in large part, to changes in race/ethnicity and age distributions between 2010 and 2060. Race/ethnicity effects would clearly reduce the value of assets from the values they would have had without the influence of the racial/ethnic dimensions. At the same time, differences in age distributions during the two time frames also reduce the relative growth in net worth and other assets shown overall but the effects are less than those for race/ethnicity. Clearly then the change projected to occur in demographic characteristics may have substantial impacts on the future socioeconomic conditions of the population of the United States.

Tables 4.18, 4.19, 4.20, 4.21, 4.22 and 4.23 examine the effects of demographic change on housing tenure, that is whether housing units are owned or rented and the characteristics associated with them including expenditures. The data in Table 4.18 show that age and race/ethnicity clearly affected ownership and median rents and values in 2010. The value of owned units was highest for nonHispanic Asian and Other ($375,800) households, followed by the value for units owned by nonHispanic Whites ($190,000) and Hispanic ($185,900) households. The value was substantially lower for nonHispanic Black households ($137,100) in 2010. Rent followed a similar pattern with the exception that Hispanic household rents were higher than those for nonHispanic White or Black households reflecting the demand resulting from larger households.

There were even larger differences in the tenure characteristics of households by race/ethnicity. Overall, 72.2% of nonHispanic White households lived in owned units compared to 44.6% of nonHispanic Black, 47.3% of Hispanic, and 55.8% of nonHispanic Asian and Other households. There are also substantial age effects, with 59.5% of householders less than 60 years of age living in owner-occupied units compared to 78.7% of those 60–64 years of age, 80.2% of those 65–74 years of age, and 74.5% of those 75 years of age or older.

Table 4.18 Median owner-occupied housing values, median monthly rents, ownership rates, and renter rates in the United States by race/ethnicity of householder, and tenure by age of householder, 2010

	Race/ethnicity				
Housing characteristic	NH[a] White	NH Black	Hispanic	NH Asian & Other	Total
Median housing values ($)	190,000	137,100	185,900	375,800	188,400
Median gross rents ($)	833	790	877	1,059	841
Tenure					
Percent owner	72.2	44.6	47.3	55.8	65.1
Percent renter	27.8	55.4	52.7	44.2	34.9
	Age group				
Housing characteristic	15–59	60–64	65–74	75+	Total
Tenure					
Percent owner	59.5	78.7	80.2	74.5	65.1
Percent renter	40.5	21.3	19.8	25.5	34.9

Source: U.S. Census Bureau, 2011b, c, d

[a]NH refers to nonHispanic; values for categories labeled NH are only for the nonHispanic persons in each category. Hispanic includes Hispanics of all races

Table 4.19 Number of households in the United States, percent change 2010–2060, and percentage of households by race/ethnicity of householder and housing tenure in 2010 and projected for 2060 using the middle projection scenario

Year/period	NH[a] White	NH Black	Hispanic	NH Asian & Other	Total
Panel A: Number of households					
All households					
2010	82,333,080	13,795,544	13,461,366	7,126,302	116,716,292
2060	82,290,325	23,680,467	41,317,810	18,933,909	166,222,511
Owner households					
2010	59,483,623	6,156,443	6,368,449	3,977,559	75,986,074
2060	60,393,109	11,579,816	21,279,747	10,971,183	104,223,855
Renter households					
2010	22,849,457	7,639,101	7,092,917	3,148,743	40,730,218
2060	21,897,216	12,100,651	20,038,063	7,962,726	61,998,656
Panel B: Percent change in households					
All households					
2010–2060	−0.1	71.7	206.9	165.7	42.4
Owner households					
2010–2060	1.5	88.1	234.1	175.8	37.2
Renter households					
2010–2060	−4.2	58.4	182.5	152.9	52.2
Panel C: Race/ethnicity of households as a percentage of households					
All households					
2010	70.5	11.8	11.5	6.2	100.0
2060	49.5	14.2	24.9	11.4	100.0
Owner households					
2010	78.3	8.1	8.4	5.2	100.0
2060	57.9	11.1	20.4	10.6	100.0
Renter households					
2010	56.1	18.8	17.4	7.7	100.0
2060	35.3	19.5	32.3	12.9	100.0

Source: Projections by the authors derived from U.S. Census Bureau, 2011c, d, 2012
[a]NH refers to nonHispanic; values for categories labeled NH are only for the nonHispanic persons in each category. Hispanic includes Hispanics of all races

Table 4.19 provides data on the number of households in the United States projected for 2060 by tenure and race/ethnicity. The data indicate that the underlying change in population would lead to decreases in the number and percentage of all households and to decreases in the percentage of all owner and renter units that have nonHispanic White householders. The number and percentage with nonHispanic Black, Hispanic, and NonHisapnic Asian and Other householders would increase. The data in this table also project that those interested in owner or renter housing change would increasingly need to analyze minority housing markets.

Table 4.20 Number and percentage of net change in the United States households by race/ethnicity of householder and housing tenure using the middle projection scenario, 2010–2060

Race/ethnicity	Number	Percent
All households		
NH[a] White	–42,755	–0.1
NH Black	9,884,923	20.0
Hispanic	27,856,444	56.3
NH Asian & Other	11,807,607	23.8
Total	49,506,220	100.0
Owner households		
NH White	909,486	3.2
NH Black	5,423,373	19.2
Hispanic	14,911,298	52.8
NH Asian & Other	6,993,624	24.8
Total	28,237,780	100.0
Renter households		
NH White	–952,241	–4.5
NH Black	4,461,550	21.0
Hispanic	12,945,146	60.9
NH Asian & Other	4,813,983	22.6
Total	21,268,438	100.0

Source: Projections by the authors derived from U.S. Census Bureau, 2011c, d, 2012

[a]NH refers to nonHispanic; values for categories labeled NH are only for the nonHispanic persons in each category. Hispanic includes Hispanics of all races

These patterns are also evident in Table 4.20, which summarizes the proportion of change in household growth due to each racial/ethnic group. Overall, 56.3% of all new households would be due to increases in the number of Hispanic households, 23.8% to nonHispanic Asian and Other, and 20.0% to nonHispanic Black households. However, the number of nonHispanic White householders would decline overall by 0.1% and for renter households by 4.5%. As with population, the future of households and housing would be determined by minority households and populations. Although nonHispanic Whites show small positive growth in owner housing, they show marked declines in the number of renter households. NonHispanic Blacks show small differences in rates of increase for renter and owner households (accounting for about 20% in both cases). NonHispanic Asian and Others would account for between 22.6 and 24.8% of the growth for all forms of housing, and Hispanics would account for between 52.8 and 60.9%. For housing as for several other factors examined in this text, minority population and housing growth would increasingly determine future patterns and markets.

Tables 4.21, 4.22 and 4.23 show the effects of household change on expenditures by race/ethnicity and time period and by household tenure. Table 4.21 provides data indicating that the single largest contributor to household expenditures would continue to be nonHispanic Whites but that their share of contribution would decline as their share of the population declines. Although nonHispanic White households accounted for 70.1% of all expenditures in 2010, they would account for 48.6% in 2060. NonHispanic Black households that accounted for 9.9% in 2010 would account for 12.0% in 2060. These values are 11.6% for Hispanics in 2010 but 24.2% in 2060, and for nonHispanic Asian and Others these values are 8.3% in 2010 and 15.3% in 2060.

What is also evident in this table is that nonHispanic White householders are expected to continue to account for a majority of owner expenditures through 2060 but would account for 35.5% of renter expenditures by 2060. All minority household groups would account for an increasing proportion of both owner- and renter-occupied housing expenditures with the total owner expenditures increasing from 6.5% in 2010 to 8.7% in 2060 for nonHispanic Black households, from 8.6 in 2010 to 20.0% in 2060 for Hispanics, and from 7.6% in 2010 to 15.2% in 2060 for non-Hispanic Asians and Others.

The expenditures for renter households show an increasing dominance of minority households. The percentage of all renter expenditures accounted for by nonHispanic White households is projected to decrease from 55.5% of all such expenditures in 2010 to 35.5% in 2060, while the comparable values for nonHispanic Black populations would be an increase from 17.0% in 2010 to 17.6% in 2060, for Hispanics would be an increase from 17.9% in 2010 to 31.5% in 2060, and for non-Hispanic Asian and Others would be an increase from 9.7% in 2010 to 15.3% in 2060. These projections clearly assume that the underlying income structure of racial/ethnic groups remains the same as in 2010, and it must be acknowledged that relative shifts may occur that could markedly alter the projected values.

The age structure of the population would also affect expenditure patterns for housing. Table 4.22 shows the patterns of such changes. As is evident in this table, whether overall expenditures or expenditures by tenure (owner or renter) are examined, the percentage of expenditures would shift toward older households. For all households as well as for owner and renter households, the percentage of all expenditures for all age groups (except renter households with householders 55–64 years of age) less than 65 years of age would decline over time, while the percentage accounted for by those 65–74 and 75+ would increase over time. The data in this table indicate that although total household expenditures would continue to be concentrated among those households with householders who are 25–64 years of age, household expenditures for those 65 years of age or older would continue to increase and would account for 24.6% of all household expenditures in 2060 compared to 15.8% in 2010.

Table 4.23 provides a final means of examining how change in the race/ethnicity and age composition of the population will affect household expenditures. The first panel of this table demonstrates the effects of race/ethnicity on owner, renter, and total housing expenditures in the United States by 2060, if the dollars of expendi-

Table 4.21 Aggregate annual expenditures and percentage of annual expenditures for housing in the United States by race/ethnicity of the householder and housing tenure in 2010 and projected to 2060 using the middle projection scenario

	NH[a] White		NH Black		Hispanic		NH Asian & Other		Total
Year	Expenditures[b]	%[c]	Expenditures	%	Expenditures	%	Expenditures	%	expenditures
All households									
2010	745,303	70.1	105,569	9.9	123,720	11.6	88,147	8.3	1,062,739
2020	760,870	65.8	121,850	10.5	163,572	14.1	109,779	9.5	1,156,072
2030	761,729	61.5	136,814	11.0	205,459	16.6	134,774	10.9	1,238,776
2040	747,101	57.1	148,697	11.4	250,865	19.2	161,705	12.4	1,308,368
2050	724,528	52.7	160,037	11.6	299,002	21.8	190,359	13.9	1,373,927
2060	700,099	48.6	172,397	12.0	348,649	24.2	220,220	15.3	1,441,365
Owner occupied									
2010	552,681	77.3	46,378	6.5	61,701	8.6	54,602	7.6	715,362
2020	563,950	73.2	53,923	7.0	83,506	10.8	68,837	8.9	770,216
2030	562,236	69.0	61,856	7.6	106,090	13.0	84,842	10.4	815,025
2040	546,648	64.6	67,745	8.0	130,144	15.4	101,754	12.0	846,291
2050	528,887	60.2	73,060	8.3	155,892	17.8	120,051	13.7	877,891
2060	513,055	56.1	79,470	8.7	182,727	20.0	139,449	15.2	914,701
Renter occupied									
2010	192,622	55.5	59,190	17.0	62,019	17.9	33,545	9.7	347,377
2020	196,920	51.0	67,928	17.6	80,067	20.8	40,942	10.6	385,856
2030	199,492	47.1	74,958	17.7	99,369	23.4	49,932	11.8	423,751
2040	200,452	43.4	80,953	17.5	120,721	26.1	59,951	13.0	462,077
2050	195,641	39.4	86,977	17.5	143,110	28.9	70,308	14.2	496,036
2060	187,044	35.5	92,927	17.6	165,922	31.5	80,772	15.3	526,664

Source: Projections by the authors derived from U.S. Census Bureau, 2011c, d, 2012; U.S. Bureau of Labor Statistics 2011b

[a]NH refers to nonHispanic; values for categories labeled NH are only for the nonHispanic persons in each category. Hispanic includes Hispanics of all races

[b]Monetary values in millions of 2010 constant dollars

[c]Percentages computed from unrounded values

Table 4.22 Proportion of annual expenditures for housing in the United States by age of householder and housing tenure in 2010 and projected to 2060 using the middle projection scenario

	Percentage of household expenditures by age of householder						
Year	15–24	25–34	35–44	45–54	55–64	65–74	75+
All households							
2010	3.0	16.8	22.9	24.7	16.8	9.1	6.7
2020	2.7	17.3	21.6	20.4	18.0	12.5	7.5
2030	2.6	15.9	22.8	19.7	15.1	13.6	10.3
2040	2.6	15.6	21.6	21.2	14.9	11.7	12.4
2050	2.5	15.8	21.5	20.3	16.1	11.7	12.0
2060	2.5	15.3	21.9	20.3	15.5	12.9	11.7
Owner households							
2010	1.0	11.9	22.9	27.7	19.5	10.8	6.1
2020	0.8	12.1	21.5	22.6	20.8	15.1	7.0
2030	0.8	11.1	22.7	22.0	17.4	16.4	9.6
2040	0.8	10.8	21.6	23.7	17.2	14.2	11.6
2050	0.8	11.0	21.4	22.8	18.7	14.3	11.1
2060	0.7	10.5	21.8	22.6	17.9	15.6	10.9
Renter households							
2010	7.2	26.9	22.9	18.5	11.3	5.4	7.8
2020	6.4	27.5	21.8	15.9	12.4	7.5	8.6
2030	6.0	25.1	23.0	15.5	10.7	8.3	11.4
2040	5.9	24.2	21.6	16.6	10.6	7.2	13.9
2050	5.7	24.3	21.6	16.0	11.6	7.2	13.7
2060	5.6	23.6	22.0	16.2	11.3	8.0	13.3

Source: Projections by the authors derived from U.S. Census Bureau, 2011c, d, 2012; U.S. Bureau of Labor Statistics 2011b

Table 4.23 Annual expenditures for housing in the United States by tenure in 2060 assuming projected patterns by race/ethnicity and age of householder and assuming 2010 distribution by race/ethnicity and age of householder using the middle projection scenario

Housing tenure	Assuming 2010 distribution in 2060	Assuming the middle scenario	Numerical difference	Percent difference
Race/ethnicity of householder				
Owner	1,018,788,837,533	914,700,749,716	−104,088,087,817	−10.2
Renter	494,719,959,929	526,663,907,704	31,943,947,775	6.5
Total	1,513,508,797,462	1,441,364,657,419	−72,144,140,043	−4.8
Age of householder				
Owner	966,457,842,929	914,700,749,716	−51,757,093,213	−5.4
Renter	573,611,063,650	526,663,907,704	−46,947,155,946	−8.2
Total	1,540,068,906,578	1,441,364,657,419	−98,704,249,159	−6.4

Source: Projections by the authors derived from U.S. Bureau of the Census, 2011b, c, d, 2012; U.S. Bureau of Labor Statistics 2011b

tures by race/ethnicity group in 2010 continue through 2060 but the racial/ethnic composition of householders changes as projected and shown in Chapter 2. The second panel shows the same effects for the projected change in the age of householders. Although projections of the total dollars of expenditures for such effects are subject to numerous potential alterations over time, they still clearly indicate how important change in demographic structure may be to housing expenditures. As shown in Table 4.23, change in the racial/ethnic composition of the population, assuming no change in expenditure differentials by race/ethnicity from 2010 to 2060, would result in a total decline of more than $72 billion in expenditures resulting from a $104 billion decrease in owner expenditures and a nearly $32 billion increase in renter expenditures for 2060 (in 2010 constant dollars). Although these represent only a 4.8% decline in overall expenditures from 2010 (in 2010 constant dollars), they demonstrate that, in the absence of increased relative housing expenditures by minority populations, housing expenditures would be negatively impacted by future patterns of racial/ethnic change.

The data in the bottom panel show (in 2010 constant dollars) even larger total net effects resulting from the aging of the population. These data show substantial negative expenditure effects for both owner and renter households due to an aging population. The data indicate a decline of nearly $52 billion for owner and $47 billion for renter housing expenditures and an overall decline of $98.7 billion (6.4%) from 2010 levels as a result of the aging population. Again, although such declines may be seen as relatively small compared to overall changes in housing markets, they nevertheless indicate that an aging population will likely reduce expenditures for housing over time.

4.3 Summary

The size, distribution and composition of the population, households, and labor force have significant implications for the economy, including both the public and private sectors.

1. Real median income was less in 2010 than in 2000, per capita income also showed real decline from 1999 to 2010, and poverty rates increased from 1999 to 2010.
2. There continue to be marked income differences among racial/ethnic groups in the United States. In 2010, median household incomes were $56,466 for nonHispanic Whites, $54,013 for nonHispanic Asian and Others, $41,543 for Hispanics, and $35,189 for nonHispanic Blacks (see Table 4.2). NonHispanic Black families had poverty rates of 21.5% in 2010; Hispanics poverty rates were 20.0%, nonHispanic Asians and Others poverty levels were 11.0%, and nonHispanic White families had poverty rates of 6.3% (Table 4.2). Clearly if such differences continue and the future rates of population growth noted in previous chapters occur, change in race/ethnicity-specific economic factors will have implications

for the economy of the nation. In fact growth in government receipts and expenditures (see Table 4.3 and 4.4) and relative levels of household wealth (see Table 4.14) were reduced in per household terms from 2000 to 2010.

3. Given the substantial differences in income and poverty among racial/ethnic groups in the nation, the patterns of projected population growth would, in the absence of change in real income for the fastest growing minority groups, lead to declines in total income at higher income levels (see Table 4.5) and to a more than $3,400 real mean household income decline (in 2010 constant dollars). Similarly, in the absence of closure in income levels among racial/ethnic groups, household poverty rates would increase by 2% (see Table 4.8) from 2010 to 2060 (based on 2010 dollars), but the rates would show little change if closure occurred in income levels between minority and nonHispanic White households.
4. Both government revenues and expenditures would also change in the absence of closure in racial/ethnic group income differences. Although the number of households is projected to increase by 48.9% from 2010 to 2060 (see Table 2.15), consumer expenditures (due to the marked racial/ethnic disparities in income) would not reach this level for any major consumer expenditure category (see Table 4.10) and the effect of racial/ethnic disparities would also suppress increases in the value of assets. Partially offsetting such declines is the aging of the population, with older households increasing as a proportion of all households and having higher net worth (see Table 4.15). Similarly, due to change in the racial/ethnic composition of the population, overall net worth would decline by –19.1% from 2010 to 2060, but this decline would be partially offset by an increase of nearly 13% due to the aging of the population (see Table 4.17).
5. Housing patterns will also be impacted by demographic change. The percentage of households with a nonHispanic White householder would decline and those with a minority householder increase. As a result, the percentage of all households with a nonHispanic White householder would decrease from 70.5 to 49.5%, while the percentage of nonHispanic Black householders would increase from 11.8 to 14.2%, the percentage of Hispanic households would increase from 11.5 to 24.9%, and the percentage of households with a nonHispanic Asian or Other householder would increase from 6.2 to 11.4% (see Table 4.19).
6. The size and percentage of household expenditures will also decrease for nonHispanic White households and increase for minority households. The percentage of total housing expenditures accounted for by nonHispanic White households is projected to decrease from 70.1% of all expenditures in 2010 to 48.6% of such expenditures in 2060, while increasing from 9.9 to 12.0% for nonHispanic Black, increasing from 11.6 to 24.2% for Hispanic, and increasing from 8.3 to 15.3% for nonHispanic Asian and Other households.
7. Both age and race/ethnicity will affect annual owner and renter household expenditures. Race/ethnicity differences in expenditure patterns lead to a total net increase in renter and a decrease in owner household expenditures while age decreases both owner and renter related expenditures.

Overall, the data in this chapter suggest that unless the economic disparities by age and those by race/ethnicity change the disparities in rates of population growth among older populations and impoverished racial/ethnic groups will not only change the distribution of total income, assets, housing-related wealth, and other economic resources among age and racial and ethnic groups but will decrease the total value of such economic resources for the total population. Although the effects of the aging of the population are clearly important to address, closing the socioeconomic differences among racial/ethnic groups is particularly essential to keep the United States from becoming poorer and less competitive. However, it is equally important to recognize that to the extent these disparities can be and are reduced or eliminated, the United States could not only become a more affluent country but could be in an advantageous position relative to many of its competitors in world markets. Many of these competitors have demographics that are likely to be even more challenging to address than those in the United States and very difficult to change (such as older age structures) while lacking large population segments with socioeconomic disparities that could be reduced or eliminated with a resultant increase in socioeconomic resources.

References

Arnott, R. D., & Chaves, D. B. (2012). Demographic changes, financial markets, and the economy. *Financial Analysts Journal, 68*(1), 23–46.

Byun, K. J., & Frey, C. (2012). The U.S. economy in 2020: Recovery in uncertain times. *Monthly Labor Review, 135*, 36.

Congressional Budget Office. (2012). *The distribution of household income and federal taxes, 2010*. http://www.cbo.gov/sites/default/files/44604-AverageTaxRates.pdf. Accessed 21 Jan 2015.

DeNavas-Walt, C., & Proctor, B. D. (2014). *Income and poverty in the United States: 2013. Current population reports P60-249 (September)*. Washington, DC: U.S. Census Bureau.

Felix, A., & Watkins, K. (2013). The impact of an aging U.S. population on state tax revenues. *Federal Reserve Bank of Kansas City Economic Review, 98*(4), 95–127.

Feyrer, J. (2008). Aggregate evidence on the link between age structure and productivity. *Population and Development Review, 34*, 78–99.

Feyrer, J. (2011). The U.S. productivity slowdown, the baby boom, and management quality. *Journal of Population Economics, 24*(1), 267–284.

King, A. G., & Knapp, C. B. (1978). Race and the determinants of lifetime earnings. *Industrial & Labor Relations Review, 31*(3), 347–355.

Lee, R. D. (2014). Macroeconomic consequences of population aging in the United States: Overview of a national academy report. *American Economic Review, 104*(5), 234–239.

Lindh, T. (1999). Age structure and economic policy: The case of saving and growth. *Population Research and Policy Review, 18*(3), 261–277.

Lindh, T., & Malmberg, B. (1999). Age structure effects and growth in the OECD, 1950–1990. *Journal of Population Economics, 12*(3), 431–449.

Lindh, T., & Malmberg, B. (2009). European Union economic growth and the age structure of the population. *Economic Change and Restructuring, 42*(3), 159–187.

Thomas, M. E. (1993). Race, class, and personal income: An empirical test of the declining significance of race thesis, 1968–1988. *Social Problems, 40*, 328–342.

U.S. Bureau of Economic Analysis. (2013). *National economic accounts*. Washington, DC: U.S. Bureau of Economic Analysis.

U.S. Bureau of Labor Statistics. (2011a). *National consumer price index*. Washington DC: U.S. Bureau of Labor Statistics.

U.S. Bureau of Labor Statistics. (2011b). *2010 consumer expenditure survey*. Washington, DC: U.S. Bureau of Labor Statistics.

U.S. Census Bureau. (1992). *1990 census of population and housing, summary file 3*. Washington, DC: U.S. Census Bureau.

U.S. Census Bureau. (1993). *1990 census of population and housing, summary file 4*. Washington, DC: U.S. Census Bureau.

U.S. Census Bureau. (2002). *2000 census of population and housing, summary file 3*. Washington, DC: U.S. Census Bureau.

U.S. Census Bureau. (2003). *2000 census of population and housing, summary file 4*. Washington, DC: U.S. Census Bureau.

U.S. Census Bureau. (2011a). *2006–2010 American community survey*. Washington, DC: U.S. Census Bureau.

U.S. Census Bureau. (2011b). *2006–2010 American community survey selected population tables*. Washington, DC: U.S. Census Bureau.

U.S. Census Bureau. (2011c). *2010 census summary file 1*. Washington, DC: U.S. Census Bureau.

U.S. Census Bureau. (2011d). *2010 census summary file 2*. Washington, DC: U.S. Census Bureau.

U.S. Census Bureau. (2012). *2012 national population projections*. Washington, DC: U.S. Census Bureau.

U.S. Census Bureau, & U.S. Bureau of Labor Statistics. (2010). *Current population survey: Survey of income and program participation*. Washington, DC: U.S. Bureau of Labor Statistics/ U.S. Census Bureau.

Chapter 5
Impacts of Future Demographic Change on Education in the United States

As noted in the introductory chapter, education is one of the key factors involved in changing the socioeconomic characteristics of populations. The future of the United States is inextricably tied to today's school children and those that follow them. Changes in the size and characteristics of the childhood population directly influence changes in the size and characteristics of enrollment in primary, secondary, and post-secondary institutions (Bare 1997; Davis and Bauman 2011; Farmer 2011; Fry and Gonzales 2008). In this chapter, we examine how education is impacted by population change. We begin by first examining key characteristics of students in the United States and then examine the long-term implications of such change.

5.1 Historic Characteristics of Students and Education in the United States

The number of people in the United States enrolled in education has increased substantially in the last two complete decades (see Table 5.1). Elementary and secondary schools have increased enrollment by 20.1% and college and universities increased enrollment by 39.6%. Overall, enrollment at both levels combined increased by 23.8%.

At the same time, it is obvious that the population of youth progressing through the system show characteristics that suggest a reduction in overall enrollment growth in the future. It is likely that the elementary and secondary growth of 14.5% from 1990 to 2000 drove much of the college increase of 28.8% from 2000 to 2010 (along with a slow growing economy that led young adults to seek higher education because employment opportunities were depressed). The recent historical increase of only 4.8% in elementary and secondary enrollment from 2000 to 2010 suggests substantial reductions (in the absence of increases in enrollment rates) in future levels of college and university enrollment.

S.H. Murdock et al., *Population Change in the United States*,
DOI 10.1007/978-94-017-7288-4_5

Table 5.1 Enrollment (in thousands) and percent change in enrollment of U.S. residents enrolled in public elementary and secondary schools and colleges, 1990–2010

				Percent change		
School level	1990	2000	2010	1990–2000	2000–2010	1990–2010
Elementary and secondary	41,217	47,204	49,484	14.5	4.8	20.1
College and university	10,845	11,753	15,143	8.4	28.8	39.6
Total	52,062	58,957	64,449	13.2	9.3	23.8

Source: U.S. Department of Education, National Center for Education Statistics, Common Core of Data (2012, 2011, 2002–2013a, 1986–1999, 1982–2011, 2002–2012)

Table 5.2 Enrollment percentages and percent change in enrollment by race/ethnicity for public elementary and secondary schools and public community colleges and universities, 2000–2010

	NH[a] White	NH Black	Hispanic	NH Asian & Other	Total enrolled
Year/time period	%	%	%	%	(in thousand)
Total public elementary and secondary					
2000	61.1	17.2	16.4	5.3	47,204
2010	52.4	16.0	23.1	8.5	49,484
% Change 2000–2010	−10.2	−2.3	48.0	67.8	4.8
Total public colleges and universities					
2000	69.7	11.6	10.8	7.9	11,753
2010	62.6	13.5	14.7	9.2	15,143
% Change 2000–2010	15.5	50.8	75.8	51.0	28.8

Source: U.S. Department of Education, National Center for Education Statistics, Common Core of Data (2012, 2011, 2002–2013a, 1986–1999, 1982–2011, 2002–2012)
[a]NH refers to nonHispanic; values for categories labeled NH are only for the nonHispanic persons in each race category. Hispanic includes Hispanics of all races

The data in Table 5.2 reflect the demographic change cited earlier in the discussion of population change. That is, at all educational levels, percentage increases are more extensive for Hispanic and nonHispanic Asian and Other populations than for nonHispanic Whites or nonHispanic Black students. Although nonHispanic White and nonHispanic Black students accounted for more than 68% of all elementary and secondary students in 2010, both groups showed decline in the numbers of elementary and secondary students from 2000 to 2010 while Hispanic and nonHispanic Asian and Other students not only increased their proportion of the total population of students from 2000 to 2010 but showed percentage increases of 48.0% and 67.8%, respectively. At the college level there was growth in enrollment among all racial and ethnic groups but particularly among Hispanics.

The extent to which different racial/ethnic groups have obtained given levels of education and the extent to which those levels have changed are shown in Table 5.3. The disparities in levels of educational attainment show large remaining differences despite substantial progress. All racial and ethnic groups showed progress in attainment during the 2000 to 2010 decade. At the high school level, an increase of roughly 5 to 6 percentage points occurred for nonHispanic Whites and nonHispanic

Table 5.3 Percentage of population 25 years of age and older in the United States who are high school graduates and higher or college graduates and higher by race/ethnicity, 2000 and 2010

Educational attainment level	NH[a] White	NH Black	Hispanic	NH Asian & Other	Total
2000					
High school graduates and higher	85.5	72.4	52.4	79.5	80.4
College graduates and higher	27.0	14.3	10.4	34.9	24.4
2010					
High school graduates and higher	90.0	81.0	61.5	85.4	85.0
College graduates and higher	30.9	17.7	13.0	42.1	27.9

Source: U.S. Census Bureau, 2003, 2011b
[a]NH refers to nonHispanic; values for categories labeled NH are only for the nonHispanic persons in each race category. Hispanic includes Hispanics of all races

Table 5.4 Public community college and university enrollment rates (per 100 persons ages 18–35) in the United States by race/ethnicity, 2000 and 2010

Year	NH[a] White	NH Black	Hispanic	NH Asian & Other	Total
Community college					
2000	8.1	7.4	6.8	8.7	7.8
2010	9.5	10.7	8.4	9.6	9.4
Public university					
2000	9.6	6.7	3.5	8.3	8.1
2010	11.6	9.0	5.6	10.8	10.0

Source: U.S. Department of Education, National Center for Education Statistics, Common Core of Data (2012, 2011, 2002–2013a, b); U.S. Census Bureau 2002, 2003, 2011c, d
[a]NH refers to nonHispanic; values for categories labeled NH are only for the nonHispanic persons in each race category. Hispanic includes Hispanics of all races

Asians and Others while increases of roughly 9 percentage points occurred for nonHispanic Blacks and Hispanics from 2000 to 2010. At the college level, increases of roughly 3% were evident for nonHispanic Whites, nonHispanic Blacks, and Hispanics, while nonHispanic Asian and Others showed an increase of more than 7%, from 34.9 to 42.1% from 2000 to 2010. Despite such change, large disparities in attainment levels continue. Even in 2010 there was a 28.5% difference in the high school graduation levels between nonHispanic Whites and Hispanics and a nearly 18% difference in college attainment levels. Despite progress large educational disparities remain among racial/ethnic groups in the United States.

The data in Table 5.4 also indicate that community colleges continue to be an important source of higher education for all students. As shown in this table, community colleges had overall enrollment rates in 2010 of 9.4% compared to 10.0% for public universities, and they show rates of 9.5% for nonHispanic Whites, 10.7% for nonHispanic Blacks, 8.4% for Hispanics, and 9.6% for nonHispanic Asians and Others in 2010. Enrollment rates in public universities in 2010 were 11.6% for

Table 5.5 Educational attainment by race/ethnicity for the United States population age 25 and older in 2010

Race/ethnicity	Population age 25 and older	Less than high school	High school diploma	Some college or associates degree	Bachelor degree or more
NH[a] White	138,362,204	10.0	29.7	29.3	31.0
NH Black	22,340,413	19.0	32.5	30.8	17.7
Hispanic	25,563,650	38.5	26.8	21.7	13.0
NH Asian & Other	13,460,392	14.6	19.8	23.5	42.1
Total	199,726,659	15.0	29.0	28.1	27.9

Source: U.S. Census Bureau, 2011b

[a]NH refers to nonHispanic; values for categories labeled NH are only for the nonHispanic persons in each race category. Hispanic includes Hispanics of all races

Table 5.6 Total (in millions of 2010 dollars) and per student expenditures for public elementary and secondary schools and public colleges and universities and percent change in expenditures, 2000–2010

	2000		2010		Percent change	
Program	Total	Per student	Total	Per student	Total	Per student
Elementary & secondary	520,208	11,020	604,215	12,210	16.1	10.8
Public colleges & universities	215,707	18,353	296,114	19,555	37.3	6.5

Source: U.S. Department of Education, National Center for Education Statistics, Common Core of Data (2012, 2011, 2002–2013a, b)

Note: Total expenditures for public elementary and secondary schools include current expenditures, interest on school debt, and capital outlay. Data for public degree-granting institutions are for total expenditures. Postsecondary data are for degree-granting institutions. Degree-granting institutions grant associate's or higher degrees and participate in Title IV federal financial aid programs

nonHispanic Whites, 9.0% for nonHispanic Blacks, 5.6% for Hispanics, and 10.8% for nonHispanic Asians and Others. Differences in college costs between community and four-year colleges continue to affect enrollment rates for America's poorest minority populations, particularly Hispanic students.

In addition, the data in Table 5.5 show that educational disparities continue to be substantial. Whereas only 10.0% of nonHispanic Whites 25 years of age or older had less than a high school level of education in 2010 while 31.0% had a bachelor's degree of more education, these value were 38.5% and 13.0% for Hispanics, 19.0% and 17.7% for nonHispanic Blacks, and 14.6% and 42.1% for nonHispanic Asians and Others. These educational disparities continue to limit the opportunities for many members of minority population groups.

The data in Table 5.6 indicate that increases in educational expenditures have not kept up with inflation, especially in the increase in expenditures for colleges and universities. While general governmental expenditures for education increased by 10.8% for elementary and secondary students and by 6.5% for public colleges and universities from 2000 to 2010, the overall inflation rate during that period was 26.6%. Clearly expenditures for education have not kept up with real costs.

5.2 Future Educational Characteristics

Tables 5.7, 5.8, 5.9 and 5.10 show projections of the number of students likely to be from each racial/ethnic group and at each educational level, assuming that age-, sex-, and race/ethnicity-specific enrollment rates for 2010 continue through 2060. The data in Table 5.7 show an overall increase of nearly 12.5 million public education students (at all levels) from 2010 to 2060 with roughly 9.7 million of the increase being in elementary and secondary enrollment and nearly 2.8 million in public colleges and university enrollment. As shown in Table 5.8 the increases would all come from minority populations because from 2010–2060 for all educational levels there are declines in the number of nonHispanic Whites enrolled in educational institutions. This reflects the projected decline in the overall number of nonHispanic Whites in the population and the older age distribution of the nonHispanic White population.

On the other hand, there are substantial increases projected for Hispanic and nonHispanic Asian and Other school populations and small increases in the number of nonHispanic Black students. For example, an examination of the percent change in the total elementary and secondary student enrollment from 2010 to 2060 indicate that (see Table 5.8), there is a 26.8% decline in the number of nonHispanic White elementary and secondary students, an 11.1% increase in the number of nonHispanic Black students, an increase of 99.3% in the number of Hispanic students, and a 105.7% increase in the number of nonHispanic Asians and Other students. In numerical terms this involves a decline from 25.9 million nonHispanic White students in 2010 to roughly 19.0 million in 2060, an increase from 7.9 million in 2010 to nearly 8.8 million nonHispanic Black students in 2060, an increase from 11.4 million in 2010 to 22.8 million Hispanic students in 2060, and an increase from 4.2 to 8.6 million nonHispanic Asian and Other students from 2010 to 2060.

At the college and university level (see Table 5.8), there is a projected decrease of 21.1% in the number of nonHispanic White students, an increase of 23.1% in the number of nonHispanic Black students, an increase of 120.4% in the number of Hispanic students, and an increase of 115.9% in the number of nonHispanic Asian and Other college students from 2010 to 2060. The roughly 2.8 million overall increase in college enrollment results from a decrease of 2.0 million nonHispanic White students from 2010 to 2060, an increase of 472,000 nonHispanic Black students, an increase of nearly 2.7 million Hispanic students, and an increase of 1.6 million nonHispanic Asian and Other students from 2010 to 2060.

As a result of such change the composition of students would change substantially (see Table 5.9). In elementary and secondary schools the percentage of nonHispanic White students is projected to decrease from 52.4% in 2010 to 32.1% in 2060, for nonHispanic Blacks the percentage of total enrollment would decline from 16.0 to 14.8, for Hispanics the enrollment increase would be from 23.1% in 2010 to 38.5% in 2060, and for nonHispanic Asians and Other the increase would be from 8.5% in 2010 to 14.6% in 2060. Overall the percentage of elementary and secondary students who are projected to be minority would exceed 50% by 2020 and would continue to increase thereafter.

Table 5.7 Total public education (all levels) enrollment (in thousands) by race/ethnicity in 2010 and projected to 2060 using the middle projection scenario

Year	NH[a] White	NH Black	Hispanic	NH Asian & Other	Total
Total public education (all levels)					
2010	35,412	9,962	13,658	5,595	64,627
2020	32,754	9,852	16,011	6,452	65,069
2030	31,788	10,413	18,825	7,769	68,795
2040	30,086	10,567	21,695	8,990	71,338
2050	28,019	10,851	24,773	10,300	73,943
2060	26,469	11,309	27,685	11,653	77,116
Public elementary and secondary schools					
2010	25,932	7,916	11,444	4,192	49,484
2020	23,812	7,735	13,398	4,867	49,812
2030	23,429	8,253	15,700	5,849	53,231
2040	21,755	8,250	17,992	6,684	54,681
2050	20,093	8,447	20,503	7,649	56,692
2060	18,991	8,791	22,806	8,624	59,212
Public community colleges					
2010	4,164	1,095	1,307	652	7,218
2020	3,893	1,127	1,534	731	7,285
2030	3,595	1,138	1,819	878	7,430
2040	3,555	1,212	2,142	1,046	7,955
2050	3,348	1,244	2,451	1,189	8,232
2060	3,130	1,295	2,778	1,345	8,548
Public universities					
2010	5,316	951	907	751	7,925
2020	5,049	990	1,079	854	7,972
2030	4,764	1,022	1,306	1,042	8,134
2040	4,776	1,105	1,561	1,260	8,702
2050	4,578	1,160	1,819	1,462	9,019
2060	4,348	1,223	2,101	1,684	9,356
Total public colleges and universities					
2010	9,480	2,046	2,214	1,403	15,143
2020	8,942	2,117	2,613	1,585	15,257
2030	8,359	2,160	3,125	1,920	15,564
2040	8,331	2,317	3,703	2,306	16,657
2050	7,926	2,404	4,270	2,651	17,251
2060	7,478	2,518	4,879	3,029	17,904

Source: Projections by the authors derived from U.S. Census Bureau, 2011c, d, 2012; 2010 Current Population Survey; U.S. Department of Education, National Center for Education Statistics, Common Core of Data (2012, 2011, 2002–2013a, b)

[a]NH refers to nonHispanic; values for categories labeled NH are only for the nonHispanic persons in each race category. Hispanic includes Hispanics of all races

Table 5.8 Percent change in projected total public education (all levels) enrollment in the United States by race/ethnicity under the middle projection scenario, 2010–2060

Time period	NH[a] White	NH Black	Hispanic	NH Asian & Other	Total
Total public education (all levels)					
2010–2020	−7.5	−1.1	17.2	15.3	0.7
2020–2030	−2.9	5.7	17.6	20.4	5.7
2030–2040	−5.4	1.5	15.2	15.7	3.7
2040–2050	−6.9	2.7	14.2	14.6	3.7
2050–2060	−5.5	4.2	11.8	13.1	4.3
2010–2060	−25.3	13.5	102.7	108.3	19.3
Public elementary and secondary schools					
2010–2020	−8.2	−2.3	17.1	16.1	0.7
2020–2030	−1.6	6.7	17.2	20.2	6.9
2030–2040	−7.1	0.0	14.6	14.3	2.7
2040–2050	−7.6	2.4	14.0	14.4	3.7
2050–2060	−5.5	4.1	11.2	12.7	4.4
2010–2060	−26.8	11.1	99.3	105.7	19.7
Public community colleges					
2010–2020	−6.5	2.9	17.4	12.1	0.9
2020–2030	−7.7	1.0	18.6	20.1	2.0
2030–2040	−1.1	6.5	17.8	19.1	7.1
2040–2050	−5.8	2.6	14.4	13.7	3.5
2050–2060	−6.5	4.1	13.3	13.1	3.8
2010–2060	−24.8	18.3	112.5	106.3	18.4
Public universities					
2010–2020	−5.0	4.1	19.0	13.7	0.6
2020–2030	−5.6	3.2	21.0	22.0	2.0
2030–2040	0.3	8.1	19.5	20.9	7.0
2040–2050	−4.1	5.0	16.5	16.0	3.6
2050–2060	−5.0	5.4	15.5	15.2	3.7
2010–2060	−18.2	28.6	131.6	124.2	18.1
Total public colleges and universities					
2010–2020	−5.7	3.5	18.0	13.0	0.8
2020–2030	−6.5	2.0	19.6	21.1	2.0
2030–2040	−0.3	7.3	18.5	20.1	7.0
2040–2050	−4.9	3.8	15.3	15.0	3.6
2050–2060	−5.7	4.7	14.3	14.3	3.8
2010–2060	−21.1	23.1	120.4	115.9	18.2

Source: Projections by the authors derived from U.S. Census Bureau, 2011c, d, 2012; 2010 Current Population Survey; U.S. Department of Education, National Center for Education Statistics, Common Core of Data (2012, 2011, 2002–2013a, b)

[a]NH refers to nonHispanic; values for categories labeled NH are only for the nonHispanic persons in each race category. Hispanic includes Hispanics of all races

Table 5.9 Percentage of total public education (all levels) enrollment by race/ethnicity in 2010 and projected to 2060 using the middle projection scenario

Year	NH[a] White	NH Black	Hispanic	NH Asian & Other	Total
Total public education (all levels)					
2010	54.8	15.4	21.1	8.7	100.0
2020	50.4	15.1	24.6	9.9	100.0
2030	46.2	15.1	27.4	11.3	100.0
2040	42.2	14.8	30.4	12.6	100.0
2050	37.9	14.7	33.5	13.9	100.0
2060	34.3	14.7	35.9	15.1	100.0
Public elementary and secondary schools					
2010	52.4	16.0	23.1	8.5	100.0
2020	47.8	15.5	26.9	9.8	100.0
2030	44.0	15.5	29.5	11.0	100.0
2040	39.8	15.1	32.9	12.2	100.0
2050	35.4	14.9	36.2	13.5	100.0
2060	32.1	14.8	38.5	14.6	100.0
Public community colleges					
2010	57.7	15.2	18.1	9.0	100.0
2020	53.4	15.5	21.1	10.0	100.0
2030	48.4	15.3	24.5	11.8	100.0
2040	44.8	15.2	26.9	13.1	100.0
2050	40.7	15.1	29.8	14.4	100.0
2060	36.7	15.1	32.5	15.7	100.0
Public universities					
2010	67.1	12.0	11.4	9.5	100.0
2020	63.4	12.4	13.5	10.7	100.0
2030	58.5	12.6	16.1	12.8	100.0
2040	54.9	12.7	17.9	14.5	100.0
2050	50.7	12.9	20.2	16.2	100.0
2060	46.4	13.1	22.5	18.0	100.0
Total public colleges and universities					
2010	62.6	13.5	14.6	9.3	100.0
2020	58.6	13.9	17.1	10.4	100.0
2030	53.7	13.9	20.1	12.3	100.0
2040	50.1	13.9	22.2	13.8	100.0
2050	45.9	13.9	24.8	15.4	100.0
2060	41.7	14.1	27.3	16.9	100.0

Source: Projections by the authors derived from U.S. Census Bureau, 2011c, d, 2012; U.S. Census Bureau and U.S. Bureau of Labor Statistics 2011; U.S. Department of Education, National Center for Education Statistics, Common Core of Data (2012, 2011, 2002–2013a, b)

[a]NH refers to nonHispanic; values for categories labeled NH are only for the nonHispanic persons in each race category. Hispanic includes Hispanics of all races

Table 5.10 Public education expenditures (in millions of 2010 dollars) in 2010 and projected for 2060 using the middle projection scenario

Year	Total public elementary and secondary	Total public colleges and universities
2010	604,200	305,147
2020	608,205	307,444
2030	649,951	313,630
2040	667,655	335,655
2050	692,209	347,625
2060	722,979	360,784

Source: Projections by the authors derived from U.S. Census Bureau, 2011c, d, 2012; U.S. Census Bureau and U.S. Bureau of Labor Statistics 2011; U.S. Department of Education, National Center for Education Statistics, Common Core of Data (2012, 2011, 2002–2013a, b, 1986–1999)
NOTE: Total expenditures for public elementary and secondary schools include current expenditures, interest on school debt, and capital outlay. Data for public degree-granting institutions are for total expenditures. Postsecondary data are for degree-granting institutions

For total college enrollment the increase in minority enrollment, given current rates, would be less than for elementary and secondary enrollment. The date at which the percentage of nonHispanic White students drops below 50% is sometime after 2040, and college enrollment rates do not come to the levels for elementary and secondary education for any other racial/ethnic group by 2060. Although there are changes in college enrollment from 62.6% of total enrollment being nonHispanic White in 2010 to 41.7% by 2060 and increases from 2010 to 2060 from 13.5% to 14.1% for nonHispanic Blacks, from 14.6% in 2010 to 27.3% in 2060 for Hispanics, and from 9.3% in 2010 to 16.9% in 2060 for nonHispanic Asian and Others, the fact that the changes remain less than the levels of attainment at the high school level show that limitations to attainment, particularly for minority populations, may continue far into the future.

5.3 Financing Public Education in the United States

The increase in the number of students noted above would require the expenditure of billions of dollars. Table 5.10 shows projections based on constant per student costs in 2010 dollars. These data indicate that at 2010 expenditure levels the costs for educating the nation's public elementary and secondary students would increase from $604 billion in 2010 to nearly $723 billion in 2060, an increase of 19.7%, and the costs of educating public college students would increase from nearly $305 billion to $361 billion in 2060, an increase of 18.2%, equaling the rate of increase in enrollment. Such costs are in constant dollars and do not account for inflation over the projection period. The data in this table indicate that education would continue to be a major public expenditure. In addition, in the absence of change that increases the readiness of minority children for full participation in academic programs,

Table 5.11 Number (in thousands) of students with financial need unmet by household resources enrolled at public colleges and universities in the United States by race/ethnicity in 2010 and projected to 2060 using the middle projection scenario

Year	NH[a] White	NH Black	Hispanic	NH Asian & Other	Total
Public community colleges					
2010	2,184	785	845	402	4,216
2020	2,056	807	994	449	4,306
2030	1,897	811	1,177	541	4,426
2040	1,867	865	1,390	643	4,765
2050	1,764	890	1,594	733	4,981
2060	1,644	923	1,806	830	5,203
Public universities					
2010	3,347	762	661	557	5,327
2020	3,209	798	789	635	5,431
2030	3,016	816	954	777	5,563
2040	3,023	882	1,146	939	5,990
2050	2,905	923	1,325	1,085	6,238
2060	2,755	975	1,533	1,251	6,514
Total public colleges and universities					
2010	5,531	1,547	1,506	959	9,543
2020	5,265	1,605	1,783	1,084	9,737
2030	4,913	1,627	2,131	1,318	9,989
2040	4,890	1,747	2,536	1,582	10,755
2050	4,669	1,813	2,919	1,818	11,219
2060	4,399	1,898	3,339	2,081	11,717

Source: Projections by the authors derived from U.S. Census Bureau, 2011c, d, 2012; U.S. Census Bureau and U.S. Bureau of Labor Statistics 2008, 2011; U.S. Department of Education, National Center for Education Statistics, Common Core of Data (2012, 2011, 2002–2013a, b)
[a]NH refers to nonHispanic; values for categories labeled NH are only for the nonHispanic persons in each race category. Hispanic includes Hispanics of all races

such costs are likely to actually be substantially greater than anticipated and may increase at much faster rates due to the requirement for additional funds for supplementary education programs.

In fact, when the data in Tables 5.11 and 5.12 are compared to those in previous tables, it is clear that the number of children requiring additional financial assistance would increase by nearly 2.2 million, by 22.8% from 2010 to 2060, compared to an increase in total enrollment of 18.2%. The increase would all be due to minority students because of the net decline projected in the number of nonHispanic White students (and therefore their decline in financial need), with the number of students with unmet financial need increasing by 22.7% from 2010 to 2060 for nonHispanic Black students, by 121.7% for Hispanic students, and by 117.0% for nonHispanic Asian and Other students.

Table 5.12 Percent change in projected number of students with financial need unmet by household resources enrolled in public colleges and universities in the United States in 2010 and projected to 2060 using the middle projection scenario

Time period	NH[a] White	NH Black	Hispanic	NH Asian & Other	Total
Public community colleges					
2010–2020	–5.9	2.8	17.6	11.7	2.1
2020–2030	–7.7	0.5	18.4	20.5	2.8
2030–2040	–1.6	6.7	18.1	18.9	7.7
2040–2050	–5.5	2.9	14.7	14.0	4.5
2050–2060	–6.8	3.7	13.3	13.2	4.5
2010–2060	–24.7	17.6	113.7	106.5	23.4
Public universities					
2010–2020	–4.1	4.7	19.4	14.0	2.0
2020–2030	–6.0	2.3	20.9	22.4	2.4
2030–2040	0.2	8.1	20.1	20.8	7.7
2040–2050	–3.9	4.6	15.6	15.5	4.1
2050–2060	–5.2	5.6	15.7	15.3	4.4
2010–2060	–17.7	28.0	131.9	124.6	22.3
Total public colleges and universities					
2010–2020	–4.8	3.7	18.4	13.0	2.0
2020–2030	–6.7	1.4	19.5	21.6	2.6
2030–2040	–0.5	7.4	19.0	20.0	7.7
2040–2050	–4.5	3.8	15.1	14.9	4.3
2050–2060	–5.8	4.7	14.4	14.5	4.4
2010–2060	–20.5	22.7	121.7	117.0	22.8

Source: Projections by the authors derived from U.S. Census Bureau, 2011c, d, 2012; U.S. Census Bureau and U.S. Bureau of Labor Statistics 2008, 2011; U.S. Department of Education, National Center for Education Statistics, Common Core of Data (2013, 2012, 2011, 2002–2013a, b)
[a]NH refers to nonHispanic; values for categories labeled NH are only for the nonHispanic persons in each race category. Hispanic includes Hispanics of all races

In addition, the data in Table 5.13 show that the students in need would increasingly be minority and particularly Black and Hispanic students. By 2060, 18.2% of Black students and 13.6% of Hispanic students in public colleges and universities would have levels of unmet financial need exceeding $15,000 (in 2010 constant dollars), and 36.9% of Black and 48.9% of Hispanic students in public colleges and universities would have levels of unmet financial need exceeding $10,000 per year (in 2010 constant dollars). Such accumulated debts would clearly make it extremely difficult for the students to meet their post-college debt obligations and would likely reduce the number who would pursue higher levels of education.

Table 5.13 Students enrolled in public colleges and universities (in thousands) with unmet financial need by need category and race/ethnicity in 2010 and projected for 2060 using the middle projection scenario

Need category	NH[a] White	NH Black	Hispanic	NH Asian & Other	Total
2010					
Public community colleges					
$15,000 or more	3.0	4.5	3.3	4.3	3.5
$10,000 to 14,999	11.8	13.4	11.7	12.9	12.2
$5,000 to 9,999	32.0	35.9	35.5	34.8	33.7
Less than $5,000	53.2	46.2	49.5	48.0	50.6
Total	2,184	785	845	402	4,216
Public universities					
$15,000 or more	21.7	32.8	25.9	32.5	25.0
$10,000 to 14,999	22.3	24.3	23.6	22.8	22.8
$5,000 to 9,999	28.8	24.0	27.5	23.9	27.4
Less than $5,000	27.2	18.9	23.0	20.8	24.8
Total	3,347	762	661	557	5,327
Total public colleges and universities					
$15,000 or more	14.4	18.4	13.3	20.6	15.5
$10,000 to 14,999	18.2	18.7	16.9	18.7	18.1
$5,000 to 9,999	30.0	30.1	32.0	28.5	30.2
Less than $5,000	37.4	32.8	37.8	32.2	36.2
Total	5,531	1,547	1,506	959	9,543
2060					
Public community colleges					
$15,000 or more	3.2	4.2	3.4	4.1	3.6
$10,000 to 14,999	11.7	13.2	11.6	13.1	12.2
$5,000 to 9,999	31.8	35.8	35.1	34.7	34.1
Less than $5,000	53.3	46.8	49.9	48.1	50.1
Total	1,644	923	1,806	830	5,203
Public universities					
$15,000 or more	21.6	31.5	25.5	32.0	26.0
$10,000 to 14,999	22.2	23.9	23.4	22.9	22.9
$5,000 to 9,999	28.9	24.7	27.7	24.2	27.1
Less than $5,000	27.3	19.9	23.4	20.9	24.0
Total	2,755	975	1,533	1,251	6,514
Total public colleges and universities					
$15,000 or more	14.7	18.2	13.6	20.9	16.1
$10,000 to 14,999	18.3	18.7	17.0	19.0	18.1
$5,000 to 9,999	30.0	30.1	31.7	28.4	30.2
Less than $5,000	37.0	33.0	37.7	31.7	35.6
Total	4,399	1,898	3,339	2,081	11,717

Source: Projections by the authors derived from U.S. Census Bureau, 2011c, d, 2012; U.S. Census Bureau and U.S. Bureau of Labor Statistics 2008, 2011; U.S. Department of Education, National Center for Education Statistics, Common Core of Data (2013, 2012, 2011, 2002–2013a, b)

[a]NH refers to nonHispanic; values for categories labeled NH are only for the nonHispanic persons in each race category. Hispanic includes Hispanics of all races

5.4 Summary

1. Nearly 50 million children were in public elementary and secondary education in the United States in 2010. More than 15 million were enrolled in public colleges and universities.
2. Public elementary and secondary school enrollment shows a pattern of decreasing growth in the 2000 to 2010 period compared to 1990 to 2000, while college and university enrollment shows a pattern of increasing growth from 2000 to 2010 compared to 1990 to 2000. This suggests that elementary and secondary enrollment growth is slowing due to reduced overall population growth in child populations in 2000–2010 compared to 1990 to 2000 and further suggests that overall college enrollment will slow in the coming years.
3. The data in this chapter also suggest that current elementary and secondary and college populations are increasingly, and would increasingly be, composed of minority population members, particularly Hispanics and nonHispanic Asians and Others in the coming decades. Whether examined in terms of numerical values or rates, minority populations would increasingly make up a majority of enrollment growth. In 2010, 52.4% of all elementary and secondary and 62.6% of all those enrolled in colleges and universities were nonHispanic Whites. By 2060, only 32.1% of those in elementary and secondary schools and 41.7% of those enrolled in higher education would be nonHispanic White. By comparison, 23.1% of those enrolled in elementary and secondary education in 2010 were Hispanic and 14.6% of those enrolled in public colleges and universities were Hispanic. By 2060 these values would be 38.5% and 27.3%, respectively. All of the increase in enrollment from 2010 to 2060 would be due to minority populations while the number of nonHispanic Whites would decline.
4. Costs (in 2010 constant dollars) for public elementary and secondary education are projected to increase from $604 billion per year in 2010 to nearly $723 billion per year in 2060. Costs for public college and university education are projected to increase from $305 billion in 2010 to nearly $361 billion per year in 2060.
5. An increasing number of college students, particularly minority populations from households with limited socioeconomic resources, would have insufficient financial resources to attend college without accumulating debt. From 2010 to 2060 the number of nonHispanic White students with unmet financial need would decrease by 20.5% while the number of nonHispanic Black students with unmet need would increase by 22.7%. The increases in the number of Hispanics with unmet needs would be 121.7% and for nonHispanic Asian and Other students 117.0%. By 2060, 55.4% of nonHispanic Black, 48.9% of Hispanic, 54.9% of nonHispanic Asian and Other, and 43.8% of nonHispanic White students attending public universities would have unmet financial need of $10,000 or more per year.

College levels of educational attainment remain essential to socioeconomic success in the United States. The data in this chapter indicate that the United States will have increasing need for educational services for its population but that the nation's population will face increasing challenges in addressing the scholastic and financial challenges necessary to attain the level of education necessary to achieve educational and financial success.

References

Bare, J. (1997). *The impact of the baby boom echo on U.S. public school enrollments. Issue brief NCES 98–039*. Washington, DC: National Center for Education Statistics.

Davis, J. W., & Bauman, K. (2011). *School enrollment in the United States: 2008. Population characteristics. Current population reports P20-564 (June)*. Washington, DC: U.S. Census Bureau.

Farmer, T. A. (2011). *The new Hispanic majority: How Texas public schools are foreshadowing national trends*. Paper presented at the annual meeting of the Pennsylvania educational research association (Philadelphia, PA, 6 Oct 2011).

Fry, R., & Gonzales, F. (2008). *One-in-five and growing fast: A profile of Hispanic public school students*. Washington, DC: Pew Hispanic Center.

U.S. Census Bureau. (2002). *2000 census of population and housing, summary file 3*. Washington, DC: U.S. Census Bureau.

U.S. Census Bureau. (2003). *2000 census of population and housing, summary file 4*. Washington, DC: U.S. Census Bureau.

U.S. Census Bureau. (2011a). *2006–2010 American community survey*. Washington, DC: U.S. Census Bureau.

U.S. Census Bureau. (2011b). *2006–2010 American community survey selected population tables*. Washington, DC: U.S. Census Bureau.

U.S. Census Bureau. (2011c). *2010 census summary file 1*. Washington, DC: U.S. Census Bureau.

U.S. Census Bureau. (2011d). *2010 census summary file 2*. Washington, DC: U.S. Census Bureau.

U.S. Census Bureau. (2012). *2012 national population projections*. Washington, DC: U.S. Census Bureau.

U.S. Census Bureau, & U.S. Bureau of Labor Statistics. (2008). *2007 current population survey: Survey of income and program participation*. Washington, DC: U.S. Bureau of Labor Statistics and U.S. Census Bureau.

U.S. Census Bureau, & U.S. Bureau of Labor Statistics. (2011). *2010 current population survey: Annual demographic survey*. Washington, DC: U.S. Bureau of Labor Statistics and U.S. Census Bureau.

U.S. Department of Education, National Center for Education Statistics. (1982–2011). *Common core of data: State nonfiscal survey of public elementary and secondary education, 1981–1982 through 2009–2010*. Washington, DC: U.S. Department of Education, National Center for Education Statistics.

U.S. Department of Education, National Center for Education Statistics. (1986–1999). *Common core of data: Integrated postsecondary education data system (IPEDS), fall enrollment survey (IPEDS-EF:86–99)*. Washington, DC: U.S. Department of Education, National Center for Education Statistics.

U.S. Department of Education, National Center for Education Statistics. (1997–2012). *Common core of data (CCD): State nonfiscal survey of public elementary/secondary education, 1996–97 through 2010–11*. Washington, DC: U.S. Department of Education, National Center for Education Statistics.

U.S. Department of Education, National Center for Education Statistics. (2002–2012). *Common core of data: Integrated postsecondary education data system (IPEDS), Spring 2001 through Spring 2011, enrollment component*. Washington, DC: U.S. Department of Education, National Center for Education Statistics.

U.S. Department of Education, National Center for Education Statistics. (2002–2013a). *Common core of data: Integrated postsecondary education data system, Spring 2001 through Spring 2012, finance component, and unpublished tabulations*. Washington, DC: U.S. Department of Education, National Center for Education Statistics.

U.S. Department of Education, National Center for Education Statistics. (2002–2013b). *Integrated postsecondary education data system Spring 2001 through Spring 2012, finance component, and unpublished tabulations*. Washington, DC: U.S. Department of Education, National Center for Education Statistics.

U.S. Department of Education, & National Center for Education Statistics. (2011). *Common core of data (CCD): National public elementary and secondary enrollment by race/ethnicity model, 1994–2010*. Washington, DC: U.S. Department of Education, National Center for Education Statistics.

U.S. Department of Education, & National Center for Education Statistics. (2012). *Common core of data (CCD): Integrated postsecondary education data system (IPEDS), Spring 2011, enrollment component, higher education general information survey*. Washington, DC: U.S. Department of Education, National Center for Education Statistics.

U.S. Department of Education, & National Center for Education Statistics. (2013). *Common core of data (CCD): 2007–08 national postsecondary student aid studies (NPSAS:08)*. Washington, DC: U.S. Dept. of Education, National Center for Education Statistics. August 2013 Revision.

Chapter 6
Implications of Population Change for Health, Health Care, and Public Assistance Programs in the United States

The demographic change cited in Chapter 2 will have dramatic implications for health and health care in the United States and other nations in the coming years (Hoque et al. 2013; Pol and Thomas 2013). This includes implications for the incidence of disease as the population grows older (Wiener and Tilly 2002) and implications for the types of diseases and disorders that are likely to occur and for the overall health of the American population (American College of Physicians 2010). In addition, it has extensive implications for health care requirements and workforces (Center for Health Workforce Studies 2006). In this chapter we examine data that indicate changes in each of these dimensions as a result of current and future change in the size and the characteristics of the population of the United States through 2060.

6.1 Change in the Incidence and Demographic Characteristics of Persons with Diseases/Disorders in the United States, 2010–2060

The data in Table 6.1 when compared to the data in Table 2.11 show the effects of the aging of the population of the United States on health incidence and conditions. Under the middle projection scenario the number of incidences of diseases and disorder would increase by 48.6% while the population would increase by 36.1%. This reflects the aging of the population from 2010 to 2060 for all racial/ethnic groups that results in a higher incidence of health events.

A comparison of the change by race/ethnicity of the persons experiencing health incidences clearly points to the effects that the aging of the population would have on the number of health incidences. This is evident in that the nonHispanic White population is projected (under the middle projection scenario) to decrease by –9.1% from 2010 to 2060 and the Black population is projected to increase by 46.8% but during this same period the nonHispanic White population would show an increase

S.H. Murdock et al., *Population Change in the United States*,
DOI 10.1007/978-94-017-7288-4_6

Table 6.1 Incidences of diseases/disorders and percent change in incidences of diseases/disorders in the United States by race/ethnicity for 2010 and projected to 2060 using the middle projection scenario

Year	NH[a] White	NH Black	Hispanic	NH Asian & Other	Total
Number of incidences					
2010	601,045,869	102,011,168	91,473,544	45,615,618	840,146,199
2020	642,712,610	121,053,645	127,029,018	59,242,274	950,037,547
2030	662,860,109	137,475,906	167,601,302	76,106,963	1,044,044,280
2040	661,051,946	153,086,695	212,617,142	94,366,779	1,121,122,562
2050	641,932,101	166,928,643	260,170,914	113,312,310	1,182,343,968
2060	623,059,888	180,887,860	310,350,113	133,778,428	1,248,076,289
Percent change of incidences					
2010–2020	6.9	18.7	38.9	29.9	13.1
2020–2030	3.1	13.6	31.9	28.5	9.9
2030–2040	–0.3	11.4	26.9	24.0	7.4
2040–2050	–2.9	9.0	22.4	20.1	5.5
2050–2060	–2.9	8.4	19.3	18.1	5.6
2010–2060	3.7	77.3	239.3	193.3	48.6

Source: Projections by the authors derived from U.S. Census Bureau, 2011b, 2011c, 2012b; National Center for Health Statistics 2009

[a]NH refers to nonHispanic; values for categories labeled NH are only for the nonHispanic persons in each race category. Hispanic includes Hispanics of all races

in the number of health incidences of 3.7% while the nonHispanic Black population is projected to show a 77.3% increase in the number of incidences. Similarly, although the Hispanic population is projected to increase by 155.1% and the non-Hispanic Asian and Other population by 140.8%, under the middle projection scenario, these populations are projected to show increases in the number of health incidences of 239.3% and 193.3%, respectively, from 2010 to 2060.

Despite substantial differences in age structures between these populations, all of their populations age (in an aggregate sense) during the projection period. For example, the percentage of the nonHispanic White population that is 65 years of age and older increases (under the middle projection scenario) from 16.4% in 2010 to 28.8% by 2060. The equivalent change for nonHispanic Blacks are from 9.1 to 20.7%, for Hispanics from 5.5 to 15.2%, and for nonHispanic Asian and Others from 8.0 to 16.8%. In fact, the percentage of persons increases in all older age groups for all racial/ethnic groups while it declines for younger ages, especially for nonHispanic Whites and nonHispanic Blacks. Age is a powerful determinant of health conditions.

Racial/ethnic status also plays a role in the determination of both the incidence of disease/disorders and the types of disorders experienced (see Table 6.2). Race/ethnicity effects are interrelated with other characteristics of these populations. For

Table 6.2 Prevalence of selected diseases/disorders in the United States by race/ethnicity and type of diseases/disorders for adults (18 years and older) in 2010 and projected to 2060 using the middle projection scenario (percentages within disease/disorder)

	NH[a] White		NH Black		Hispanic		NH Asian & Other	
Disease/disorder	2010	2060	2010	2060	2010	2060	2010	2060
High blood pressure	69.3	47.2	14.8	17.2	10.2	24.2	5.7	11.4
Coronary heart disease	76.4	55.8	9.7	11.5	7.7	19.7	6.2	13.0
Angina pectoris	78.7	57.3	7.4	9.2	7.6	20.6	6.3	13.0
Heart attack	77.9	57.2	9.3	11.2	6.8	18.5	5.9	13.2
Other heart condition/disease	79.5	61.0	9.4	12.2	6.4	16.7	4.6	10.1
Stroke	70.3	48.4	15.1	18.0	9.3	23.0	5.3	10.6
Emphysema	83.1	63.8	6.5	10.1	5.3	14.4	5.1	11.7
Asthma	67.5	47.3	14.1	16.1	11.6	24.2	6.8	12.4
Asthma attack past year	66.8	45.2	13.1	14.6	11.7	25.5	8.3	14.8
Ulcer	73.4	51.1	10.3	13.0	10.1	23.4	6.2	12.5
Ulcer past year	64.5	38.6	12.3	13.8	16.1	32.7	7.1	15.0
Cancer	85.6	68.7	6.5	9.9	4.9	13.9	3.0	7.4
Diabetes	62.9	38.1	15.1	16.5	14.9	32.8	7.2	12.6
Hayfever past year	75.4	54.7	9.7	11.9	8.2	20.2	6.7	13.1
Sinusitis past year	72.2	51.3	12.9	16.2	9.5	21.7	5.4	10.8
Chronic bronchitis past year	75.7	56.5	10.8	13.5	9.0	20.8	4.5	9.2
Weak/failing kidneys past year	65.1	41.9	17.6	21.7	13.9	29.8	3.3	6.7
Liver condition past year	64.3	38.1	11.1	12.5	17.3	37.5	7.3	11.9
Pregnancy related	51.7	31.5	14.0	13.7	26.2	42.3	8.1	12.5
Ever worn hearing aid	86.9	70.3	4.6	5.8	5.5	16.3	3.0	7.6
Vision impairment	68.0	45.6	14.8	17.4	12.1	27.0	5.1	9.9
blindness	62.8	42.6	20.9	20.8	6.6	14.6	9.7	22.0
Lost all teeth	75.3	52.9	11.7	15.7	8.5	22.1	4.4	9.4
Sad past month	60.5	37.1	15.4	15.2	18.7	38.5	5.4	9.3
Nervous past month	69.8	45.3	9.7	11.3	16.1	35.6	4.4	7.9
Restless past month	67.6	46.0	14.1	15.7	12.8	27.9	5.5	10.4
Hopeless past month	61.7	36.8	13.2	12.9	19.4	40.8	5.8	9.4
Everything an effort past month	59.7	39.5	18.7	19.0	14.7	29.3	6.9	12.1
Worthlessness past month	65.0	41.2	13.7	14.6	16.4	35.8	4.9	8.5
Total	71.1	49.7	12.6	14.8	10.7	24.4	5.6	11.0

Source: Projections by the authors derived from U.S. Census Bureau, 2011b, 2011c, 2012b; National Center for Health Statistics 2009

[a]NH refers to nonHispanic; values for categories labeled NH are only for the nonHispanic persons in each race category. Hispanic includes Hispanics of all races

example, the older nonHispanic White population has higher rates of prevalence for cancer, emphysema, heart, and related conditions more closely associated with older populations because they have an older median age. In fact, when examined in terms of who is likely to be the patient populations in the future, it is evident that nonHispanic Whites who formed the largest percentage of patients for all conditions in 2010 would also do so for nearly all diseases/disorders in 2060. These results for 2010 reflect the numerical size of the nonHispanic White population relative to other populations, while those for 2060 also reflect the older age structure of the nonHispanic White population. The exceptions are for pregnancy-related cases and incidences of depression (as indicated by the "sad past month" category), for which Hispanics would account for the largest percentage of cases in 2060. The overall extent to which minority populations would come to play a larger role in health incidences is evident in that nonHispanic Whites account for more than 50% of the total number of incidences for all 29 disease/disorder categories in 2010, but for only 12 categories in 2060, and these 12 categories include disease/disorder categories such as heart-related incidences and cancer, which are clearly more prevalent at older ages.

There are exceptions, however, in which minority population groups show incidence rates that are higher than would be expected given their age and other demographic characteristics. An example of this is the incidence of diabetes for Hispanics. In 2060, Hispanics would account for 30.6% of the total population but 32.8% of all diabetes cases. NonHispanic Blacks would account for 16.5% of all diabetes incidences (even as they accounted for only 13.2% of the total population). Minority populations would account for 61.9% of all incidences of diabetes in 2060 while nonHispanic Whites would account for 38.1%. A similar difference between these groups occurs for pregnancy-related disorders and for nearly all the disorders suggesting depression and related conditions. Among minority populations, nonHispanic Blacks and nonHispanic Asians and Others would have a higher share of incidences related to blindness than their respective shares of the total population. The highest incidence rate for Hispanics is that related to pregnancy-related conditions. In addition nonHispanic Blacks show high rates of kidney disease. What such differences suggest is that genetic and behavioral factor differences among racial/ethnic groups may lead to different forms of disease/disorder incidence rates and would likely change the future demand for treatment of different disease/disorders.

6.1.1 Prevalence of Disabilities

Table 6.3 provides projections of the prevalence of conditions associated with disabilities in the United States by race/ethnicity of those experiencing such disabilities. These data show much higher incidence rates for Hispanics and nonHispanic Asians and Others for every time period and declines (associated with population decline) occurring for nonHispanic Whites in 2040–2050 and 2050–2060. The 86.8% increase in the total number of conditions associated with disabilities, when compared to the overall 48.6% increase in the number of all incidences of disease and disorder, clearly indicates that the aging of the population would also result in a marked increase in the number of persons with life-limiting disabilities.

Table 6.3 Prevalence of conditions associated with disabilities in the United States by race/ethnicity in 2010 and projected to 2060 using the middle projection scenario

Year	NH[a] White	NH Black	Hispanic	NH Asian & Other	Total
Number of incidences					
2010	45,549,306	8,465,606	5,826,867	3,466,481	63,308,260
2020	52,063,902	10,749,918	9,001,314	4,983,320	76,798,454
2030	58,052,800	13,046,251	13,141,370	7,036,704	91,277,125
2040	60,512,173	15,291,635	18,023,083	9,234,283	103,061,174
2050	58,671,984	16,945,469	23,205,857	11,444,891	110,268,201
2060	57,161,711	18,532,754	28,649,083	13,923,893	118,267,441
Percent change of incidences					
2010–2020	14.3	27.0	54.5	43.8	21.3
2020–2030	11.5	21.4	46.0	41.2	18.9
2030–2040	4.2	17.2	37.1	31.2	12.9
2040–2050	−3.0	10.8	28.8	23.9	7.0
2050–2060	−2.6	9.4	23.5	21.7	7.3
2010–2060	25.5	118.9	391.7	301.7	86.8

Source: Projections by the authors derived from U.S. Census Bureau, 2011b, 2011c, 2012b; National Center for Health Statistics 2009

[a]NH refers to nonHispanic; values for categories labeled NH are only for the nonHispanic persons in each race category. Hispanic includes Hispanics of all races

6.2 Health Care Personnel, Health Care Services, and Uninsured Persons

Table 6.4 indicates the number of health care personnel of a variety of types in 2010 and projected to 2060. This table includes data on physicians as well as dentists, optometrists, pharmacists, registered nurses, veterinarians, and podiatrists. Based on current occupational rates relative to the respective population bases, these data project a 7.4% increase in the number of health professionals from 2010 to 2060, but the increase in the number of incidences and disorders is projected to be 48.6%. Although a given patient may have more than a single incidence of disease and increased and improved technology may impact patient to health professional requirements, these data still point to a likely future shortage of health care professionals.

Table 6.4 further illustrate the degree to which nonHispanic Whites currently dominate selected healthcare professions and the disparity in representation of minority population groups in many of these same professions. In all of the professions shown, nonHispanic Whites account for more than 80% of those employed in such professions in 2010. The date in Panels B and C show numbers needed so that each profession had the same proportions of each race/ethnic group as was present in 2010 and projected for 2060 (using the middle projection scenario). These data indicate that the fastest growing groups are already under represented in the number of healthcare professionals.

Table 6.4 Health care personnel in the United States by specialty and race/ethnicity in 2010 (actual) and simulated to reflect 2010 and projected 2060 population distribution by race/ethnicity using the middle projection scenario

Health personnel	NH[a] White	NH Black	Hispanic	NH Asian & Other	Total
Panel A: 2010 actual					
Physicians	619,526	43,180	42,204	44,147	749,057
Dentists	134,188	6,338	8,472	6,268	155,266
Optometrists	27,942	1,032	1,351	3,027	33,352
Pharmacists	207,883	14,821	9,077	16,506	248,287
Registered Nurses	2,359,086	297,267	119,252	40,923	2,816,528
Veterinarians	73,132	2,058	2,667	703	78,560
Podiatrists	7,608	353	408	92	8,461
Total	3,429,365	365,049	183,431	111,666	4,089,511
Simulated to reflect population race/ethnicity distribution					
Panel B: 2010 distribution					
Physicians	477,899	91,385	122,096	57,677	749,057
Dentists	99,061	18,942	25,308	11,955	155,266
Optometrists	21,279	4,069	5,436	2,568	33,352
Pharmacists	158,407	30,291	40,471	19,118	248,287
Registered Nurses	1,796,945	343,616	459,094	216,873	2,816,528
Veterinarians	50,122	9,584	12,805	6,049	78,560
Podiatrists	5,399	1,032	1,379	651	8,461
Total	2,609,112	498,919	666,589	314,891	4,089,511
Panel C: 2060 distribution					
Physicians	358,115	110,965	257,238	114,328	840,646
Dentists	71,576	22,178	51,414	22,850	168,018
Optometrists	16,041	4,971	11,523	5,121	37,656
Pharmacists	116,584	36,125	83,744	37,219	273,672
Registered Nurses	1,271,166	393,882	913,091	405,818	2,983,957
Veterinarians	33,232	10,297	23,871	10,609	78,009
Podiatrists	3,705	1,148	2,662	1,183	8,698
Total	1,870,419	579,566	1,343,543	597,128	4,390,656

Source: Projections by the authors derived from U.S. Census Bureau, 2012a , 2012b; Ruggles et al. 2010

[a]NH refers to nonHispanic; values for categories labeled NH are only for the nonHispanic persons in each race category. Hispanic includes Hispanics of all races

This premise is further strengthened when data in Table 6.5 are examined. The data in this table indicate the likely enrollment in medical and other health-related schools in 2010 and projected to 2060. These data suggest an increase of slightly less than 14,000 (13,975) United States medical students from 2010 to 2060, an increase of 18.6%, while the projected increase in those with disease incidence is projected to be 48.6%. Even with increased use of technology, without further enhancement in the number of national or international medical professionals, there is likely to be an insufficient number of such persons available to treat patients in the coming years.

Table 6.5 Persons in the United States enrolled in health-related[a] institutions by race/ethnicity in 2010 and numeric and percent change in projected enrollment to 2060 using the middle projection scenario

Year	NH[b] White	NH Black	Hispanic	NH Asian & Other	Total
Health related institutions					
2010	45,442	5,512	6,209	18,070	75,233
2020	42,714	5,685	7,302	20,314	76,015
2030	39,154	5,688	8,602	24,004	77,448
2040	38,455	6,001	10,087	28,465	83,008
2050	36,091	6,175	11,504	32,206	85,976
2060	33,573	6,382	12,978	36,275	89,208
Numeric change					
2010–2020	−2,728	173	1,093	2,244	782
2020–2030	−3,560	3	1,300	3,690	1,433
2030–2040	−699	313	1,485	4,461	5,560
2040–2050	−2,364	174	1,417	3,741	2,968
2050–2060	−2,518	207	1,474	4,069	3,232
2010–2060	−11,869	870	6,769	18,205	13,975
Percent change					
2010–2020	−6.0	3.1	17.6	12.4	1.0
2020–2030	−8.3	0.1	17.8	18.2	1.9
2030–2040	−1.8	5.5	17.3	18.6	7.2
2040–2050	−6.1	2.9	14.0	13.1	3.6
2050–2060	−7.0	3.4	12.8	12.6	3.8
2010–2060	−26.1	15.8	109.0	100.7	18.6

Source: Projections by the authors derived from U.S. Census Bureau, 2011b, 2011c, 2012a, 2012b; Association of American Medical Colleges 2012a, 2012b

Note: Enrollment does not include students who were graduated, dismissed, withdrawn, deceased, never enrolled, completed fifth pathway, did not complete fifth pathway, or degree revoked

[a]Does not include foreign students

[b]NH refers to nonHispanic; values for categories labeled NH are only for the nonHispanic persons in each race category. Hispanic includes Hispanics of all races

Table 6.6 indicates that some of the physician shortage could be improved if the rates of residency for minority groups were to become equal to 2010 rates for non-Hispanic Whites. The difference between the total number of physicians shown in the first column of this table, which assumes a continuation of current race/ethnicity specific rates, and the second column, which assumes that nonHispanic White rates of enrollment in medical school apply to all persons in all race/ethnicity groups in the United States population, indicate that if this change were to occur there would be an additional 23,657 medical residencies in 2060, an increase of 26.5%. This is the number occurring in a single year (2060). Clearly the expansion of the number of minority medical students over the projection period from 2010 to 2060 could ensure the nation's ability to meet the physician needs of its growing population. In fact, maintaining the number of persons per physician at 2010 levels in 2060 would require the addition of 179,421 physicians more than the 840,646 projected to exist

Table 6.6 Projected enrollment of United States residents in United States health related institutions by race/ethnicity in 2060 using alternative enrollment rate assumptions

Race/ethnicity	Assuming 2010 enrollment differentials	Assuming NH[a] White enrollment rates for minority groups
NH White	33,573	33,573
NH Black	6,382	11,866
Hispanic	12,978	31,151
NH Asian & Other	36,275	36,275
Total	89,208	112,865

Source: Projections by the authors derived from U.S. Census Bureau, 2011b, 2011c, 2012a, 2012b; and Association of American Medical Colleges 2012a, 2012b, 2012 National Population Projections , 2012–2060, and 2010 American Community Survey; and Association of American Medical Colleges

[a]NH refers to nonHispanic; values for categories labeled NH are only for the nonHispanic persons in each race category. Hispanic includes Hispanics of all races

Note: Enrollment does not include students who were graduated, dismissed, withdrawn, deceased, never enrolled, completed fifth pathway, did not complete fifth pathway, or degree revoked. Because rates for nonHispanic Asian and Other exceeded nonHispanic Whites in 2010, values for nonHispanic Asian & Other are the same for both scenarios

in Table 6.4. Thus the increase in the number of minority medical students indicated above (of 23,657 per year) could address that need, although the loss of physicians from practice due to aging and other factors would clearly require additional new physicians. The point however is that increasing medical education opportunities for minority students is likely to be important if the nation's future need for physicians is to be addressed. This is also true in other categories of health care professionals.

Table 6.7 indicates the number of physician contacts and hospital days and related costs projected for medical care in the United States in the coming decades. The data in this table indicate a significant increase in both the total number of events (contacts or days of hospitalization) and the total costs for physician services and hospital services. While the population is projected to increase by 36.1%, the total number of contacts is projected to increase by 54.1% from 3.2 contacts per person per year in 2010 to 3.6 contacts per person per year in 2060. At the same time, hospital days are projected to increase by 76.0%. These data indicate that physician contacts are likely to increase more extensively than the number of incidences, reflecting an aging population base in which the number of health occurrences per person increase. At the same time they suggest that increases in costs associated with physician contacts would increase at a rate higher than total contacts. This reflects the potential impact of an aging population with more specialized needs than a younger population.

The results shown in the data in Table 6.8 clearly reflect the aging of the population. In 2010 there were a total of 1,392,000 persons in nursing homes or one nursing home resident per 221.8 people in the population, while in 2060 (under the middle projection scenario) there are projected to be 3,805,851 people in nursing homes or one nursing home resident per 110.4 people in the population. Reflecting this growth in the number of nursing home residents would be a 173.4% increase in

Table 6.7 Physician contacts and days of hospital care in the United States by age of patient and associated costs for 2010 (in thousands) and projected for 2060 using the middle projection scenario

Panel A:			Panel B:	
	Physician contacts and total costs		Hospital days and associated costs	
Age of patient	Number	Costs	Number	Costs
2010				
<18	145,241,599	$ 21,893,823	10,992,527	$ 15,926,356
18–44	228,348,245	46,828,420	35,573,784	71,184,004
45–54	150,245,132	34,023,330	49,370,284	191,113,414
55–64	169,219,015	39,506,309	29,329,808	36,223,771
65–74	148,951,976	34,854,164	29,890,481	39,654,703
75+	141,054,033	32,285,734	17,501,612	26,367,411
Total	983,060,000	209,391,780	172,658,496	380,469,659
2060				
<18	174,818,258	$ 26,352,230	13,231,104	$ 19,169,684
18–44	286,517,349	58,757,425	44,309,797	88,665,739
45–54	168,193,471	38,087,769	59,103,881	228,784,725
55–64	218,099,443	50,918,060	58,676,175	72,471,434
65–74	297,036,250	69,505,288	70,166,839	93,083,304
75+	370,471,175	84,796,824	58,447,659	88,047,385
Total	1,515,135,946	328,417,596	303,935,455	590,222,271

Source: Projections by the authors derived from U.S. Census Bureau, 2011b, 2011c, 2012b; National Center for Health Statistics 2011, 2012a, 2012b, 2012 National Population Projections, 2012–2060; National Center for Health Statistics, Medical Expenditure Panel Survey, Healthcare Cost and Utilization Project, Nationwide Inpatient Sample, and Health, United States, 2011: *With Special Feature on Socioeconomic Status and Health*

total nursing home related monthly costs from $4.4 billion per month to more than $12.0 billion per month in 2060 (under the middle projection scenario). The aging of the population as noted above would clearly impact the healthcare service infrastructure and the fiscal resources of the nation.

Tables 6.9, 6.10, 6.11 and 6.12 examine the projected effects of projected population change on enrollment and expenditures for Medicaid/CHIP programs (for youth and adults) and for Medicare (for elderly persons) in the United States under current rates of use by age and race/ethnicity and per capita costs as of 2010 for the period from 2010 through 2060.

The data in Table 6.9 show substantial levels of change in enrollment and expenditures in these programs in the 2005–2010 time period, with Medicaid enrollment expanding by 21.0%, CHIP enrollment by 26.9%, and Medicare enrollment by 11.5%. However, expenditures in these programs increased by 27.8%, 59.5%, and 39.4%, respectively. Given that overall population growth during this period was approximately 4.9%, it is evident that not only population change but also the aging of the population and other factors are leading to increased enrollment and costs in these programs.

Table 6.8 Number of nursing home residents in the United States by age of patient and associated costs for 2010 (in thousands of dollars) and projected for 2060 using the middle projection scenario

Nursing home residents and monthly costs		
Age of patient	Number	Costs (in $thousands)
2010		
<21	2,784	8,811
21–64	204,624	647,635
65–74	203,232	643,229
75–84	382,800	1,211,562
85–94	492,768	1,559,611
95+	105,792	334,832
Total	1,392,000	4,405,680
2060		
<21	3,305	10,460
21–64	253,683	802,907
65–74	405,280	1,282,711
75–84	895,249	2,833,463
85–94	1,460,710	4,623,147
95+	787,624	2,492,830
Total	3,805,851	12,045,518

Source: Projections by the authors derived from U.S. Census Bureau, 2011b, 2011c, 2012b; Center for Medicare and Medicaid Services, 2012 and Cowles 2011, 2012 National Population Projections, 2012–2060; Centers for Medicare and Medicaid Services, 2012 *Nursing Home Data Compendium*, and C. Cowles, 2010 Nursing Home Statistical Yearbook

The data in Table 6.10 show projected growth by race/ethnicity of recipients in Medicaid and CHIP programs from 2010 to 2060.[1] These data show declines in the number of nonHispanic White recipients after 2030 for Medicaid and CHIP but increases in the number of recipients in all other racial/ethnic groups, with total 2010–2060 increases of 42.7% for nonHispanic Blacks, 148.4% for Hispanics, and 156.7% for nonHispanic Asians and Others. Overall because of the relative size of the projected populations in each racial/ethnic group, the percentage of all recipients in 2060 is projected to be 25.9% nonHispanic White, 19.2% nonHispanic Black, 41.5% Hispanic, and 13.4% nonHispanic Asian and Other. Of the total net increase in the number of recipients, nonHispanic Whites are projected to show a 5.0% decrease in their proportion of the net change in the total number of recipients, while nonHispanic Black populations would account for 15.6%, Hispanics for 67.2%, and nonHispanic Asians and Others for 22.2% of the net increase in the number of recipients from 2010 to 2060. Clearly the underlying change in the characteristics of the population would change the number and characteristics of recipients in these programs.

Table 6.11 shows the same type of data for Medicare. However, because of differences in age structure between nonHispanic White and other population groups,

[1] These projections use as a starting point Medicaid/CHIP enrollment rates prior to the full implementation of the Affordable Care Act.

Table 6.9 Enrollment and change in enrollment (in thousands), federal and state expenditures (in millions of 2010 dollars), and per recipient costs in Medicaid programs, the Children's Health Insurance Program (CHIP), and Medicare in the United States, 2005–2010

Area	2005	2006	2007	2008	2009	2010	Change 2005–2010	
							Numeric	Percent
Medicaid								
Enrollment	42,580.0	42,239.9	42,733.6	44,793.5	48,733.2	51,522.2	8,942.2	21.0
Expenditures (in $millions)								
Total	$304,637.3	$303,639.6	$320,243.0	$338,552.2	$366,486.2	$389,208.0	$84,570.7	27.8
Federal	174,430.8	173,251.5	182,587.1	193,169.3	243,012.7	263,998.5	89,567.7	51.3
State	130,206.5	130,388.2	137,655.9	145,382.8	123,473.4	125,209.5	–4,997.0	–3.8
Expenditures per recipient								
Total	$7,154.5	$7,188.5	$7,493.9	$7,558.1	$7,520.3	$7,554.2	399.7	5.6
Federal	4,096.5	4,101.6	4,272.7	4,312.4	4,986.6	5,124.0	1,027.5	25.1
State	3,057.9	3,086.8	3,221.3	3,245.6	2,533.7	2,430.2	–627.7	–20.5
CHIP								
Enrollment	4,043.9	4,078.2	4,397.5	4,835.6	4,966.0	5,132.1	1,088.2	26.9
Expenditures (in $millions)								
Total	$5,274.0	$5,958.1	$6,512.1	$7,461.3	$7,881.0	$8,411.1	$3,137.1	59.5
Federal	3,665.6	4,094.6	4,492.9	5,173.3	5,508.8	5,840.3	2,174.7	59.3
State	1,608.4	1,863.4	2,019.2	2,288.0	2,372.3	2,570.8	962.4	59.8
Expenditures per recipient								
Total	$1,304.2	$1,461.0	$1,480.9	$1,543.0	$1,587.0	$1,638.9	$ 334.7	25.7
Federal	906.5	1,004.0	1,021.7	1,069.8	1,109.3	1,138.0	231.5	25.5
State	397.7	456.9	459.2	473.2	477.7	500.9	103.2	25.9
Medicare								
Beneficiaries	42,606.0	43,436.0	44,368.0	45,500.0	46,575.0	47,492.0	4,886.0	11.5
Expenditures (in $millions)	$369,936.0	$434,160.0	$446,460.0	$466,216.0	$512,346.0	$515,800.0	$145,864.0	39.4
Expenditures per recipient	$8,682.7	$9,995.4	$10,062.7	$10,246.5	$11,000.5	$10,860.8	$ 2,178.1	25.1

Source: Centers for Medicare and Medicaid Services, Medicaid Financial Management Report 2010, Health Management Associates for the Kaiser Commission on Medicaid and the Uninsured, 2012a, b; and 2006–2011 Annual Reports of The Boards of Trustees of the Federal Hospital Insurance and Federal Supplementary Medical Insurance Trust Funds

Table 6.10 Medicaid/CHIP recipients, percent change in projected recipients, percent recipients by race/ethnicity, and net change in recipients in 2010 and projected to 2060 using the middle projection scenario

Year/period	NH[a] White	NH Black	Hispanic	NH Asian & Other	Total
Panel A: Medicaid/CHIP recipients					
2010	24,884,522	12,062,538	15,006,503	4,700,758	56,654,321
2020	25,770,059	13,369,113	18,986,183	5,963,577	64,088,932
2030	26,041,045	14,489,821	23,166,165	7,397,795	71,094,826
2040	25,423,605	15,346,609	27,747,110	8,875,772	77,393,096
2050	24,316,462	16,248,240	32,548,844	10,436,096	83,549,642
2060	23,231,197	17,215,896	37,270,538	12,066,575	89,784,206
Panel B: Percent change in Medicaid/CHIP recipients					
2010–2020	3.6	10.8	26.5	26.9	13.1
2020–2030	1.1	8.4	22.0	24.0	10.9
2030–2040	–2.4	5.9	19.8	20.0	8.9
2040–2050	–4.4	5.9	17.3	17.6	8.0
2050–2060	–4.5	6.0	14.5	15.6	7.5
2010–2060	–6.6	42.7	148.4	156.7	58.5
Panel C: Percent of Medicaid/CHIP recipients by race/ethnicity					
2010	43.9	21.3	26.5	8.3	100.0
2020	40.2	20.9	29.6	9.3	100.0
2030	36.6	20.4	32.6	10.4	100.0
2040	32.8	19.8	35.9	11.5	100.0
2050	29.1	19.4	39.0	12.5	100.0
2060	25.9	19.2	41.5	13.4	100.0
Panel D: Number and percent of net change in Medicaid/CHIP recipients, 2010–2060					
Race/ethnicity			Number	Percent	
NH White			–1,653,325	–5.0	
NH Black			5,153,358	15.6	
Hispanic			22,264,035	67.2	
NH Asian & Other			7,365,817	22.2	
Total			33,129,885	100.0	

Source: Projections by the authors derived from U.S. Census Bureau, 2012a, 2012b; Center for Medicare and Medicaid Services 2013; Boards of Trustees, Federal Hospital Insurance and Federal Supplementary Medical Insurance Trust Funds 2006–2011; Health Management Associates 2012a, 2012b; Ruggles et al. 2010

[a]NH refers to nonHispanic; values for categories labeled NH are only for the nonHispanic persons in each race category. Hispanic includes Hispanics of all races

Table 6.11 Medicare beneficiaries, percent change in projected beneficiaries, percent beneficiaries by race/ethnicity, and net change in beneficiaries in 2010 and projected to 2060 using the middle projection scenario

Year/period	NH[a] White	NH Black	Hispanic	NH Asian & Other	Total
Panel A: Medicare beneficiaries					
2010	37,207,601	4,664,369	3,423,364	2,196,666	47,492,000
2020	45,975,034	6,402,537	5,435,049	3,312,363	61,124,983
2030	55,114,945	8,583,386	8,606,457	4,795,984	77,100,772
2040	55,752,500	9,917,315	12,245,453	6,258,067	84,173,335
2050	53,642,505	10,976,148	15,977,459	7,799,334	88,395,446
2060	53,767,865	12,763,094	20,040,676	9,673,309	96,244,944
Panel B: Percent change in Medicare beneficiaries					
2010–2020	23.6	37.3	58.8	50.8	28.7
2020–2030	19.9	34.1	58.4	44.8	26.1
2030–2040	1.2	15.5	42.3	30.5	9.2
2040–2050	−3.8	10.7	30.5	24.6	5.0
2050–2060	0.2	16.3	25.4	24.0	8.9
2010–2060	44.5	173.6	485.4	340.4	102.7
Panel C: Percent of Medicare beneficiaries by race/ethnicity					
2010	78.3	9.8	7.2	4.7	100.0
2020	75.2	10.5	8.9	5.4	100.0
2030	71.5	11.1	11.2	6.2	100.0
2040	66.2	11.8	14.5	7.5	100.0
2050	60.7	12.4	18.1	8.8	100.0
2060	55.9	13.3	20.8	10.0	100.0
Panel D: Number and percent of net change in Medicare beneficiaries, 2010–2060					
Race/ethnicity			Number	Percent	
NH White			16,560,264	34.0	
NH Black			8,098,725	16.6	
Hispanic			16,617,312	34.1	
NH Asian & Other			7,476,643	15.3	
Total			48,752,944	100.0	

Source: Projections by the authors derived from U.S. Census Bureau, 2012a, 2012b; Center for Medicare and Medicaid Services 2013; Boards of Trustees, Federal Hospital Insurance and Federal Supplementary Medical Insurance Trust Funds 2006–2011; Health Management Associates 2012a, 2012b; Ruggles et al. 2010

[a]NH refers to nonHispanic; values for categories labeled NH are only for the nonHispanic persons in each race category. Hispanic includes Hispanics of all races

although minority populations show the largest percentage increases in the total number of recipients, nonHispanic White populations retain large proportions of those receiving benefits from such programs. The total percent change from 2010 to 2060 is 44.5% for nonHispanic Whites, 173.6% for nonHispanic Blacks, 485.4% for Hispanics, and 340.4% for nonHispanic Asians and Other. Of the net change in the number of recipients, nonHispanic Whites would account for 34.0%, nonHispanic Blacks for 16.6%, Hispanics for 34.1%, and nonHispanic Asians and Others for 15.3%. As with other programs addressing the needs of the elderly, the older age structure of nonHispanic Whites results in their continuing to play a larger role in Medicare programs than in overall population growth and change.

Table 6.12 provides data on the projected increase in costs for the projection period (2010–2060) for Medicaid/CHIP and Medicare. The data in Panel A for Medicaid and CHIP show an increase of more than $205 billion from 2010 to 2060 while Medicare costs are projected to increase by more than $529 billion. These values are increases of 58.4% for Medicaid/CHIP and 102.7% for Medicare. Given that Medicare's total costs are projected to increase by more than $488 billion more than the costs for Medicaid/CHIP, the fact that nonHispanic Whites would account

Table 6.12 Total costs (in millions of 2010 constant dollars) for CHIP/Medicaid and Medicare by race/ethnicity of recipients in 2010 and projected to 2060 using the middle projection scenario

Year	NH[a] White	NH Black	Hispanic	NH Asian & Other	Total
Panel A: Medicaid/CHIP					
2010	$ 154,388.4	$ 74,838.3	$ 93,103.3	$ 29,164.4	$ 351,494.4
2020	159,882.4	82,944.6	117,794.0	36,999.2	397,620.2
2030	161,563.7	89,897.7	143,727.4	45,897.4	441,086.1
2040	157,733.0	95,213.3	172,148.5	55,067.0	480,161.8
2050	150,864.0	100,807.2	201,939.3	64,747.6	518,358.2
2060	144,130.9	106,810.8	231,233.6	74,863.4	557,038.6
Panel B: Medicare					
2010	$ 404,103.4	$ 50,658.7	$ 37,180.4	$ 23,857.5	$ 515,800.0
2020	499,324.6	69,536.5	59,028.9	35,974.8	663,864.8
2030	598,591.1	93,222.2	93,472.8	52,088.1	837,374.3
2040	605,515.4	107,709.7	132,995.1	67,967.5	914,187.8
2050	582,599.3	119,209.5	173,527.6	84,706.8	960,043.2
2060	583,960.8	138,617.1	217,657.3	105,059.6	1,045,294.8

Source: Projections by the authors derived from U.S. Census Bureau, 2012a, 2012b; Center for Medicare and Medicaid Services 2013; Boards of Trustees, Federal Hospital Insurance and Federal Supplementary Medical Insurance Trust Funds 2006–2011; Health Management Associates 2012a, 2012b; Ruggles et al. 2010

[a]NH refers to nonHispanic; values for categories labeled NH are only for the nonHispanic persons in each race category. Hispanic includes Hispanics of all races

for more than 34% of the costs of Medicare costs clearly indicates how important age as well as race/ethnicity characteristics will be in impacting governmental costs. Whereas minority racial/ethnic groups play a disproportionate role in other social programs, in programs for the elderly such as Medicare, nonHispanic Whites would clearly have a disproportionate (to their overall percentage of the total population) impact.

Although the introduction of the Affordable Care Act (Health Care and Education Reconciliation Act 2010; and Patient Protection and Affordable Care Act 2010) may change the number of uninsured, it is useful to examine the numbers likely to remain uninsured in the absence of the complete implementation of some forms of inclusive health care insurance. The data in Table 6.13 show the projected number and characteristics of the uninsured without the ACA or other legislation. An examination of the data in this table show that, in the absence of major changes, the total number of uninsured would increase by more than 23.8 million persons, or by 49.6%, between 2010 and 2060. Because of a decrease in the total number of nonHispanic Whites, the number of uninsured nonHispanic Whites would decrease by 4.6 million, but the number of uninsured nonHispanic Blacks would increase by 2.2 million, the number of uninsured Hispanics would increase by 21.4 million, and the number of uninsured nonHispanic Asians and Others would increase by 4.8 million between 2010 and 2060. With their rapid growth, minority populations would come to account for 76.6% of all uninsured persons by 2060. Overall, because they are more likely to be uninsured, the rapid growth in minority populations leads to a percentage increase in the number of uninsured of 49.6% compared to at 36.1% increase in the total population between 2010 and 2060.

6.3 Social Service Usage: Supplemental Nutrition Assistance Program (SNAP) and Temporary Assistance to Needy Families (TANF)

In this section we examine the effects of population size and characteristics and population growth and change in population characteristics on a selected set of social programs. Specifically we examine the impacts on the Supplemental Nutrition Assistance Program (SNAP) and the Temporary Assistance to Needy Families (TANF) programs.

The data in Table 6.14 show recent changes in the two programs noted above. The data show that enrollment in SNAP increased by 56.7% in the short period from 2005 to 2010, a period of an economic recession, and that enrollment in TANF declined by 3.2% due to program changes and tightened eligibility requirements. Expenditures increased by $1.7 billion (33.1%) for SNAP and by $9.9 billion (42.7%) for TANF. Whereas federal funds accounted for the largest share of the increase for SNAP, state funds accounted for the largest proportion of TANF increases.

Table 6.13 Medically uninsured in the United States by race/ethnicity in 2010 and projected to 2060 using the middle projection scenario and without implementation of the Affordable Care Act

Year/period	NH[a] White	NH Black	Hispanic	NH Asian & Other	Total
Number uninsured					
2010	21,453,113	7,122,625	15,597,577	3,849,856	48,023,171
2020	20,480,935	7,723,430	19,396,892	4,587,237	52,188,494
2030	19,214,499	8,012,210	23,443,925	5,512,556	56,183,190
2040	18,567,290	8,533,764	27,865,152	6,551,942	61,518,148
2050	17,846,164	9,006,830	32,406,996	7,609,162	66,869,152
2060	16,835,139	9,354,111	36,971,772	8,663,784	71,824,806
Numeric change					
2010–2020	−972,178	600,805	3,799,315	737,381	4,165,323
2020–2030	−1,266,436	288,780	4,047,033	925,319	3,994,696
2030–2040	−647,209	521,554	4,421,227	1,039,386	5,334,958
2040–2050	−721,126	473,066	4,541,844	1,057,220	5,351,004
2050–2060	−1,011,025	347,281	4,564,776	1,054,622	4,955,654
2010–2060	−4,617,974	2,231,486	21,374,195	4,813,928	23,801,635
Percent change					
2010–2020	−4.5	8.4	24.4	19.2	8.7
2020–2030	−6.2	3.7	20.9	20.2	7.7
2030–2040	−3.4	6.5	18.9	18.9	9.5
2040–2050	−3.9	5.5	16.3	16.1	8.7
2050–2060	−5.7	3.9	14.1	13.9	7.4
2010–2060	−21.5	31.3	137.0	125.0	49.6
Percent of the uninsured					
2010	44.7	14.8	32.5	8.0	100.0
2020	39.2	14.8	37.2	8.8	100.0
2030	34.2	14.3	41.7	9.8	100.0
2040	30.2	13.9	45.3	10.6	100.0
2050	26.7	13.5	48.5	11.3	100.0
2060	23.4	13.0	51.5	12.1	100.0
Percent uninsured					
2010	10.9	18.9	30.9	16.2	15.6
2020	10.3	18.5	30.4	15.8	15.6
2030	9.7	17.6	29.8	15.5	15.7
2040	9.6	17.5	29.4	15.4	16.2
2050	9.6	17.3	29.0	15.3	16.7
2060	9.4	16.9	28.7	15.1	17.1

Source: Projections by the authors derived from U.S. Census Bureau, 2011b, 2011c, 2012a, 2012b; Ruggles et al. 2010

[a]NH refers to nonHispanic; values for categories labeled NH are only for the nonHispanic persons in each race category. Hispanic includes Hispanics of all races

Table 6.14 Enrollment and change in enrollment (monthly in thousands), expenditures (in millions of 2010 dollars), and per recipient costs in the Supplemental Nutrition Assistance Program (SNAP) and in Temporary Assistance for Needy Families (TANF) in the United States, 2005–2010

Area	2005	2006	2007	2008	2009	2010	Change 2005–2010	
							Numeric	Percent
Supplemental Nutrition Assistance Program (SNAP)								
Enrollment	25,717.8	26,548.8	26,316.0	28,222.6	33,490.0	40,301.9	14,584.0	56.7
Expenditures								
Total	$ 5,206.3	$ 5,532.6	$ 5,708.2	$ 6,179.4	$ 6,576.4	$ 6,930.4	1,724.1	33.1
Federal	2,493.2	2,667.0	2,761.7	2,977.6	3,181.9	3,482.9	989.7	39.7
State	2,713.1	2,865.6	2,946.5	3,201.8	3,394.4	3,447.5	734.4	27.1
Expenditures per recipient								
Total	$ 202.4	$ 208.4	$ 216.9	$ 219.0	$ 196.4	$ 172.0	–30.4	–15.0
Federal	96.9	100.5	104.9	105.5	95.0	86.4	–10.5	–10.8
State	105.5	107.9	112.0	113.4	101.4	85.5	–20.0	–19.0
Temporary Assistance for Needy Families (TANF)								
Enrollment	4,548.5	4,148.5	3,896.8	3,795.0	4,154.4	4,402.9	–145.6	–3.2
Expenditures								
Total	$ 23,311.8	$ 22,684.3	$ 24,026.4	$ 24,997.1	$ 29,505.4	$ 33,255.5	9,943.7	42.7
Federal	14,163.7	13,570.1	13,636.8	14,473.9	15,178.6	18,064.7	3,901.1	27.5
State	9,148.1	9,114.2	10,389.7	10,523.2	14,326.9	15,190.7	6,042.7	66.1
Expenditures per recipient								
Total	$ 5,125.1	$ 5,468.1	$ 6,165.6	$ 6,586.8	$ 7,102.3	$ 7,553.0	2,427.9	47.4
Federal	3,113.9	3,271.1	3,499.5	3,813.9	3,653.6	4,102.9	989.0	31.8
State	2,011.2	2,197.0	2,666.2	2,772.9	3,448.6	3,450.2	1,439.0	71.5

Source: U.S. Census Bureau, 2011b, 2011c; U.S. Department of Agriculture, 2012, 2005–2010; U.S. Department of Health & Human Services, 2013a, b

Table 6.15 TANF enrollment in the United States, percent change in projected enrollment, percent enrollment by race/ethnicity in 2010 and projected to 2060 using the middle projection scenario

Year/period	NH[a] White	NH Black	Hispanic	NH Asian & Other	Total
Panel A: TANF enrollment					
2010	1,400,130	1,404,531	1,320,875	277,385	4,402,921
2020	1,408,931	1,599,655	1,630,072	329,294	4,967,952
2030	1,334,469	1,635,769	1,974,720	393,879	5,338,837
2040	1,282,305	1,721,160	2,363,862	469,854	5,837,181
2050	1,235,840	1,824,382	2,746,925	543,385	6,350,532
2060	1,162,549	1,900,987	3,137,266	615,998	6,816,800
Panel B: Percent change in projected TANF enrollment					
2010–2020	0.6	13.9	23.4	18.7	12.8
2020–2030	−5.3	2.3	21.1	19.6	7.5
2030–2040	−3.9	5.2	19.7	19.3	9.3
2040–2050	−3.6	6.0	16.2	15.6	8.8
2050–2060	−5.9	4.2	14.2	13.4	7.3
2010–2060	−17.0	35.3	137.5	122.1	54.8
Panel C: Percent of TANF projected enrollment by race/ethnicity					
2010	31.8	31.9	30.0	6.3	100.0
2020	28.4	32.2	32.8	6.6	100.0
2030	25.0	30.6	37.0	7.4	100.0
2040	22.0	29.5	40.5	8.0	100.0
2050	19.4	28.7	43.3	8.6	100.0
2060	17.1	27.9	46.0	9.0	100.0

Source: Projections by the authors derived from U.S. Census Bureau, 2011b, 2011c, 2012b; U.S. Department of Health & Human Services 2013a, 2013b

[a]NH refers to nonHispanic; values for categories labeled NH are only for the nonHispanic persons in each race category. Hispanic includes Hispanics of all races

Tables 6.15 and 6.16 show the projected change in the number and characteristics of TANF and SNAP recipients, respectively. The number of TANF recipients is projected to increase by 54.8% and the number of SNAP recipients by 48.1% from 2010 to 2060. Both programs show dramatic declines in the number and the percentage of all recipients who are nonHispanic White and increases in the number of recipients from all other racial/ethnic groups. These data indicate the largest numerical increases (of nearly 1.8 million of 2.4 million for TANF and 14.3 million of 19.3 million for SNAP) would be due to the increase in the number of Hispanic recipients. By 2060, 17.1% of recipients of TANF would be nonHispanic White compared to 31.8% in 2010, 27.9% would be nonHispanic Black compared to 31.9% in 2010, 46.0% would be Hispanic in 2060 compared to 30.0% in 2010, and 9.0% would be nonHispanic Asian and Other in 2060 compared to 6.3% in 2010.

Table 6.16 SNAP recipients in the United States, percent change in projected recipients, percent of recipients by race/ethnicity in 2010 and projected to 2060 using the middle projection scenario

Year/period	NH[a] White	NH Black	Hispanic	NH Asian & Other	Total
Panel A: SNAP recipients					
2010	16,557,953	10,903,842	9,934,692	2,905,391	40,301,878
2020	16,270,227	11,807,265	12,352,647	3,531,265	43,961,404
2030	15,868,534	12,598,532	15,087,261	4,306,395	47,860,722
2040	15,251,584	13,286,516	18,072,517	5,116,603	51,727,220
2050	14,561,199	14,022,576	21,148,715	5,970,649	55,703,139
2060	13,849,216	14,776,372	24,215,037	6,845,425	59,686,050
Panel B: Percent change in projected SNAP recipients					
2010–2020	−1.7	8.3	24.3	21.5	9.1
2020–2030	−2.5	6.7	22.1	22.0	8.9
2030–2040	−3.9	5.5	19.8	18.8	8.1
2040–2050	−4.5	5.5	17.0	16.7	7.7
2050–2060	−4.9	5.4	14.5	14.7	7.2
2010–2060	−16.4	35.5	143.7	135.6	48.1
Panel C: Percent of SNAP projected recipients by race/ethnicity					
2010	41.0	27.1	24.7	7.2	100.0
2020	37.0	26.9	28.1	8.0	100.0
2030	33.2	26.3	31.5	9.0	100.0
2040	29.5	25.7	34.9	9.9	100.0
2050	26.1	25.2	38.0	10.7	100.0
2060	23.1	24.8	40.6	11.5	100.0

Source: Projections by the authors and U.S. Census Bureau, 2011b, 2011c, 2012b; U.S. Department of Agriculture, 2012, 2005–2010

[a]NH refers to nonHispanic; values for categories labeled NH are only for the nonHispanic persons in each race category. Hispanic includes Hispanics of all races

These changes in values for SNAP would be from 41.0% of all recipients being nonHispanic White in 2010 to 23.1% in 2060. Value changes for other racial/ethnic groups are from 27.1% for nonHispanic Blacks, 24.7% for Hispanics, and 7.2% for nonHispanic Asian and Others in 2010 to projections of 24.8%, 40.6%, and 11.5% for nonHispanic Blacks, Hispanics, and nonHispanic Asians and Others, respectively, in 2060. Clearly for both TANF and SNAP, recipients would increasingly be members of minority populations. In fact, as shown in Table 6.17, all of the increase would be due to minority populations with the number of nonHispanic White recipients decreasing for both TANF and SNAP from 2010 to 2060.

Finally, reflecting the overall growth in the number of recipients, the data in Table 6.18 show that expenditures would increase from roughly $33.3 billion in 2010 to $51.5 billion in 2060 for TANF and from $6.9 billion in 2010 to $10.3 billion in 2060 for SNAP. The faster growth of populations with lower incomes, which currently are largely the Hispanic and nonHispanic Black populations, would substantially increase the costs associated with these programs.

Table 6.17 Number and percent of net change in enrollment in TANF and SNAP by race/ethnicity, 2010–2060 using the middle projection scenario

Race/ethnicity	Number	Percent
Panel A: Number and percent of net change in TANF enrollment		
NH[a] White	−237,581	−9.8
NH Black	496,456	20.6
Hispanic	1,816,390	75.2
NH Asian & Other	338,613	14.0
Total	2,413,878	100.0
Panel B: Number and percent of net change in SNAP recipients		
NH[a] White	−2,708,737	−14.0
NH Black	3,872,530	20.0
Hispanic	14,280,345	73.7
NH Asian & Other	3,940,034	20.3
Total	19,384,172	100.0

Source: Projections by the authors derived from U.S. Census Bureau, 2011b, 2011c, 2012b; U.S. Department of Health & Human Services, 2013a, b; U.S. Department of Agriculture, 2005–2010

[a]NH refers to nonHispanic; values for categories labeled NH are only for the nonHispanic persons in each race category. Hispanic includes Hispanics of all races

6.4 Summary

1. The demographic change described in this volume will have substantial implications for population-related change in the incidence and type of diseases/disorders that occur, the characteristics of health care provision and training and education, and the demand for a variety of public assistance programs in the United States between now and 2060.
2. A comparison of the change by age and race/ethnicity in the populations experiencing health incidences clearly points to the effects that the aging and racial/ethnic diversification of the population will have on the number of health incidences and other health related factors.
3. For example, the percentage of the nonHispanic White population 65 years of age and older increases (under the middle projection scenario) from 16.4% in 2010 to 28.8% by 2060. The equivalent rates of change for the nonHispanic Black population are from 9.1 to 20.7%, for Hispanics from 5.5 to 15.2%, and for nonHispanic Asians and Others from 8.0 to 16.8%.
4. Race/ethnicity differences are also of critical importance for other factors as well. This is evident in that the nonHispanic White population is projected to decrease by −9.1% from 2010 to 2060 but the nonHispanic Black population to increase by 46.8%, the Hispanic population by 155.1%, and the nonHispanic Asian and Other population by 140.8%. By comparison the nonHispanic White population would show an increase in the number of health incidences of 3.7% while the nonHispanic Black population is projected to show a 77.3% increase,

Table 6.18 Total costs (in 2010 constant dollars) for TANF and SNAP by race/ethnicity of recipients in 2010 and projected to 2060 using the middle projection scenario

Year	NH[a] White	NH Black	Hispanic	NH Asian & Other	Total
Panel A: TANF					
2010	$10,575,247,453	$10,608,488,411	$ 9,976,638,279	$2,095,101,894	$33,255,476,037
2020	10,641,655,843	12,082,194,215	12,311,933,816	2,487,157,582	37,522,941,456
2030	10,079,244,357	12,354,963,257	14,915,060,160	2,974,968,087	40,324,235,861
2040	9,685,249,665	12,999,921,480	17,854,249,686	3,548,807,262	44,088,228,093
2050	9,334,299,520	13,779,557,246	20,747,524,525	4,104,186,905	47,965,568,196
2060	8,780,732,597	14,358,154,811	23,695,770,098	4,652,632,894	51,487,290,400
Panel B: SNAP					
2010	$2,847,329,980	$ 1,875,040,727	$ 1,708,384,266	$ 499,615,315	$ 6,930,370,288
2020	2,798,479,044	2,030,849,580	2,124,655,284	607,377,580	7,561,361,488
2030	2,729,387,848	2,166,947,504	2,595,008,892	740,699,940	8,232,044,184
2040	2,623,272,448	2,285,280,752	3,108,472,924	880,055,716	8,897,081,840
2050	2,504,526,228	2,411,883,072	3,637,578,980	1,026,951,628	9,580,939,908
2060	2,382,065,152	2,541,535,984	4,164,986,364	1,177,413,100	10,266,000,600

Source: Projections by the authors derived from U.S. Census Bureau, 2011b, 2011c, 2012b; U.S. Department of Health & Human Services, 2013a, b; U.S. Department of Agriculture, 2005–2010

[a]NH refers to nonHispanic; values for categories labeled NH are only for the nonHispanic persons in each race category. Hispanic includes Hispanics of all races

the Hispanic population an increase of 239.3%, and the nonHispanic Asian and Other population a 193.3% increase from 2010 to 2060.

5. Rates and the number of persons with disabilities would also change. The data presented here show an 86.8% increase in the number of cases involving disabilities compared to an overall 48.6% increase in the number of incidences of all diseases and disorders. This disparity is largely a result of higher rates of disabilities for Hispanics and nonHispanic Asians and Others.
6. The data presented in this chapter indicate a potential future shortage in the number of health care personnel. Based on 2010 occupational participation rates, there would be a 7.4% increase in the number of health care professionals from 2010 to 2060. However the disease incidence is projected to increase by 48.6% from 2010 to 2060. Increases in the number of minority health professionals to the levels of nonHispanic Whites could increase the number of physicians by nearly 24,000 per year and would, if continued across the projection period, result in nearly complete closure between the demand for, and supply of, health care professionals by 2060.
7. Because of the aging of the population and the increased level of disability that often accompanies conditions of the elderly the number of contacts are expected to increase by 54.1% over the projection period while hospital days are projected to increase by 76.0%. Physician contacts per person will change from 3.2 to 3.6. At the same time, physician costs will increase by 56.8%, while hospital related costs will increase by 55.1% (in 2010 constant dollars).
8. Due to the aging of the population and the lower incomes and higher levels of poverty of minority populations, the number of nursing home patients, enrollment and expenditures for Medicaid/CHIP, and Medicare enrollment and expenditures are projected to increase from 2010 to 2060. Whereas there were 1.4 million persons in nursing homes in 2010, there are projected to be 3.8 million in 2060. Nursing home costs are projected to increase by 173.4% from $4.4 billion per month in 2010 to $12.1 billion per month.
9. Enrollment in Medicaid/CHIP programs is projected to increase by 58.5% from 2010 to 2060 with 25.9% of recipients in 2060 being nonHispanic White, 19.2% nonHispanic Black, 41.5% Hispanic, and 13.4% nonHispanic Asian and Other compared to 43.9, 21.3, 26.5, and 8.3% being from these racial/ethnic categories in 2010. Overall the absolute number of nonHispanic Whites would decline, and the largest single category of recipients (making up two of every three recipients in 2060) would be Hispanic. Costs would more than double to more than $557 billion per year by 2060.
10. The number of Medicare beneficiaries would increase by 102.7%, by nearly 49 million persons from 2010 to 2060. Unlike Medicaid, because Medicare is designed to assist the elderly, it would remain (despite a decrease from 78.3% of those receiving benefits being nonHispanic White in 2010 to 55.9% of all recipients in 2060) a program whose recipients are largely nonHispanic White. Of the total number of more than 96 million recipients in 2060, 55.9% would be nonHispanic White, 13.3% would be nonHispanic Black, 20.8% Hispanic, and 10.0% would be nonHispanic Asian and Other. Given the current benefit patterns, the program costs would increase to more than $1 trillion in 2060.

11. Despite the projected growth in Medicaid and Medicare enrollees, the number of persons likely to remain uninsured (in the absence of the Affordable Care Act or other legislation) would increase from 48 million in 2010 to 71.8 million in 2060 (an increase of more than 23 million from 2010 to 2060).
12. Enrollments in, and associated costs for, the Supplemental Nutrition Assistance Program (SNAP) and Temporary Assistance to Needy Families (TANF) programs are also projected to increase. The number of TANF recipients is projected to increase by 54.8% from 2010 to 2060 to 6.8 million in 2060, and the number in SNAP is projected to increase by 48.1% from 2010 to 2060 to 59.7 million in 2060. The number of nonHispanic Whites in both of these programs would decrease from 2010 to 2060, and by 2060 more than 40% of those in both programs are projected to be Hispanic. Costs for TANF are projected to increase from $33.3 billion in 2010 to $51.5 billion in 2060 while the costs for SNAP would increase from $6.9 billion in 2010 to $10.3 billion in 2060.

Overall, the data in this chapter indicate that health and welfare programs are likely to increase substantially in both enrollment and costs as a result of population growth and aging and the characteristics (of reduced financial resources) of the fastest growing population segments. These data also indicate that substantial governmental financial and personnel investments will be essential if we are going to address the health care and social service needs of people in the United States in the coming decades. These needs will represent substantial challenges for the individuals directly impacted and for the nation.

References

American College of Physicians. (2010). *Racial and ethnic disparities in health care, update 2010*. Washington, DC. http://www.acponline.org/advocacy/current_policy_papers/assets/racial_disparities.pdf. Accessed 21 Jun 2014.

Association of American Medical Colleges. (2012a). *Data warehouse: student file*. Washington, DC: Association of American Medical Colleges. Accessed on 7 Feb 2012.

Association of American Medical Colleges. (2012b). *Data warehouse: applicant matriculant file*. Washington, DC: Association of American Medical Colleges. Accessed 7 Feb 2012.

Boards of Trustees of the Federal Hospital Insurance and Federal Supplementary Medical Insurance Trust Funds. (2006–2011). *2006–2011 annual reports of the boards of trustees*. Washington, DC: Federal Hospital Insurance and Federal Supplementary Medical Insurance Trust Funds.

Center for Health Workforce Studies. (2006). *The impact of the aging population on the health workforce in the United States: summary of key findings*. Report. Center for health workforce studies. http://www.albany.edu/news/pdf_files/impact_of_aging_excerpt.pdf. Accessed 15 Jan 2015.

Centers for Medicare and Medicaid Services. (2012). *2012 Nursing home data compendium*. Baltimore: Centers for Medicare and Medicaid Services.

Centers for Medicare and Medicaid Services. (2013). *Medicaid statistical information system (MSIS), Medicaid financial management reports, 2002–2010*. Baltimore: Centers for Medicare and Medicaid Services. http://medicaid.gov/Medicaid-CHIP-Program-Information/By-Topics/Data-and-Systems/MBES/CMS-64-Quarterly-Expense-Report.html. Accessed 21 Jan 2013.

Cowles, C. M. (2011). *2010 nursing home statistical yearbook.* McMinnville: Cowles Research Group.
Health Care and Education Reconciliation Act (ACA). (2010). Public Law 111–152.
Health Management Associates. (2012a). CHIP enrollment: June 2011; data snapshot. *Kaiser Commission on Medicaid and the Uninsured, 2012.* Naples, FL: Health Management Associates. http://www.kff.org/medicaid/enrollmentreports.cfm. Accessed 23 Feb 2012.
Health Management Associates. (2012b). Medicaid enrollment: June 2011; data snapshot. *Kaiser Commission on Medicaid and the Uninsured, 2012.* Naples: Health Management Associates. http://www.kff.org/medicaid/enrollmentreports.cfm. Accessed 23 Feb 2012.
Hoque, N., McGehee, M. A., & Bradshaw, B. S. (2013). *Applied demography and public health.* New York: Springer.
National Center for Health Statistics. (2009). *United States national health interview survey.* Atlanta: Centers for Disease Control and Prevention.
National Center for Health Statistics. (2011). *Health, United States, 2011: With special feature on socioeconomic status and health.* Atlanta: Centers for Disease Control and Prevention.
National Center for Health Statistics. (2012a). United States healthcare cost and utilization project, nationwide inpatient sample. In *2010 national statistics for outcomes by patient and hospital characteristics.* http://www.cdc.gov/nchs/data/hus/hus11.pdf. Accessed 10 Nov 2012.
National Center for Health Statistics. (2012b). *United States medical expenditure panel survey.* Atlanta: Centers for Disease Control and Prevention, Agency for Healthcare Research and Quality.
National Center for Health Statistics. (2012c). *United States national health interview survey.* Atlanta: Centers for Disease Control and Prevention.
Patient Protection and Affordable Care Act (ACA). 2010. Public Law 111–148.
Pol, L. G., & Thomas, R. K. (2013). *The demography of health and healthcare* (3rd ed.). Dordrecht: Springer Science+Business Media.
Ruggles, S. J., Alexander, T., Genadek, K., Goeken, R., Schroeder, R. B., & Sobek, M. (2010). *Integrated public use microdata series: Version 5.0.* Minneapolis: University of Minnesota.
U.S. Census Bureau. (2011a). *2010 American community survey.* Washington, DC: U.S. Census Bureau.
U.S. Census Bureau. (2011b). *2010 census summary file 1.* Washington, DC: U.S. Census Bureau.
U.S. Census Bureau. (2011c). *2010 census summary file 2.* Washington, DC: U.S. Census Bureau.
U.S. Census Bureau. (2012a). *2009–2011 American community survey.* Washington, DC: U.S. Census Bureau.
U.S. Census Bureau. (2012b). *2012 national population projections.* Washington, DC: U.S. Census Bureau.
U.S. Department of Agriculture. (2012). *Food stamp program participation and costs.* Washington, DC: U.S. Department of Agriculture.
U.S. Department of Agriculture. (2005–2010). *Supplemental nutrition assistance program (SNAP) state activity reports, 2005–2010.* Food and Nutrition Service Program Accountability and Administration Division. Washington, DC: U.S. Department of Agriculture.
U.S. Department of Health and Human Services. (2010). *2009 HCFA statistics.* Washington, DC: U.S. Department of Health and Human Services.
U.S. Department of Health and Human Services. (2013a). *Administration for children and families, caseload data for 2005–2010.* Washington, DC: U.S. Department of Health and Human Services.
U.S. Department of Health and Human Services. (2013b). *TANF financial data fiscal year reports, 2005–2010.* Washington, DC: U.S. Department of Health and Human Services.
Wiener, J. M., & Tilly, J. (2002). Population ageing in the United States of America: Implications for public programmes. *International Journal of Epidemiology, 31*(4), 776–781.

Chapter 7
The Effects of Demographic Change on Selected Transportation Services and Demand

Most households in the United States own at least one vehicle. Population growth will increase demand for more roadway infrastructure and increase congestion, air pollution, and energy use. But vehicle ownership and driver licensing rates differ by age, sex, and race/ethnicity partly due to household and other socioeconomic differences. Thus changes in the underlying demographic characteristics of the population, absent improvements in the socioeconomic resources of minority households, are likely to affect the magnitude of change as well as impact the demand for alternative transportation modes. In this chapter we analyze the effects of population growth and change in the demographic characteristics of the population on change in vehicle ownership, drivers, and transportation mode choice on the work commute. In addition, we explore the impacts of growth in the number of drivers and changes in the age structure of the driving population on change in the number of vehicular crashes.

7.1 Historic Changes in Licensed Drivers

Recent trends suggest that the United States, like many other developed countries, may have reached saturation in car ownership and use (The Economist 2012; Goodwin 2012; U.S. Department of Transportation 2011a; Dargay et al. 2007). In 2010 most adults were licensed to drive (Table 7.1) and the licensure rate has remained fairly constant over the last three decades (at around 670 to 680 drivers per 1,000 people). With the exception of the last decade, percentage growth in licensed drivers exceeded growth in the population as a whole, although the rate of growth attenuated over time. Several factors influenced the explosive growth in automobile use in the mid to late twentieth century. First, changes in household preferences coincided with change in the development of urban infrastructure that was more conducive to vehicular travel than any other transportation modes (Cline 2014a; Pisarski 2006). The automobile enabled the development of suburban communities

S.H. Murdock et al., *Population Change in the United States*,
DOI 10.1007/978-94-017-7288-4_7

Table 7.1 Total population, total licensed drivers, licensed drivers per 1,000 people in the United States and percent change, 1950–2010

	Number (in millions)		Percent change from previous time		Licensed drivers per 1,000 population	
Year	Population	Drivers	Population	Drivers	Drivers	Percent change
1950	152	62	–	–	407.9	–
1960	180	87	18.4	40.3	483.3	18.5
1970	204	112	13.3	28.7	549.0	13.6
1980	227	145	11.3	29.5	638.8	16.4
1990	248	167	9.3	15.2	673.4	5.4
2000	281	191	13.3	14.4	679.7	0.9
2010	309	210	10.0	9.9	679.6	0.0

Source: U.S. Department of Transportation, Federal Highway Administration, Office of Highway Policy Information, Highway Statistics Series

further from central business districts. The change in urban infrastructure, in turn, reinforced the preference and necessity for owning the automobile to access most daily activities. Increases in household incomes during this period also meant that more households could afford more than one vehicle. More importantly, the explosive growth in licensed drivers occurring from the 1950s through the 1980s coincided during a period when women entered the labor force at greater numbers than in the past (Cline 2014a; Greene 1987; Lave 1991; Pisarski 2006). Most of these factors will have very little influence on growth in automobile use in the future, which means that, absent major technological advances that would replace the automobile as the major form of transportation or change in the socioeconomic conditions of the underlying population, growth in licensed drivers will continue to be a function primarily of growth in the population as a whole (Greene 1987; Lave 1991; Polzin et al. 2004).

Although the change in the number of drivers has grown more slowly in the last few decades, the number of elderly drivers (drivers age 65 years and older) has increased substantially. There were 6.4 million elderly drivers added between 2000 and 2010, more than three times the increase in the number of young drivers (drivers less than age 30 [Table 7.2]). One third of the growth in all drivers was accounted for by the addition of elderly drivers. This rapid growth in older drivers can be attributed to the growth in the elderly population overall as well as the entry of recent cohorts of elderly people (and women in particular) who had comparatively higher licensing rates prior to reaching age 65 than previous cohorts (Cline 2014b; Greene 1987; Lave 1991; Pisarski 2006:35).

By 2010, there were 33.7 million elderly drivers, 7.9 million of whom were in the oldest ages (age 80 and above). Continued growth in the elderly population, including growth in the oldest old, will lead to increases in the number of elderly drivers in the United States. This has many implications for transportation policy.

Table 7.2 Licensed drivers by age and numeric and percent change in licensed drivers by age, 2000–2010

	Licensed drivers		2000–10 change	
Age	2000	2010	Numeric	%
<30	43,295,053	45,455,689	2,160,636	5.0
30–64	120,004,160	130,927,632	10,923,472	9.1
65+	27,325,809	33,731,618	6,405,809	23.4
80+	5,561,217	7,874,804	2,313,587	41.6
Total	190,625,022	210,114,939	19,489,917	10.2

Source: U.S. Department of Transportation, Federal Highway Administration, Highway Statistics Series, 2000, 2010

For instance, elderly drivers (age 65 years and older) take more trips but drive fewer miles than younger drivers and their travel patterns are less predictable than younger drivers (Cline 2014b; Rosenbloom 2001; Rosenbloom and Herbel 2009). This is due to the fact that most elderly drivers are retired and are able to arrange their daily vehicle trips during times outside of the typical work commute. In the aggregate, this helps to alleviate congestion during peak commute hours but increases the number of people on roads during off-peak times. In addition to impacts to demands on the transportation system, the growth in the elderly population will have implications for traffic safety. Although accident rates per driver are lower for the elderly than those for the youngest drivers, there is a slight increase in crash rates with increasing age, particularly for crashes involving fatalities (Highway Loss Data Institute 2005, United States Department of Transportation, National Highway Safety Administration 2010). Thus, growth in the elderly population will increase the number of elderly drivers involved in crashes, even as the overall accident rate declines due to the fact that a smaller proportion of drivers will be in the youngest ages when crash rates are at the highest levels (Highway Loss Data Institute 2012).

7.2 Vehicle Ownership

In most communities in the United States, a car is necessary in order to access jobs, school, healthcare, and other services and activities. Because of this, most households today own at least one vehicle (Table 7.3). Those who do not own a vehicle may use public transportation to access services and activities and thus a large number of households without vehicles (zero vehicle households) can indicate a need for public transportation and related services within a community. In the United States, the proportion of households without vehicles in 2010 remained approximately the same as in 2000, although there was a slight increase in the proportion of zero vehicle households for households headed by someone younger than 65. Not surprisingly, the likelihood of household vehicle ownership increases with increasing

Table 7.3 Households and households without vehicles in the United States in 2000 and 2010

Age of householder	2000 households			2010 households		
		Without vehicles			Without vehicles	
	Total	Number	%	Total	Number	%
15–64	82,845,411	6,901,306	8.3	90,896,456	8,151,097	9.0
65+	22,634,690	3,959,761	17.5	25,819,836	4,602,975	17.8
All households	105,480,101	10,861,067	10.3	116,716,292	12,754,072	10.9

Source: U.S. Census Bureau, 2000, and 2010 Censuses; 2006–2010 American Community Survey

household income (Giuliano and Dargay 2006). Due to differences in household income, minorities are more likely to live in zero vehicle households (Giuliano 2003; Pisarski 2006). Thus, continued growth in minority households without concomitant improvement in socioeconomic resources would result in a larger proportion of zero vehicle households.

In addition to racial and ethnic change, the aging of the population is likely to impact the number of zero vehicle households. In 2010, 17.8% or 4.6 million elderly households had no vehicle present. Many people choose to give up driving altogether and may sell their car as they age and deteriorating physical and cognitive abilities compromise their driving skills (D'Ambrosio et al. 2008; Donorfio et al. 2008). The increase in older households without vehicles may challenge the delivery of social and healthcare services to populations aging in places where no public transportation services are available (Countouris et al. 2014; Ryser and Halseth 2012). Without access to transportation, elderly people in these households will become increasingly isolated, leading to additional deterioration in their mental and physical health (Curl et al. 2014; Marottoli et al. 2000; Oxley and Whelan 2008).

Workers who live in vehicle owning households are more likely to drive or ride in a car on the commute to work (Paulley et al. 2006; Polzin et al. 2001; Pucher and Renne 2003). Since most households own at least one car, it is not surprising that in 2010, 87% of all workers either drove alone or carpooled to work (Table 7.4). This was essentially the same percentage using a car on the journey to work in 2000. At the same time, the proportion of workers using public transportation remained about the same (at about 4.9% of all commuters in 2010) with a slight increase in the proportion of workers using other forms of transportation or working from home (about 8.6% of all commuters in 2010 – an increase of 1.2% over 2000).

Transportation mode use varies between racial/ethnic groups due to differences in socioeconomic resources, geographic distribution, and group preferences (Giuliano 2003; Pisarski 2006: 70; Polzin et al. 2001). Thus, changes in the racial/ethnic characteristics of commuters will likely change the magnitude of the demand for various transportation modes. In 2010, 80% of nonHispanic White workers drove alone on the journey to work – more than any other racial/ethnic group (Table 7.4). At the same time, a larger proportion of nonHispanic Blacks rode on public transportation than any other group due to the fact that a larger proportion of nonHispanic Black

Table 7.4 Percent of all United States commuters by transportation mode on the journey to work, 2000 and 2010

Mode	NH White	NH Black	Hispanic	NH Asian & Other	Total
2000					
Drove alone	79.7	66.2	60.6	66.9	75.7
Carpooled	10.0	15.9	22.5	15.7	12.2
Public transit	2.9	12.0	8.9	8.9	4.7
Other	7.4	5.9	8.0	8.5	7.4
Total	100.0	100.0	100.0	100.0	100.0
2010					
Drove alone	80.1	72.4	68.0	68.3	76.7
Carpooled	8.1	9.8	15.6	13.0	9.8
Public transit	2.9	11.0	7.9	9.1	4.9
Other	8.9	6.8	8.5	9.6	8.6
Total	100.0	100.0	100.0	100.0	100.0
Difference					
Drove alone	0.4	6.2	7.4	1.4	1.0
Carpooled	−1.9	−6.1	−6.9	−2.7	−2.4
Public transit	0.0	−1.0	−1.0	0.2	0.2
Other	1.5	0.9	0.5	1.1	1.2

Source: U.S. Census Bureau, Census 2000, 2009–2011 American Community Survey; Ruggles et al. 2010

households lack the resources to purchase and maintain a vehicle and most African-Americans live in major urban areas in neighborhoods accessible to public transportation (Bhat and Naumann 2013; Giuliano 2003; Polzin et al. 2001).

Hispanics are more likely to carpool than any other group (15.6% of Hispanic commuters carpooled 2010). As with the nonHispanic Black population, there is a larger proportion of low income Hispanic households than nonHispanic White households and thus Hispanics are less likely to own a vehicle and must seek transportation alternatives. Since the Hispanic population is more dispersed than the nonHispanic Black population, a larger proportion of Hispanics live in areas where public transportation may not be available, and thus workers who own no vehicles may share rides with friends, family, or co-workers or negotiate arrangements with informal taxi services (Cline 2014c; Cline et al. 2009; Lovejoy and Hardy 2011). In addition, Hispanic households are larger and thus workers may share a ride with another family member (Pisarski 2006: 87). Finally, Hispanics are more likely to be working in occupations, such as construction, that are conducive to carpooling to a specific job site (Cline et al. 2009).

7.3 Effects of Future Demographic Change on Future Transportation Use

The previous sections of this chapter highlighted selected trends in transportation use and demographic factors that have influenced those trends. These demographic factors when combined with the projected demographic change outlined in Chapters 2 and 3, will substantially impact transportation use, demand for transportation infrastructure, and change in traffic safety, among other things. In this section, we summarize the results of projections of selected transportation factors. We begin with the effects of demographic change on the number and characteristics of licensed drivers and subsequent effects on change in aggregate vehicle miles of travel and demand for roadway infrastructure. Then we explore the consequences of an aging driving population on traffic safety. We then summarize the change in household vehicle ownership and worker's mode of commute as a result of these demographic changes. Finally, we show alternative scenarios of future transportation use and related factors assuming that all race/ethnic groups use transportation in the same ways as nonHispanic Whites did in 2010.

Projections of licensed drivers were derived by combining information from the 2009 National Household Transportation Survey (NHTS [U.S. Department of Transportation 2011b]) and licensure data reported to the U.S. Department of Transportation from state administrative records (U.S. Department of Transportation 2011a). From these data, licensure rates by age, sex, and race/ethnicity were calculated for 2010 and applied to the population projections. The projections of licensed drivers assume no change in licensure rate by age, sex, and race/ethnicity and use the middle population projection scenario. These projections show that the number of licensed drivers would continue to grow but at a pace slower than total population change (Tables 7.5, 7.6, 7.7 and 7.8). Under this projection scenario, the population would increase by 36.1% between 2010 and 2060 compared to just 34.1% for licensed drivers. Still, as with today, most adults would be licensed drivers so that by 2060 there would be 282.2 million licensed drivers (72.1 million more than was in 2010).

This growth in the number of drivers will increase the demand for transportation-related infrastructure. As the number of drivers in the United States increases by more than one third, the number of miles driven on streets, freeways, and highways will increase. Vehicle miles traveled (VMT) measures the distance a vehicle travels on a yearly basis. In 2010, drivers drove an estimated 2.1 trillion vehicle miles (an average of 12,888 per driver [Table 7.6]). Assuming average rates of VMT by race/ethnicity in 2009, the projected number of yearly VMT would increase to 3.3 trillion by 2060 (an increase of 57.1%) even as VMT per driver declines. This would increase congestion, affecting air quality and demand for maintenance on and expansion of existing transportation networks. In 2010, there were 19.1 road miles for every 1,000 drivers in the United States (U.S. Department of Transportation 2011a). In order to maintain this same capacity, another 1.4 million local street, freeway, and highway miles would need to be added by 2060.

Table 7.5 Projected number of licensed drivers in the United States by race/ethnicity and year using the middle projection scenario

Year	NH White	NH Black	Hispanic	NH Asian & Other	Total
Panel A: Number of drivers					
2010	146,425,531	22,213,101	26,853,597	14,622,710	210,114,939
2020	150,613,276	25,258,317	35,026,951	18,091,686	228,990,230
2030	150,395,950	27,570,334	43,980,790	22,274,431	244,221,505
2040	147,209,683	29,832,314	53,710,883	26,808,815	257,561,695
2050	142,103,303	32,011,281	63,805,919	31,531,223	269,451,726
2060	137,308,814	34,137,138	74,277,696	36,449,946	282,173,594
Panel B: Percent by race/ethnicity					
2010	69.7	10.6	12.8	6.9	100.0
2020	65.8	11.0	15.3	7.9	100.0
2030	61.6	11.3	18.0	9.1	100.0
2040	57.2	11.6	20.9	10.3	100.0
2050	52.7	11.9	23.7	11.7	100.0
2060	48.7	12.1	26.3	12.9	100.0
Panel C: Numeric change					
2010–20	4,187,745	3,045,216	8,173,354	3,468,976	18,875,291
2020–30	−217,326	2,312,017	8,953,839	4,182,745	15,231,275
2030–40	−3,186,267	2,261,980	9,730,093	4,534,384	13,340,190
2040–50	−5,106,380	2,178,967	10,095,036	4,722,408	11,890,031
2050–60	−4,794,489	2,125,857	10,471,777	4,918,723	12,721,868
2010–60	−9,116,717	11,924,037	47,424,099	21,827,236	72,058,655
Panel D: Percent change					
2010–20	2.9	13.7	30.4	23.7	8.2
2020–30	−0.1	9.2	25.6	23.1	6.2
2030–40	−2.1	8.2	22.1	20.4	5.2
2040–50	−3.5	7.3	18.8	17.6	4.4
2050–60	−3.4	6.6	16.4	15.6	4.5
2010–60	−6.2	53.7	176.6	149.3	34.3

Source: Projections by the authors derived from U.S. Census Bureau, 2010 Census, 2012 National Population Projections, 2012–2060; U.S. Department of Transportation, Federal Highway Administration, Highway Statistics Series, 2010; and National Household Travel Survey 2009

The changing racial/ethnic and age characteristics result in slower growth in the number of licensed drivers, drivers per 1,000 people, and average VMT. In 2010, the majority of all licensed drivers were nonHispanic White (69.7%), but by 2060, this group would account for less than half of all licensed drivers. In fact, if current trends continue, nonHispanic White drivers would decline by 9.1 million between 2010 and 2060. All other racial/ethnic groups would see growth in the number of drivers, with the most rapid growth occurring among Hispanic (176.6%) and Asian and Other drivers (149.3%). Assuming current licensure rates by age, sex, and race/

Table 7.6 Population, licensed drivers, and yearly vehicle miles of travel (in billions) in 2010 and projected to 2060 using the middle projection scenario

				Yearly vehicle miles of travel	
Year	Population	Drivers	Drivers per 1,000 population	Per driver	Total (in billions)
2010	309,000,000	210,114,939	679.6	12,888	2,094.1
2020	333,895,553	228,990,230	685.8	12,365	2,831.5
2030	358,471,142	244,221,505	681.3	12,048	2,942.3
2040	380,015,683	257,561,695	677.8	11,859	3,054.3
2050	399,803,369	269,451,726	674.0	11,790	3,177.0
2060	420,267,733	282,173,594	671.4	11,682	3,296.4

Source: Projections by the authors derived from U.S. Census Bureau, 2010 Census, 2012 National Population Projections, 2012–2060; U.S. Department of Transportation, Federal Highway Administration, Highway Statistics Series, 2010; and National Household Travel Survey 2009

Table 7.7 Number of licensed drivers in the United States by age and race/ethnicity in 2010 and projected for 2060 using the middle projection scenario

Age	NH White	NH Black	Hispanic	NH Asian & Other	Total
2010					
<30	27,869,845	5,519,378	8,209,879	3,856,587	45,455,689
30–64	90,158,749	14,541,097	16,854,642	9,373,143	130,927,632
65+	28,396,937	2,152,626	1,789,076	1,392,980	33,731,619
80+	7,021,793	351,738	313,741	187,532	7,874,804
Total	146,425,531	22,213,101	26,853,597	14,622,710	210,114,939
2060					
<30	20,774,419	6,374,314	17,189,551	7,896,875	52,235,159
30–64	71,944,834	20,654,547	44,827,098	21,825,582	159,252,061
65+	44,589,561	7,108,277	12,261,047	6,727,489	70,686,374
80+	14,191,834	1,560,502	3,022,170	1,333,759	20,108,265
Total	137,308,814	34,137,138	74,277,696	36,449,946	282,173,594
Numeric change, 2010–2060					
<30	−7,095,426	854,936	8,979,672	4,040,288	6,779,470
30–64	−18,213,915	6,113,450	27,972,456	12,452,439	28,324,429
65+	16,192,624	4,955,651	10,471,971	5,334,509	36,954,755
80+	7,170,041	1,208,764	2,708,429	1,146,227	12,233,461
Total	−9,116,717	11,924,037	47,424,099	21,827,236	72,058,655
Percentage change, 2010–2060					
<30	−25.5	15.5	109.4	104.8	14.9
30–64	−20.2	42.0	166.0	132.9	21.6
65+	57.0	230.2	585.3	383.0	109.6
80+	102.1	343.7	863.3	611.2	155.3
Total	−6.2	53.7	176.6	149.3	34.3

Source: Projections by the authors derived from U.S. Census Bureau, 2010 Census, 2012 National Population Projections, 2012–2060; U.S. Department of Transportation, Federal Highway Administration, Highway Statistics Series, 2010; and National Household Travel Survey 2009

Table 7.8 Percentage of licensed drivers by age and race/ethnicity in 2010 and projected for 2060 using the middle projection scenario (percentages within race/ethnicity and within age)

Age	NH White	NH Black	Hispanic	NH Asian & Other	Total
2010					
Percent of drivers by age (within race/ethnicity)					
<30	19.0	24.8	30.6	26.4	21.6
30–64	61.6	65.5	62.8	64.1	62.3
65+	19.4	9.7	6.6	9.5	16.1
80+	4.8	1.6	1.2	1.3	3.7
Total	100.0	100.0	100.0	100.0	100.0
Percent of drivers by race/ethnicity (within age)					
<30	61.3	12.1	18.1	8.5	100.0
30–64	68.9	11.1	12.9	7.1	100.0
65+	84.2	6.4	5.3	4.1	100.0
80+	89.2	4.5	4.0	2.3	100.0
Total	69.7	10.6	12.8	6.9	100.0
2060					
Percent of drivers by age (within race/ethnicity)					
<30	15.1	18.7	23.1	21.7	18.5
30–64	52.4	60.5	60.4	59.9	56.4
65+	32.5	20.8	16.5	18.4	25.1
80+	10.3	4.6	4.1	3.7	7.1
Total	100.0	100.0	100.0	100.0	100.0
Percent of drivers by race/ethnicity (within age)					
<30	39.8	12.2	32.9	15.1	100.0
30–64	45.2	13.0	28.1	13.7	100.0
65+	63.1	10.1	17.3	9.5	100.0
80+	70.6	7.8	15.0	6.6	100.0
Total	48.7	12.1	26.3	12.9	100.0

Source: Projections by the authors derived from U.S. Census Bureau, 2010 Census, 2012 National Population Projections, 2012–2060; U.S. Department of Transportation, Federal Highway Administration, Highway Statistics Series, 2010; and National Household Travel Survey 2009

ethnicity, the number of drivers per 1,000 people would increase from 679.6 to 685.8 by 2020, and then begin to decline with increasing diversity of the underlying population (Table 7.6). By 2060, the licensure rate, assuming current trends, would be lower than the rate in 2010 (671.4 per 1,000 people compared to 679.6 per 1,000 people in 2010). In addition to these lower licensure rates, those who are licensed to drive would drive fewer miles on average in 2060 than in 2010 (11,682 miles per year compared to 12,888 in 2010).

7.3.1 Age Effects on Transportation

The aging of the population would affect the age characteristics of licensed drivers. Between 2010 and 2060, the number of elderly drivers would increase by 109.6% compared to a 14.9% increase in the number of drivers younger than 30 (Table 7.7). By 2060, 25.1% of all drivers would be elderly, up from 16.1% in 2010; and, due to an increase in the number of people living longer, there would be an increase in the oldest of drivers (Table 7.8). In fact, of the projected 37.0 million elderly drivers added between 2010 and 2060, 12.2 million of those would be 80 years old and older. Thus by 2060, 7.1% of drivers in the United States would be at least 80 years old (compared to just 3.7% in 2010).

The confluence of the changing age structure and racial/ethnic diversity of the underlying population can be seen in the change in the driving population between 2010 and 2060. The largest percentage and numeric increases among all but elderly drivers would occur for drivers who are Hispanic or of nonHispanic Asian and Other descent. During the same period, the number of nonHispanic White drivers under age 65 would decline by 25.1 million drivers, which would lead to a nonelderly driving population that is majority minority by 2060. This would not be the case for elderly drivers. In 2060, elderly drivers are projected to be 63.1% nonHispanic White (44.6 million of the projected 70.7 million drivers age 65 and older). Among all nonHispanic White drivers, 32.5% would be 65 years of age or older.

This increase in the number of drivers, including increases in elderly drivers, would impact the changes in the number of crashes occurring. The projections of the number of drivers by age involved in crashes by crash severity are shown in Table 7.9. These projections were derived by applying estimated crash rates by age and sex for 2010 to the licensed driver projections. Assuming no changes in these rates, the number of drivers involved in crashes would increase by 2.7 million between 2010 and 2060 (Table 7.9). This would include an increase of 14,598 drivers involved in fatality related crashes. By 2060, there would be 12.2 million drivers involved in crashes, including 58,287 drivers involved in crashes where at least one person died (up from 9.5 million and 43,689 in 2010, respectively). Because younger drivers are less experienced and take greater risks, they will continue to over-represent the proportion of vehicle accidents relative to their representation in the driving population. In 2060, 18.5% of all licensed drivers would be younger than 30, and they would account for 34.8% of all crashes and 29.6% of all fatality related accidents.

As a result of the aging of the population, the riskiest drivers (young drivers) will account for a decreasing share of all drivers influencing a decline in crash rates over time, from 4,541.5 per 100,000 licensed drivers in 2010 to 4,333.9 in 2060. Although crash rates would decline overall, crashes involving elderly drivers would increase with concomitant increases in elderly drivers (Table 7.9). By 2060, 1.9 million or 15.8% of all crashes would involve an elderly driver (up from 847,560 or 8.9% in 2010). At the same time, elderly drivers would account for approximately 21.8% of all fatal accidents (up from 12.7% in 2010).

Table 7.9 Drivers involved in crashes by age and severity of crash in 2010 and projected to 2060 using the middle projection scenario

Age	Fatality	Injury	Non-injury	Total
Panel A: 2010 crashes by age				
15–19	3,750	291,400	774,600	1,069,750
20–29	9,752	684,600	1,641,900	2,336,252
30–44	11,583	786,000	1,910,500	2,708,083
45–64	13,044	761,000	1,806,000	2,580,044
65+	5,560	258,000	584,000	847,560
Total	43,689	2,781,000	6,717,000	9,541,689
Panel B: 2060 crashes by age				
15–19	2,511	195,129	518,693	716,333
20–29	14,767	1,036,584	2,486,076	3,537,427
30–44	12,663	859,282	2,088,623	2,960,568
45–64	15,631	911,944	2,164,220	3,091,795
65+	12,715	590,032	1,335,577	1,938,324
Total	58,287	3,592,971	8,593,189	12,244,447
Panel C: percent by age in 2010				
15–19	8.6	10.5	11.5	11.2
20–29	22.3	24.6	24.4	24.5
30–44	26.5	28.3	28.4	28.4
45–64	29.9	27.4	26.9	27.0
65+	12.7	9.3	8.7	8.9
Total	100.0	100.0	100.0	100.0
Panel D: percent by age in 2060				
15–19	4.3	5.4	6.0	5.9
20–29	25.3	28.9	28.9	28.9
30–44	21.7	23.9	24.3	24.2
45–64	26.8	25.4	25.2	25.3
65+	21.8	16.4	15.5	15.8
Total	100.0	100.0	100.0	100.0

Source: Projections by the authors derived from U.S. Census Bureau, 2010 Census, 2012 National Population Projections, 2012–2060; U.S. Department of Transportation, Federal Highway Administration, Highway Statistics Series, 2010; and National Household Travel Survey 2009; U.S. Department of Transportation, National Highway Traffic Safety Administration, Traffic Safety Facts 2010

7.3.2 Impact of Demographic Change on Vehicle Ownership

The effects of demographic changes on household vehicle ownership are shown in Table 7.10. In these projections, we assume that the rates of household vehicle ownership by race/ethnicity and age of the householder prevail throughout the projection period. Because the absence of a car has implications for public transportation and service delivery, we focus our analysis on household ownership of at least one

Table 7.10 Households and households without vehicles in 2010 and projected for 2060 using the middle projection scenario

Age, race/ethnicity of householder	Households				
		Without vehicles		Percent of households	
	Total	Number	Percent	All	Without vehicles
2010					
15–34 years:	23,358,174	2,607,608	11.2	20.0	20.4
NH White	14,335,542	920,335	6.4	12.3	7.2
NH Black	3,159,538	753,352	23.8	2.7	5.9
Hispanic	4,006,709	672,404	16.8	3.4	5.3
NH Asian & Other	1,856,385	261,517	14.1	1.6	2.0
35–64 years:	67,538,282	5,543,489	8.2	57.9	43.5
NH White	46,928,989	2,155,596	4.6	40.2	16.9
NH Black	8,342,822	1,789,515	21.4	7.1	14.0
Hispanic	7,958,736	1,175,296	14.8	6.8	9.2
NH Asian & Other	4,307,735	423,082	9.8	3.8	3.4
65 years and older:	25,819,836	4,602,975	17.8	22.1	36.1
NH White	21,068,549	3,072,742	14.6	18.1	24.1
NH Black	2,293,184	808,418	35.3	2.0	6.3
Hispanic	1,495,921	462,249	30.9	1.3	3.6
NH Asian & Other	962,182	259,566	27.0	0.7	2.1
Total	116,716,292	12,754,072	10.9	100.0	100.0
2060					
15–34 years:	27,988,145	3,665,445	13.1	16.8	14.9
NH White	11,546,390	734,453	6.4	6.9	3.0
NH Black	4,029,259	955,280	23.7	2.4	3.9
Hispanic	8,523,283	1,428,442	16.8	5.1	5.8
NH Asian & Other	3,889,213	547,270	14.1	2.4	2.2
35–64 years:	81,335,007	8,481,977	10.4	48.9	34.6
NH White	36,909,637	1,700,527	4.6	22.2	6.9
NH Black	11,903,477	2,543,306	21.4	7.2	10.4
Hispanic	22,334,031	3,243,424	14.5	13.4	13.2
NH Asian & Other	10,187,862	994,720	9.8	6.1	4.1
65 years and older:	56,899,359	12,382,080	21.8	34.3	50.5
NH White	33,834,298	5,075,723	15.0	20.4	20.7
NH Black	7,747,731	2,729,931	35.2	4.7	11.1
Hispanic	10,460,496	3,243,450	31.0	6.3	13.2
NH Asian & Other	4,856,834	1,332,976	27.4	2.9	5.5
Total	166,222,511	24,529,502	14.8	100.0	100.0

Source: Projections by the authors derived from U.S. Census Bureau, 2012 National Population Projections, 2012–2060; 2006–2010 American Community Survey, and 2010 Census

vehicle. In 2010, the overwhelming majority of households owned at least one vehicle. This is not expected to change over the course of the next fifty years. Still, there are many households that owned no vehicle in 2010, a majority of which were headed by a nonHispanic Black, Hispanic, or nonHispanic Asian or Other householder (Table 7.10). Changes in the racial/ethnic and age characteristics of the population, absent improvements in socioeconomic resources and related patterns of purchasing, would lead to a greater proportion of households that own no vehicle (from 10.9% in 2010 to 14.8% by 2060).

What is more significant is the change in age characteristics of zero vehicle households. The last two columns in Table 7.10 show the proportional share accounted for by each race/ethnicity and age householder groups. Households headed by persons age 65 years and older (elderly households) accounted for 36.1% of all zero vehicle households in 2010. This proportional share would increase so that by 2060 the majority (50.5%) of all zero vehicle households would be headed by an elderly householder.

Other forms of transportation will be needed so that people in these households are able to access healthcare and other services and generally interact with others in their community. This will also have implications for the ways in which transit systems serve their local populations as they will find themselves not only serving primarily workers on their work commute, but also finding ways to best serve populations (including frail elderly) who have no other means of transportation.

7.3.3 Impact of Demographic Change on Worker's Modes of Commuting

The effects of demographic changes on commuting transportation mode choice are shown in Tables 7.11 and 7.12. These projections were derived by applying the 2010 commuting rates for workers by mode choice, race/ethnicity, sex, and age of the worker to the labor force projections shown in Chapter 3. Under these assumptions, the number of commuters would increase by 25.2% between 2010 and 2060. Of the different modes of travel to work, all modes except driving alone would increase at a faster rate than the total number of commuters. Between 2010 and 2060, the number of commuters riding public transit on the journey to work would increase by 55.6% (3.7 million commuters [Table 7.12]). During the same period, the number of commuters carpooling to work would increase by 42.0% (or 5.6 million commuters). This would lead to a slightly smaller proportion of commuters driving alone on the journey to work (at 74.1% in 2060 down from 76.6% in 2010 [Table 7.12]). In addition to the changes in transportation mode, the characteristics of commuters using each mode would change considerably. In 2010, the majority of all commuters for each transportation mode except public transit were nonHispanic White. By 2060, the majority of all commuters regardless of transportation mode would be minority.

Table 7.11 Journey to work by race/ethnicity of commuter and transportation mode in 2010 and projected to 2060 using the middle projection scenario

Mode	NH White	NH Black	Hispanic	NH Asian & Other	Total
2010					
Drove alone	73,819,579	10,353,207	13,783,998	6,823,949	104,780,733
Carpooled	7,505,357	1,402,262	3,165,631	1,301,183	13,374,433
Public transit	2,668,664	1,566,632	1,593,626	910,638	6,739,560
Other	8,161,486	969,662	1,720,045	957,195	11,808,388
Total	92,155,086	14,291,763	20,263,300	9,992,965	136,703,114
2060					
Drove alone	61,061,484	14,647,772	35,199,113	15,864,230	126,772,599
Carpooled	6,149,382	1,925,725	7,877,248	3,041,797	18,994,152
Public transit	2,204,377	2,157,847	4,023,221	2,103,457	10,488,902
Other	6,924,431	1,353,423	4,408,534	2,237,971	14,924,359
Total	76,339,674	20,084,767	51,508,116	23,247,455	171,180,012
Numeric change, 2010–60					
Drove Alone	−12,758,095	4,294,565	21,415,115	9,040,281	21,991,866
Carpooled	−1,355,975	523,463	4,711,617	1,740,614	5,619,719
Public Transit	−464,287	591,215	2,429,595	1,192,819	3,749,342
Other	−1,237,055	383,761	2,688,489	1,280,776	3,115,971
Total	−15,815,412	5,793,004	31,244,816	13,254,490	34,476,898
Percent change, 2010–60					
Drove alone	−17.3	41.5	155.4	132.5	21.0
Carpooled	−18.1	37.3	148.8	133.8	42.0
Public transit	−17.4	37.7	152.5	131.0	55.6
Other	−15.2	39.6	156.3	133.8	26.4
Total	−17.2	40.5	154.2	132.6	25.2

Source: Projections by the authors derived from U.S. Census Bureau, 2009–2011 American Community Survey and 2012 National Population Projections, 2012–2060; Ruggles et al. 2010

Of all transportation modes, public transportation was the most racially/ethnically diverse in 2010, with 40% of all workers riding public transportation being nonHispanic White, 23% nonHispanic Black, and 24% Hispanic. As was the case in 2010, public transit would have the most diverse population of any mode in 2060. Whereas the largest racial/ethnic group represented was nonHispanic Whites in 2010, by 2060, the largest racial/ethnic group to take public transit on the journey to work would be Hispanic.

7.4 Alternative Projection Scenarios

As the previous sections have shown, demographic changes without improvement in the socioeconomic resources of Hispanics and nonHispanic Blacks will impact transportation use in a variety of different ways. Table 7.13 compares the results of

Table 7.12 Journey to work mode as a percent of all commuters by race/ethnicity in 2010 and projected to 2060 using the middle projection scenario

Mode	NH White	NH Black	Hispanic	NH Asian & Other	Total
Commute as a percent of all commuters (within race/ethnicity)					
2010					
Drove alone	80.1	72.4	68.0	68.3	76.6
Carpooled	8.1	9.8	15.6	13.0	9.8
Public transit	2.9	11.0	7.9	9.1	4.9
Other	8.9	6.8	8.5	9.6	8.7
Total	100.0	100.0	100.0	100.0	100.0
2060					
Drove alone	80.0	72.9	68.3	68.2	74.1
Carpooled	8.1	9.6	15.3	13.1	11.1
Public transit	2.9	10.7	7.8	9.0	6.1
Other	9.0	6.8	8.6	9.7	8.7
Total	100.0	100.0	100.0	100.0	100.0
Commute as a percent of all commuters (across race/ethnicity)					
2010					
Drove alone	70.5	9.9	13.2	6.4	100.0
Carpooled	56.1	10.5	23.7	9.7	100.0
Public transit	39.6	23.2	23.6	13.6	100.0
Other	69.1	8.2	14.6	8.1	100.0
Total	67.4	10.5	14.8	7.3	100.0
2060					
Drove alone	48.2	11.6	27.8	12.4	100.0
Carpooled	32.4	10.1	41.5	16.0	100.0
Public transit	21.0	20.6	38.4	20.0	100.0
Other	46.4	9.1	29.5	15.0	100.0
Total	44.6	11.7	30.1	13.6	100.0

Source: Projections by the authors derived from U.S. Census Bureau, 2009–2011 American Community Survey and 2012 National Population Projections, 2012–2060; Ruggles et al. 2010

projections of selected transportation factors previously presented to an alternative scenario that assumes that all race/ethnic groups use transportation in the same way and extent as nonHispanic Whites did in 2010. The first column of data shows the previous projections assuming no change in race/ethnicity specific rates. This is compared to the second column where it is assumed that all race/ethnic groups would use the transportation system in the same way as nonHispanic Whites did in 2010. The last column shows the differences for these two different simulations.

In general, this table shows that increasing racial/ethnic diversity (the baseline scenario) would attenuate the growth in dependence on the automobile and increase demand for public transportation. Under the baseline scenario, there would be 23.8 million fewer drivers and each driver would drive an average of 2.8 miles less than if all drivers drove the same as nonHispanic Whites in 2010.

Table 7.13 Drivers, vehicle ownership, and commute mode in 2060 using alternative rate assumptions

Factor	Current rates	NH White rates	Difference
Drivers (millions)	282.2	306.0	–23.8
Vehicle miles traveled	–	–	
Yearly aggregate (millions)	3,296,400	3,890,600	–594,200
Yearly per driver	11,682	12,717	–1,034
Daily per driver	32.0	34.8	–2.8
Zero vehicle households (millions)	24.5	16.5	8.1
Commuters (millions)	171.2	175.6	–4.4
Driving alone (millions)	126.8	140.3	–13.5
Carpooling (millions)	19.0	14.4	4.6
Riding public transit (millions)	10.5	5.2	5.3
Percent commuters using:			
Driving alone	74.1	79.9	–5.8
Carpooling	11.1	8.2	2.9
Riding public transit	6.1	2.9	3.2

These demographic changes, without concomitant improvements in socioeconomic resources of minorities, would impact the number of households owning vehicles as well as effect changes in the intensity of use of forms of transportation other than the personal vehicle. There would be 8.1 million more zero vehicle households in 2060 than there would be if all households owned vehicles at the same rate as nonHispanic Whites in 2010. Vehicle ownership impacts transportation mode choice. Thus, under the baseline projections, there would be 4.4 million fewer commuters overall and 13.5 million fewer commuters driving alone on the journey to work. At the same time, the baseline scenario shows the number of public transit users on the work commute to be more than double the use if all commuters use public transportation at the same level as nonHispanic Whites did in 2010.

7.5 Summary

In this chapter we highlighted the effects of future demographic change on driving, vehicle ownership, traffic safety, and public transportation in the United States. Unlike the factors presented in previous chapters, many of the impacts on transportation would have different values depending upon particular policy perspectives. For instance, in previous chapters we showed that race/ethnic changes without concomitant improvements in education and other factors would lead to a lower average household income than in 2010. This would have negative consequences. For transportation, some may see fewer drivers and more carpoolers and transit riders as a positive impact on the transportation system while others may have a different perspective. We summarize the potential impacts of these changes on the implications for public policy below:

1. The most significant demographic factor impacting future transportation use would be overall population growth. As a result of the growing population, the number of licensed drivers would increase by over one third from 210.1 million in 2010 to 282.2 million by 2060. Maintaining the same level of road infrastructure as today, federal, state, and local governments would need to add an additional 1.4 million more roadway miles between now and 2060. There would be a 25.2% increase in the number of workers commuting on an average day, from 136.7 million in 2010 to 171.2 million in 2060. Use of every transportation mode would expand concurrently with growth in the number of commuters, with faster rates of increase in the number of commuters carpooling or riding public transit. By 2060, there would be 126.8 million commuters driving alone, 19.0 million carpoolers, and 10.5 million public transit users on the work commute (an increase of 21.0, 42.0, and 55.6%, respectively). These increases in use in all forms of transportation will put pressure on an already stressed transportation infrastructure.
2. Population growth will help to increase roadway congestion and diminish air quality, but demographic compositional change will work to limit these overall impacts. Race/ethnicity change will work to attenuate the growth in transportation use highlighted above. Absent changes in licensure rates, average vehicle miles travelled, vehicle ownership rates, and other factors for minorities, there would be 23.8 million fewer drivers and 594.2 billion fewer vehicle miles driven in 2060 than if all race/ethnic groups were licensed and drove at the same level as nonHispanic Whites did in 2010.
3. On a per driver basis, the average vehicle miles travelled would decrease from 12,888 in 2010 to 11,682 by 2060. The United States will not experience the explosive growth in the number of licensed drivers as was experienced from the 1950s into the 1980s in the future decades examined here. Licensed drivers will grow at a pace slower than the population as a whole. Combining these two factors (lower average VMT and slower growth in licensed drivers) with continued improvements in gas mileage will negatively impact the current state and federal highway financing structure that is dependent upon a gas tax.
4. Race/ethnicity change without changes in the ways in which these groups use transportation will lead to increases in demand for public transportation. The number of zero vehicle households would increase from 12.8 million in 2010 to 24.5 million in 2060, an increase of 91.4%. Of all households present in 2060, 14.8% would own no vehicle (up from 10.9 in 2010). The number of public transit riders on the work commute would increase by 55.6% from 6.7 million people in 2010 to 10.5 million in 2060.
5. An aging and more racially/ethnically diverse elderly population with limited economic resources will impact service delivery of health and social services. Agencies will need to find ways to deliver services to populations aging in place in urban and rural areas where transportation options may be limited or not available at all. In 2010, 17.8% of all elderly households had no vehicle present (a

total of 4.6 million households). By 2060, 21.8% of all elderly households would have no vehicle present (12.4 million households). While elderly households without vehicles accounted for a little more than a third of zero vehicle households in 2010, the majority of such households would be headed by someone 65 years of age or older by 2060.

6. Changes in racial/ethnic composition of the population, without changes in transportation behaviors, will increase the proportion of commuters carpooling on a typical workday. If current carpooling rates remain in 2060, 11.1% of all commuters would carpool in 2060 (compared to 9.8% in 2010). Thus 19.0 million commuters would carpool on the work commute in 2060. If all commuters used the same transportation modes as nonHispanic Whites in 2010, then there would be 4.6 million fewer carpoolers and the share of commuters carpooling would fall from 11.1% to 8.2%.
7. The aging of the population will effectively decrease the overall crash rate (due to a decrease in the share of drivers at younger ages) while at the same time increasing the number of elderly drivers involved in crashes. While the number of drivers would increase by 34.3% between 2010 and 2060, fatality and all crashes would increase by 33.4 and 28.3%, respectively. Because of growth in elderly drivers, 15.8% of all drivers involved in accidents in 2060 would be elderly (up from 8.9% in 2010). Due primarily to frailty, the elderly drivers share of all fatality accidents would change from 12.8% in 2010 to 21.8% by 2060. Thus with these increases in elderly drivers, public policies to enhance traffic safety for elderly drivers may be necessary.

In summary, the changing demographic composition of the U.S. population will have substantial impacts on the transportation system. Although population growth will mean that there will be an increase in demand for all transportation modes; the demographic changes will lead to fewer drivers, fewer vehicle miles travelled, and greater demand for public transit in 2060 than what would otherwise occur if minority transportation behaviors changed to match those of nonHispanic Whites in 2010. Since transportation use is influenced by household income and wealth, improvements in the socioeconomic characteristics of minority populations will work to increase car use and diminish public transportation demand.

References

Bhat, G., & Naumann, R. B. (2013). Travel-related behaviors, opinions, and concerns of U.S. adult drivers by race/ethnicity, 2010. *Journal of Safety Research, 47*, 93–97.

Cline, M. (2014a). Driving licensing rates. In M. Garrett (Ed.), *Encyclopedia of transportation: Social science and policy* 4, 451–453.

Cline, M. (2014b). Automobile drivers, elderly. In M. Garrett (Ed.), *Encyclopedia of transportation: Social science and policy* 4, 209–211.

Cline, M. (2014c). Carpooling. In M. Garrett (Ed.), *Encyclopedia of transportation: Social science and policy* 4, 360–362.

Cline, M., Sparks, C., & Eschbach, K. (2009). Understanding carpool use among Hispanics in Texas. *Transportation Research Record, 2118*, 39–46.

Countouris, M., Gilmore, S., & Yonas, M. (2014). Exploring the impact of a community hospital closure on older adults: A focus group study. *Health & Place, 26*, 143–148.

Curl, A. S., Stowe, J., Cooney, T., & Proulx, C. (2014). Giving up the keys: How driving cessation affects engagement in later life. *The Gerontologist, 54*(3), 423–433.

D'Ambrosio, L. A., Donorfio, L. K. M., Coughlin, J. F., Mohyde, M., & Meyer, J. (2008). Gender differences in self-regulation patterns and attitudes toward driving among older adults. *Journal of Women & Aging, 20*(3–4), 265–282.

Dargay, J. D., Gately, D., & Sommer, M. (2007). Vehicle ownership and income growth, worldwide: 1960–2030. *Energy Journal, 28*(4), 143–170.

Donorfio, L. K. M., D'Ambrosio, L. A., Coughlin, J. F., & Mohyde, M. (2008). Health, safety, self-regulation and the older driver: It's not just a matter of age. *Journal of Safety Research, 39*(6), 555–561.

Giuliano, G. (2003). Travel, location and race/ethnicity. *Transportation Research Part A, 37*, 351–372.

Giuliano, G., & Dargay, J. (2006). Car ownership, travel and land use: A comparison of the U.S. and Great Britain. *Transportation Research Part A: Policy and Practice, 40*(2), 106–124.

Goodwin, P. (2012). Peak travel, peak car and the future of mobility: Evidence, unresolved issues, policy implications, and a research agenda. International transport forum discussion paper. http://www.econstor.eu/handle/10419/97079. Accessed 14 Dec 2014.

Greene, D. L. (1987). Long-run vehicle travel prediction from demographic trends. *Transportation Research Record, 1135*, 1–9.

Highway Loss Data Institute. (2005). *Insurance losses by driver age. Insurance special report A-70*. Arlington: Highway Loss Data Institute.

Highway Loss Data Institute. (2012). Estimating the effect of projected changes in the driving population on collision claim frequency. *Highway Loss Data Institute Bulletin, 29*(8), 1–9.

Lave, C. (1991). *Things won't get a lot worse: the future of U.S. traffic congestion*. Working paper 33. Berkeley: The University of California Transportation Center.

Lovejoy, K., & Hardy, S. (2011). Social networks as a source of private-vehicle transportation: The practice of getting rides and borrowing vehicles among Mexican immigrants in California. *Transportation Research Part A: Policy and Practice, 45*(4), 248–257.

Marottoli, R. A., et al. (2000). Consequences of driving cessation: Decreased out-of-home activity levels. *The Journals of Gerontology Series B: Psychological Sciences and Social Sciences, 55*(6), S334–S340.

Oxley, J., & Whelan, M. (2008). It cannot be all about safety: The benefits of prolonged mobility. *Traffic Injury Prevention, 9*(4), 367–378.

Paulley, N., et al. (2006). The demand for public transport: The effects of fares, quality of service, income and car ownership. *Transport Policy, 13*, 295–306.

Pisarski, A. (2006). *Commuting in America III*. Washington, DC: Transportation Research Board.

Polzin, S. E., Chu, X., & Rey, J. R. (2001). Mobility and mode choice of people of color for non-work travel. *TRB Transportation Research Circular E-CO26*, 391–412.

Polzin, S. E., Chu, X., & Toole-Holt, L. (2004). Forecasts of future vehicle miles of travel in the United States. *Transportation Research Record, 1895*, 147–155.

Pucher, J., & Renne, J. L. (2003). Socioeconomics of urban travel: Evidence from the 2001 NHTS. *Transportation Quarterly, 57*(3), 49–77.

Rosenbloom, S. (2001). Sustainability and automobility among the elderly: An international assessment. *Transportation, 28*, 375–408.

Rosenbloom, S., & Herbel, S. (2009). The safety and mobility patterns of older women: Do current patterns foretell the future? *Public Works Management & Policy, 13*(4), 338–353.

Ruggles, S. J., Alexander, T., Genadek, K., Goeken, R., Schroeder, R. B., & Sobek, M. (2010). *Integrated public use microdata series: Version 5.0*. Minneapolis: University of Minnesota.

Ryser, L., & Halseth, G. (2012). Resolving mobility constraints impeding rural seniors' access to regionalized services. *Journal of Aging & Social Policy, 24*(3), 328–344.

The Economist. (2012, September 22). Seeing the back of the car. *The Economist, 404*(8803), 29–32.

U.S. Census Bureau. (2002). *2000 census summary file 3*. Washington, DC: U.S. Census Bureau.

U.S. Census Bureau. (2011a). *2010 census summary file 1*. Washington, DC: U.S. Census Bureau.

U.S. Census Bureau. (2011b). *2010 census summary file 2*. Washington, DC: U.S. Census Bureau.

U.S. Census Bureau. (2011c). *2006–2010 American community survey selected population tables*. Washington, DC: U.S. Census Bureau.

U.S. Census Bureau. (2012a). The 2012 statistical abstract: Pdf version. Washington DC: U.S. Census Bureau. http://www.census.gov/compendia/statab/2012edition.html. Accessed on 13 Sept 2014.

U.S. Census Bureau. (2012b). *2009–2011 American community survey*. Washington, DC: U.S. Census Bureau.

U.S. Census Bureau. (2012c). *2012 national population projections*. Washington, DC: U.S. Census Bureau.

U.S. Department of Transportation. (1991, 2000–2011). *Highway statistics series*. Washington, DC: U.S. Department of Transportation, Office of Highway Policy Information (OHPI).

U.S. Department of Transportation. (2011a). *Highway statistics 2011*. Washington, DC: U.S. Department of Transportation, Office of Highway Policy Information (OHPI).

U.S. Department of Transportation. (2011b). *2009 national household travel survey*. Washington, DC: Federal Highway Administration.

U.S. Department of Transportation, National Highway Safety Administration. (2010). *Traffic safety facts 2010*. Washington, DC: U.S. Department of Transportation, National Highway Safety Administration.

Chapter 8
Summary and Implications

In this final chapter, we first provide a brief synopsis of the key findings noted in previous chapters. We then examine the implications of projected demographic change, and of the complex of socioeconomic and service-related factors affected by such change, for the future population of the nation as a whole and for key segments of that population in the coming decades. We then project what such effects are likely to mean to the socioeconomic future of the United States in the absence of policies and actions to change them. Finally, we demonstrate the change in these effects likely to occur if the socioeconomic characteristics associated with these demographic and related socioeconomic factors were to be altered. We thus examine what population-related socioeconomic effects are likely to occur in the absence of policy changes to address them and what could result from effective interventions to change the socioeconomic effects associated with projected patterns of future demographic change. Although the effects of future demographic change on socioeconomic dimensions have been recognized and described by the lead author in numerous earlier works (see Murdock 1995; 1997; 2003 and 2014) and have recently been highlighted in works by Frey (2015) and by Mather and Jarosz (2014) and others (see any current demography text), it is evident that these efforts will now and for decades form continuing challenges to the socioeconomic conditions of the population of the United States.

8.1 Summary

This volume has examined the Census Bureau's 2012 projections of the United States population and the implications of the projected patterns for demographic and socioeconomic change, and change in the types and levels of demand for critical services in the United States through 2060. Summaries for each of the major chapters are provided below as essential background for the remainder of the chapter.

S.H. Murdock et al., *Population Change in the United States*,
DOI 10.1007/978-94-017-7288-4_8

8.1.1 Chapters 1 and 2: Historical and Projected Population and Household Patterns

1. Many demographic characteristics including age, household type, and race/ethnicity are related to income and other socioeconomic factors and service usage with middle ages, family households and nonHispanic White racial/ethnic status being related to higher income and other socioeconomic resources and differential rates of use of a variety of public and private services.
2. Analysis of historic patterns of population change from the first census in 1790 through 2010 show that natural increase (the difference between the number of births and the number of deaths) has been the major source of population growth in every census decade except that from 1900 to 1910 in which the other major component of population growth, immigration from other nations, was the largest contributor to total population growth.
3. Immigration from Europe was the largest source of immigrants for all decades from 1790 through the 1950s after which Latin America and Asia have been the major contributors to overall net immigration (Table 2.2).
4. The United States population (similar to the population of other developed nations) has become increasingly older and has more females than males. Thus, in 1900 the median age was 22.9 years and there were 104 males for every 100 females but, by 2010, the median age was 37.2 and there were 96.7 males per 100 females (Table 2.4).
5. The population of the United States is projected by the United States Census Bureau (Table 2.7) to increase from the 308.7 million that it was in 2010 to almost 420.3 million in 2060 (under the Census Bureau's middle projection scenario).
6. The United States population has become increasingly diverse and will become more so in the future. NonHispanic Whites accounted for 63.7% of the total population in 2010 while nonHispanic Blacks accounted for 12.2% of the population, Hispanics for 16.4% of the population and nonHispanic Asians and Others for 7.7% of the total population. By 2060 (under the Census Bureau's middle projection scenario), 42.6% of the population of the United States will be nonHispanic White, 13.2% nonHispanic Black, 30.6% Hispanic, and 13.6% nonHispanic Asian and Other (Table 2.10). Of the net increase of more than 111.5 million from 2010 to 2060, 70.2% is projected to be accounted for by Hispanics, 15.8% by nonHispanic Blacks, and 30.0% by nonHispanic Asian and Others while the proportion accounted for by nonHispanic Whites is projected to decrease by 16% (under the middle projection scenario).
7. The population of the United States will also become older with the percentage of the population 65 years of age or older increasing from 13% in 2010 to nearly 21.9% by 2060 under the middle projection scenario. The substantial variation in the age structure of different racial/ethnic groups is projected to continue. For example, in 2010 16.4% of nonHispanic Whites were 65 years of age or older compared to 9.1% of nonHispanic Blacks, 5.5% of Hispanics, and 8.0% of non-

Hispanic Asians and Others. In 2060 (under the middle projection scenario), 28.8% of nonHispanic Whites, 20.7% of nonHispanic Blacks, 15.2% of Hispanics and 16.8% of nonHispanic Asians and Others will be 65 years of age or older (Table 2.11).

8. Households will show patterns of change similar to those for population. The number of households will increase under the middle projection scenario from 116.7 to 166.2 million (Table 2.14) and will show an increased number of minority headed households. The percent of all householders who are nonHispanic White decreases from 70.6% in 2010 to 49.5% in 2060 (Table 2.16) and with all of the 2010–2060 increase in households being due to minority households (Table 2.18). In 2010, 22.2% of all households were headed by someone 65 years of age or older but, by 2060, 34.2% of all householders will be 65 years of age or older. Households will also change form with the percent of family households (households with two or more people related by kinship, marriage or adoption) decreasing (Table 2.19).

8.1.2 Chapter 3: Labor Force

9. As a result of the change in demographic characteristics noted above, the labor force of the United States will also increase, age and diversify racially and ethnically. The labor force increased from 62.2 million in 1950 to 153.9 million in 2010 and is projected to grow to 196.2 million in 2060 (under the middle projection scenario) (see Tables 3.1 and 3.4). Reflecting change in the population, the labor force is also projected to become more diverse with the percentage of the labor force composed of nonHispanic Whites decreasing from 66.1% in 2010 to 43.4% in 2060 (under the middle projection scenario, Table 3.5). The percentage of the labor force that is nonHispanic Black will increase from 11.4 to 12.5%, that for Hispanics from 15.2 to 30.6% and that for nonHispanic Asians and Others from 7.3% in 2010 to 13.5% of the labor force of the United States in 2060 (under the middle projection scenario).
10. As with the population, the labor force will also age (Table 3.8) with the percentage of persons in the labor force 60 years of age and older increasing from 12.1% in 2010 to 17.4% in 2060 for nonHispnic Whites (under the middle projection scenario). The nonHispanic Black labor force 60 years of age or older will increase from 7.3 to 13.0%, the Hispanic labor force from 4.8 to 10.4% and the nonHispanic Asian and Other labor force from 7.6% to 12.0%. Overall the labor force will increase from 10.0% who are 60 years of age or older in 2010 to 14.0% of that age in 2060.
11. Given current differentials in the educational achievement of racial/ethnic groups, patterns of population growth, if continued (in the absence of improvements in nonHispanic Black and Hispanic educational levels) will lead to a generally less well-educated workforce. Whereas 10.0% of the workforce had less than a high school degree in 2010, by 2060 this number is projected to

increase to 14.0% while the percentage with a bachelor's degree or higher level of education could decrease from 29.7% in 2010 to 27.5% in 2060 (Tables 3.10 and 3.11). Although these latter differences are not large, historical patterns suggest that, due to projected patterns of increased educational attainment in the labor forces in other nations, any decline will be detrimental to the competitiveness of the United States.

12. Data on occupational shifts also suggest that minority achievement involving employment in management, business and financial occupations will increase from 25.6% in 2010 to 46.4% in 2060 while the percentage of all workers who are unemployed will increase from 10.8% to 11.2% (Tables 3.12 and 3.13). Although these levels of change are small they stand in marked contrast to historical patterns and clearly suggest that improvement in minority education and in occupational attainment continue to be essential to the overall improvement of the competitiveness of the labor force of the United States. Similarly, data on wages and earning show an overall reduction in average salaries and levels of earnings in the absence of improvements in minority education and occupational attainment.

8.1.3 Chapter 4: Income and Poverty: Implications for Household Wealth, Consumer Expenditures, Home Ownership, Net Worth, and Tax Revenues

13. In constant 2010 dollars median household income decreased and per capita income increased from 1989 to 2010 (see Table 4.1) while poverty rates increased for all including persons, families and children (see Table 4.2). Similarly, tax receipts declined from 2000 to 2010. Only the elderly have experienced a decline in poverty over this time period due, in large part, to the indexing of social security to rates of inflation.
14. Due to differentials in income patterns by age and race/ethnicity when 2010 patterns are projected forward they indicate a decline in overall income levels in the future leading to real dollar declines in average household income from 2010 to 2060 (see Table 4.6). Simulations demonstrate that closure of income for all racial/ethnic groups to those for nonHispanic Whites in 2010 will lead to an overall increase in aggregate income of nearly $1.6 trillion by 2060 indicating that improvements in minority household incomes are essential to maintaining the overall wealth of the United States (Table 4.6). Data in Tables 4.7 and 4.8 show that, in the absence of income increases for minority populations, poverty will increase for nearly all household types but that closure to nonHispanic White rates will significantly reduce poverty. Data in Table 4.9 show that federal tax revenues will not keep pace with population growth and data in Table 4.14 show that consumer expenditures will be reduced due to change in household structure and the racial/ethnic composition of the population.

15. Projections for a variety of economic factors including assets, net worth, housing values, and rents (see Tables 4.15–4.23) indicate that, in the absence of additional closure of minority populations' financial characteristics to those for nonHispanic Whites, increases in total assets, net worth, housing values, rents, and similar financial factors will not keep pace with historical patterns and the per household values for such factors will decline over time. In sum, in the absence of improvements in the economic competitiveness for nonHispanic Black and Hispanic households the United States will become poorer and less competitive in the future than it is today.

8.1.4 Chapter 5: Impacts of Demographic Change on Education in the United States

16. One of the key factors at the heart of the socioeconomic disparities associated with racial/ethnic differences lies in differentials in education. Although nonHispanic Black and Hispanic students represent an increasing percentage of all students at all educational levels, disparities in educational attainment remain substantial. In 2010, nearly 31.0% of nonHispanic Whites and more than 42.0% of nonHispanic Asians and Others had a college degree or higher level of education but only 17.7% of nonHispanic Blacks and 13.0% of Hispanics (see Table 5.3).
17. Projections of future enrollment show that school populations will increasingly be composed of minority students. In fact, more than 50% of elementary and secondary students were minority (in 2015) but, by 2060, 32.1% of elementary and secondary students are projected to be nonHispanic White, 14.8% to be nonHispanic Black, 38.5% to be Hispanic, and 14.6% to be nonHispanic Asian and Other (see Table 5.9). College enrollment will change more slowly but, by 2060, 41.7% of all college students will be nonHispanic White, 14.1% nonHispanic Black, 27.3% Hispanic, and 16.9% nonHispanic Asian and Other (see Table 5.9).
18. Because of the underlying socioeconomic characteristics of the fastest growing minority populations, the number of such students requiring financial assistance to attend college will increase. Although the percentage of nonHispanic White students needing assistance will decline (because their absolute numbers will decline) the percentage increase in the number of nonHispanic Black students needing financial assistance is projected to increase by 22.7%, the percentage of Hispanic students needing financial assistance will increase by 121.7% and the percent of nonHispanic Asian and Other students needing financial assistance is projected to increase by 117.0% from 2010 to 2060 (see Table 5.12). The percentage of those requiring financial assistance who are nonHispanic White will decline from 58.0% in 2010 to 37.5% of all those needing assistance in 2060. These values for nonHispanic Black, Hispanic, and nonHispanic Asian and Other students were 16.2, 15.8 and 10.0% respectively in 2010 but are projected to be 16.2, 28.5 and 17.8% respectively in 2060.

8.1.5 Chapter 6: Health and Health Care and Social Services in the United States

19. The demographic change projected for the United States will also impact the demand for medical and health services in the coming decades. Because of the aging of the population, the incidences of disease and disorder are projected to increase faster than the population. Whereas the total population of the United States is projected to increase by 36.1% the total number of disease and disorder incidences is projected to increase by 48.6% from 2010 to 2060 (see Table 6.1).
20. As with other phenomena examined in this work there will be a marked shift from occurrences among nonHispanic Whites to occurrences among minority populations. In 2010, over 50% of incidences, for all 29 different disease/disorder categories shown in Table 6.2, were among nonHispanic Whites while by 2060 only 12 of the categories will have more than 50% of the occurrences being among nonHispanic Whites. The projected percentage of persons experiencing these events who are nonHispanic White will decline from 71.1% to 49.7%. The patient population, like the population as a whole is projected to become more diverse.
21. Because of the aging of the population, particularly the nonHispanic White and nonHispanic Black populations, the increase in the number of persons with incidences that are disabling will be substantial, increasing by 86.8% from 2010 to 2060 compared to a 36.1% increase in the total population (see Table 6.3).
22. As a result of such changes, it is clear that the future population of the United States will have greater levels of need for health care services and that this will lead to increases in the number of health care personnel and services and to increased total costs. These will include an increase of more than 91,000 physicians and an overall increase of more than 300,000 medical personnel of all types (see Table 6.4).
23. Reflecting the aging of the population, the number of persons in nursing homes and the associated costs will increase substantially (see Table 6.8). The number of nursing home residents is projected to increase from nearly 1.4 million in 2010 to more than 3.8 million in 2060 and monthly nursing home costs are projected to increase from $4.4 billion in 2010 to $12.0 billion in 2060 (in 2010 constant dollars). Similarly the total number of Medicare beneficiaries is projected to increase by nearly 103% (under the middle projection scenario, see Table 6.11) from 2010 to 2060 compared to an overall population increase of 36.1%.
24. Reflecting the increasing size of minority populations, which due to a variety of historical, discriminatory and other factors tend to have lower levels of socioeconomic resources, the growth of such populations leads to large increases in the number of participants and in the costs related to TANF, SNAP, CHIP, Medicare, and Medicaid, and a variety of related programs (see Tables 6.10–6.12).

8.1.6 Chapter 7: Transportation

25. Because of the disproportionate extent to which automobile ownership and use involve nonHispanic White drivers, many of the implications for automobile and nonautomobile transportation reflect patterns for this population group.
26. The number of licensed drivers increased more rapidly than the population as a whole from 1950 to 1990 but, since1990, slowed to a pace approximately equal to total population growth. In addition, as with other factors examined in this volume, the driving population has aged so that the number of drivers under 30 years of age increased by only 5% from 2000 to 2010 while the number over 65 and the number over 80 years of age increased by 23.4% and 41.6% respectively (see Table 7.1).
27. Because minorities are less likely to own vehicles and to be drivers, the more rapid growth of minority populations does not lead to as substantial an increase in the driver population as in other substantive areas examined in this work. Whereas the total population is projected to increase by 36.1% from 2010 to 2060, the number of drivers is projected to increase by 34.3% (see Table 7.5). The percentage of all drivers who are minority group members will increase and the percent who are nonHispanic White will decrease. The total number of nonHispanic White drivers will decrease by 6.2% while the number of nonHispanic Black drivers will increase by 53.7%, the number of Hispanic drivers by 176.6%, and the number of nonHispanic Asian and Other drivers by 149.3% from 2010 to 2060. Thus, minority drivers will account for all of the 72.1 million drivers added from 2010 to 2060.
28. The level and the forms of commuting are also projected to change due to the projected change in population. Because of the decrease in the size of the non-Hispanic White population commuting to work, the number of this population driving to work alone, carpooling, taking public transportation, and involved in other forms of transit, decreases for each of these commuting types while the number increases for all other racial and ethnic groups. For example, the percentage of Hispanics driving alone, and taking public transit are projected to increase from 2010 to 2060 by 155.4% and 152.5%, respectively. These same rates for nonHispanic Asians and Others increase by 132.5 and 131.0% and those for nonHispanic Blacks by 41.5 and 37.7% while for nonHispanic Whites there are projected 2010 to 2060 changes of -17.3% and -17.4%. In the absence of increased rates of driving and commuting among minority populations, there will be an absolute decline in the rates of drivers in the population in the coming decades (see Tables 7.3–7.8).

8.2 The Implications of an Alternative Future

Overall, the analyses in the prior chapters in this volume, as summarized above, suggest that future patterns of population growth, racial/ethnic diversification and the aging of the population will change the total number and characteristics of people involved in the substantive areas noted above. Because the fastest growing population segments are generally ones with reduced socioeconomic resources, projected future patterns of population change are of critical importance to the determination of the competitiveness and the overall socioeconomic characteristics of the future population of the United States. This demographic change, if related to socioeconomic factors in the manner that they are currently related, will alter a wide variety of factors including the size, characteristics, and value of the nation's housing stock; the size, characteristics and competitiveness of its labor force; the income, wealth and poverty of its population; the number of persons enrolled in and obtaining given levels of education, the health and health care characteristics of its population, and the number of drivers and other transportation characteristics of the United States.

This analysis has also suggested that, due to a variety of historical, discriminatory and other factors, in the absence of change in socioeconomic differentials among population groups, the change in the characteristics of the population of the United States is likely to lead to a population that is poorer, less competitive and increasingly disadvantaged. It further demonstrates how the pervasive nature of these effects is likely to change the overall levels of wealth, education, and competitiveness of the population of the United States making its population simply poorer overall and less competitive internationally.

Despite the apparent pervasive nature of these changes we do not believe that they are inevitable. Thus, in the sections that follow we demonstrate how closure between minority and nonHispanic White patterns, produced in large part by closure in educational levels, could alter the socioeconomic implications of the projected patterns of change for the United States.

8.2.1 Addressing the Socioeconomic Differences Among Racial/Ethnic Groups in the United States

Given the projected change in the characteristics of the future population, in the remainder of this chapter we address the issue of what types of change might lead to an alternative, and more positive, socioeconomic future for the population of the United States. We assert that although the demographic changes described above may vary somewhat, alternative patterns of demographic change are unlikely to reverse what would otherwise be reduced levels of socioeconomic resources for the population of the United States. We argue that the socioeconomic changes likely to be necessary to alter the nation's socioeconomic future are unlikely to come from projected patterns of change in the population structure or components of that change but from changes made in the socioeconomic characteristics associated with given population characteristics.

Although we have emphasized the central importance of demographic change for the future of the United States, we have further argued that socioeconomic changes likely to be necessary to alter the nation's socioeconomic future are unlikely to come from projected patterns of change in the population structure alone or from components of that change but from changes made in the socioeconomic characteristics associated with given population characteristics. We examine this premise in detail below. The analysis presented suggests that the closing socioeconomic gaps through demographic change will simply not sufficiently mitigate projected long term changes so as to sufficiently reverse the effects described above for the nation's minority populations.

8.2.2 The Current Demographic State of Minority Populations in the United States

The rationale for this assertion can be determined by examining the current state and likely future population patterns for the different racial/ethnic groups in the United States population. For example, the expected reduction in the size of the relatively wealthier and better educated nonHispanic White population is unlikely to be altered by higher rates of nonHispanic White population growth. NonHispanic White populations have had fertility levels below replacement levels for more than two decades. The average nonHispanic White woman was 42 years of age (and is thus past the prime child bearing ages) as of the 2010 Census and immigration has failed to bring large numbers of nonHispanic Whites to the United States because the countries of origin of this population segment have among the oldest populations in the world with very low levels of fertility and total population growth. Key among these areas is Europe, which has one of the oldest populations of any region of the world. Substantial renewed growth of nonHispanic White populations through immigration to the United States is highly unlikely.

The nonHispanic Asian and Other population is growing relatively rapidly with a projected growth rate of nearly 140% from 2010 to 2060 and a net increase of nearly 33.5 million for this period, under the middle projection scenario. Such change is clearly significant and important but, under all of the alternative projection scenarios (see Chapter 2), the nonHispanic Asian and Other population is projected to account for 30% of the total growth in the population of the United States from 2010 to 2060. This is consequential but not enough to offset patterns of slow growth for other larger population segments.

Similar to nonHispanic Whites, nonHispanic Black populations show fertility levels that are below replacement. Although extensive immigration from African countries is possible, the socioeconomic characteristics of recent immigrants show patterns associated with higher levels of socioeconomic resources including reduced fertility patterns. In sum, then, although it is possible that increased immigration from a broad range of population segments from Africa could change the potential rate of growth in this population, there is little to suggest that such patterns are likely to occur or, if they do occur, that they would bring with them populations who will have high levels of fertility and hence the extensive growth that will substantially alter the socioeconomic future of the United States.

It is also likely that Hispanic growth rates will decline because their immigration level is decreasing and their fertility levels have also begun to decline. Nevertheless they continue to have the highest rates of immigration and the highest birth rates of any racial and ethnic group in the United States and have a relatively young population (e.g., the average Hispanic woman was 27 years of age in 2010) and all current projections show this population's numerical increase is likely to exceed that for any other group.

Given that ratios of population change from different racial/ethnic groups are unlikely to change substantially and given the sobering socioeconomic differentials evident among different population groups, as noted in the preceding chapters of this book, we suggest that factors that can directly alter the socioeconomic characteristics of the fastest growing population segments must be addressed if we are to change the socioeconomic future of the United States. That is, assistance to our minority populations, (particularly, because of their projected level of growth and socioeconomic characteristics, the Hispanic and nonHispanic Black populations), to change their socioeconomic characteristics is critical to changing the socioeconomic effects associated with future population change in the United States.

8.2.3 Can We Obtain Desired Socioeconomic Growth Rates if Recent Relationships to Race/Ethnicity Specific Patterns Continue into the Future?

Among the factors that can be seen as potentially altering socioeconomic outcomes associated with the projected population change is change in the levels of education among racial/ethnic groups. Education is one of the most widely acknowledged and strongly supported sources of socioeconomic success (see the discussion in Chapter 1). It is a factor that increases socioeconomic success for all racial/ethnic groups. This is evident in the data in Table 8.1 that shows average (mean) incomes for four educational levels of attainment for four racial/ethnic groups. The pervasive effect of education in increasing income is obvious. In every occupation for every racial/ethnic group income increases with higher levels of education. Even for those in operative, fabricator and laborer positions income increases with increased levels of education. The data in this table show average household income of nonHispanic Whites in this occupational category increasing nearly linearly from $45,859 for householders with less than a high school education to $80,478 for those with professional degrees. These values for nonHispanic Blacks are $35,403 and $62,621;

Table 8.1 Mean household income by race/ethnicity, educational attainment, and occupation in 2010

Occupation	Less than high school	High school	Bachelor's degree	Graduate professional
NH[a] White				
Management & professional	$70,989	$85,796	$112,871	$144,569
Technical, sales, & administrative	46,579	65,504	102,983	126,081
Service	34,694	50,098	72,379	88,343
Farming, forestry, & fishing	46,370	60,981	81,517	96,543
Precision production, craft, and repair	52,102	68,145	83,517	97,980
Operatives, fabricators, and laborers	45,859	57,393	69,929	80,478
Total	46,738	66,254	105,026	139,704
NH Black				
Management & professional	47,139	60,069	80,789	103,818
Technical, sales, & administrative	29,363	45,830	69,280	84,474
Service	27,189	37,365	62,115	71,773
Farming, forestry, & fishing	27,715	35,311	56,088	64,559
Precision production, craft, and repair	42,590	56,529	73,968	79,073
Operatives, fabricators, and laborers	35,403	46,909	62,430	62,621
Total	31,692	46,558	74,726	99,043
Hispanic				
Management & professional	61,002	72,488	93,560	123,830
Technical, sales, & administrative	43,661	57,180	81,358	94,998
Service	37,565	46,560	64,445	69,498
Farming, forestry, & fishing	37,823	43,092	50,379	57,571
Precision production, craft, and repair	47,107	58,701	64,984	71,173
Operatives, fabricators, and laborers	44,940	51,972	55,626	54,422
Total	43,014	56,155	83,324	114,184
NH Asian & Other				
Management & professional	73,587	79,266	105,244	139,147
Technical, sales, & administrative	51,164	62,039	92,077	117,248
Service	41,952	48,761	63,598	77,234
Farming, forestry, & fishing	43,987	51,343	67,192	92,512
Precision production, craft, and repair	53,063	67,493	79,889	101,770
Operatives, fabricators, and laborers	48,979	55,219	67,725	71,154
Total	48,922	61,802	95,897	132,649

Source: U.S. Census Bureau, 2011a; Ruggles et al. 2010

Note: Race/Ethnicity, educational attainment, and occupation of the householder. Excludes householders who were unemployed or not in the civilian laborforce

[a]NH refers to nonHispanic; values for categories labeled NH are only for the nonHispanic persons in each race category. Hispanic includes Hispanics of all races

for Hispanics $44,940 and $54,422, and for nonHispanic Asians and Others $48,979 for those with less than a high school level of education and $71,154 for those with a graduate level of education. Clearly, income differences remain between racial/ethnic groups in similar occupations (in part because the income shown is from all sources and there are differences in the extent to which different racially and ethnically specific populations are likely to also have inherited and obtained other sources of wealth). But, for all racial/ethnic groups, increased levels of education lead to increased income.

The data in Tables 8.2, 8.3 and 8.4 further address the issue of whether socioeconomic change is likely to occur if current patterns of relationships between racial/ethnic groups and changes in socioeconomic factors continue over time. Table 8.2 indicates that, although the period from 1980 through 2010 showed positive average improvements, significant closure between racial/ethnic group incomes, particularly those between Hispanics and nonHispanic Black populations and other racial/ethnic groups did not occur. Although varying by income type, the average change for mean household income was quite small, ranging from 4.4% for Hispanics and 5.0% for nonHispanic Blacks to 9.0% for nonHispanic Asians and Others and 8.7% for nonHispanic Whites.

Table 8.3 shows similar data for education by race/ethnicity. Concentrating on change in levels of education likely to improve socioeconomic resource bases the findings reflect those for income. Although percentage change for some population groups show relatively substantial average rates of growth, the absolute values continue to be quite limited. For example, the increase in the number of Hispanics and the number of nonHispanic Black persons with a Bachelor's degree or higher level of education were quite different, in absolute terms, from those for nonHispanic Whites and nonHispanic Asians and Others. For Hispanics the percentage increase was 549.2% for the three decades from 1980 to 2010 and was 164.5% for nonHispanic Black students for the1980 to 2010 period. However, the numerical increase for Hispanics with these levels of education was only 2.8 million and was 2.9 million for nonHispanic Blacks. The 1980–2010 increase was 4.9 million or 648.8% for nonHispanic Asians and Others and 23.6 million or 123.0% for nonHispanic Whites. Such absolute levels of numerical growth leave Hispanics and nonHispanic Blacks with very low levels of overall educational attainment compared to other populations after three decades of change.

The data in Table 8.4 show similar patterns for occupational change. The data in this table show improvement in the number of Hispanic and nonHispanic Black minorities in managerial and professional positions but again improvements that fail to bring substantial closure with nonHispanic Whites and nonHispanic Asians and Others. For example, the percent of Hispanics in management and professional positions increased from 2.8% of all persons in such positions in 1980 to 7.1% in 2010. The similar values for nonHispanic Black workers were from 5.7% of Black workers in this category in 1980 to 8.1% in 2010. Although such changes are significant this percent is still far less than the percentage of the total labor force they represent. Hispanics were 15.2% and nonHispanic Blacks were 11.4% of the labor force in 2010.

Table 8.2 Median, mean, and per capita income levels (in 2010 dollars) by race/ethnicity for 1980–2010 and percent change for 1980–1990, 1990–2000, 2000–2010, average change for the three decades, and the largest decade growth for any period from 1980 to 2010

Race/ethnicity	1980	1990	2000	2010	1980–1990	1990–2000	2000–2010	Avg	Largest
Median household income									
NH[a] White	53,508	54,609	59,379	56,466	2.1	8.7	−4.9	2.0	8.7
NH Black	32,723	33,764	38,539	35,189	3.2	14.1	−8.7	2.9	14.1
Hispanic	40,292	42,204	44,077	41,543	4.7	4.4	−5.7	1.1	4.7
NH Asian & Other	51,315	55,770	68,018	54,013	8.7	22.0	−20.6	3.4	22.0
Total	50,459	51,922	54,964	51,914	2.9	5.9	−5.5	1.1	5.9
Mean household income									
NH[a] White	61,879	68,635	79,045	76,543	10.9	15.2	−3.2	7.6	15.2
NH Black	41,857	44,519	51,327	47,942	6.4	15.3	−6.6	5.0	15.3
Hispanic	48,127	52,182	57,172	54,456	8.4	9.6	−4.8	4.4	9.6
NH Asian & Other	61,585	71,384	76,872	79,555	15.9	7.7	3.5	9.0	15.9
Total	59,122	65,116	73,931	70,883	10.1	13.5	−4.1	6.5	13.5
Per capita income									
NH[a] White	23,207	27,378	32,485	32,136	18.0	18.7	−1.1	11.9	18.7
NH Black	13,442	15,476	18,964	18,342	15.1	22.5	−3.3	11.5	22.5
Hispanic	13,411	14,544	15,852	15,638	8.4	9.0	−1.3	5.4	9.0
NH Asian & Other	18,470	21,392	28,655	30,122	15.8	34.0	5.1	18.3	34.0
Total	21,328	24,629	28,254	27,334	15.5	14.7	−3.3	9.0	15.5
Aggregate income (in $billions)									
NH[a] White	4,190	5,147	6,331	6,325	18.0	18.7	−1.1	11.9	18.7
NH Black	353	452	632	691	15.1	22.5	−3.3	11.5	22.5
Hispanic	198	318	553	789	8.4	9.0	−1.3	5.4	9.0
NH Asian & Other	97	194	437	716	15.8	34.0	5.1	18.3	34.0
Total	4,839	6,111	7,953	8,439	26.3	30.1	6.1	20.9	30.1

Source: U.S. Census Bureau, 1982, 1983, 1992, 1993, 2002, 2003, 2011a; U.S. Bureau of Labor Statistics 2011; Ruggles et al. 2010

[a]NH refers to nonHispanic; values for categories labeled NH are only for the nonHispanic persons in each race category. Hispanic includes Hispanics of all races

The data in Table 8.5 indicate the level of projected change in different types of income under three alternatives of projected rates of growth. One alternative shown in the second and third columns indicates income levels in 2030 and 2060 if average (mean) percent change per decade (derived from the average for the three decades from 1980 to 2010) were to occur for each of the decade periods from 2010 to 2030 and 2010 to 2060. The second set of two columns assumes that the largest percent change from the three decades of 1980–90, 1990–2000, and 2000–2010 would occur each decade throughout the period from 2010 through 2060. The final two

Table 8.3 Number and percent persons 25 years of age and older in the United States by race/ethnicity and educational level, 1980–2010, and change for 1980–1990, 1990–2000, 2000–2010, average percent change 1980–2010, and largest decade percent change 1980–2010

	Decade numeric and percent change												
	1980		1990		2000		2010		Percent change 1980–2010				
Race/ethnicity	Number	%	Number	%	Number	%	Number	%	1980–1990	1990–2000	2000–2010	Average	Largest
Less than high school diploma/GED													
NH[a] White	33,582,580	30.5	26,297,000	20.9	19,483,380	14.6	13,843,239	10.0	−21.7	−25.9	−28.9	−25.5	−21.7
NH Black	6,328,560	48.8	6,011,515	36.7	5,375,402	27.5	4,237,270	19.0	−5.0	−10.6	−21.2	−12.3	−5.0
Hispanic	3,755,760	55.9	5,603,315	50.0	8,688,431	47.6	9,812,109	38.4	49.2	55.1	12.9	39.1	55.1
NH Asian & Other	843,600	29.8	1,307,492	24.7	2,176,584	20.5	1,947,094	14.5	55.0	66.5	−10.5	37.0	66.5
Total	44,510,500	33.5	39,219,322	24.7	35,723,797	19.6	29,839,712	14.9	−11.9	−8.9	−16.5	−12.4	−8.9
High school diploma/GED													
NH[a] White	57,455,480	52.1	71,675,385	57.0	78,256,825	58.5	81,725,237	59.1	24.7	9.2	4.4	12.8	24.7
NH Black	5,563,260	42.9	8,502,375	51.9	11,372,068	58.2	14,148,934	63.3	52.8	33.8	24.4	37.0	52.8
Hispanic	2,442,760	36.4	4,571,080	40.8	7,653,812	41.9	12,400,998	48.5	87.1	67.4	62.0	72.2	87.1
NH Asian & Other	1,228,480	43.4	2,318,499	43.9	4,743,301	44.6	5,843,666	43.4	88.7	104.6	23.2	72.2	104.6
Total	66,689,980	50.2	87,067,339	54.9	102,026,006	56.0	114,118,835	57.1	30.6	17.2	11.9	19.9	30.6
Bachelor degree													
NH[a] White	13,352,640	12.1	17,850,811	14.2	22,934,856	17.1	26,874,987	19.4	33.7	28.5	17.2	26.5	33.7
NH Black	745,280	5.7	1,238,870	7.6	1,858,026	9.5	2,590,283	11.6	66.2	50.0	39.4	51.9	66.2
Hispanic	327,900	4.9	654,431	5.8	1,213,060	6.6	2,283,293	8.9	99.6	85.4	88.2	91.1	99.6
NH Asian & Other	462,640	16.3	1,029,238	19.5	2,277,332	21.4	3,425,347	25.4	122.5	121.3	50.4	98.1	122.5
Total	14,888,460	11.2	20,773,350	13.1	28,283,274	15.5	35,173,910	17.6	39.5	36.2	24.4	33.4	39.5

Graduate/professional degree													
NH[a] White	5,829,840	5.3	9,815,446	7.9	13,077,254	9.8	15,906,487	11.5	68.4	33.2	21.6	41.1	68.4
NH Black	338,360	2.6	636,990	3.8	941,817	4.8	1,359,028	6.1	88.3	47.9	44.3	60.2	88.3
Hispanic	186,440	2.8	367,920	3.4	697,736	3.9	1,055,592	4.2	97.3	89.6	51.3	79.4	97.3
NH Asian & Other	295,320	10.5	630,881	11.9	1,432,330	13.5	2,250,320	16.7	113.6	127.0	57.1	99.2	127.0
Total	6,649,960	5.1	11,451,237	7.3	16,149,137	8.9	20,571,427	10.4	72.2	41.0	27.4	46.9	72.2
High school/GED or higher													
NH[a] White	76,637,960	69.5	99,341,642	79.1	114,268,935	85.4	124,506,711	90.0	29.6	15.0	9.0	17.9	29.6
NH Black	6,646,900	51.2	10,378,235	63.3	14,171,911	72.5	18,098,245	81.0	56.1	36.6	27.7	40.1	56.1
Hispanic	2,957,100	44.1	5,593,431	50.0	9,564,608	52.4	15,739,883	61.6	89.2	71.0	64.6	74.9	89.2
NH Asian & Other	1,986,440	70.2	3,978,618	75.3	8,452,963	79.5	11,519,333	85.5	100.3	112.5	36.3	83.0	112.5
Total	88,228,400	66.5	119,291,926	75.3	146,458,417	80.4	169,864,172	85.1	35.2	22.8	16.0	24.7	35.2
Bachelor degree or higher													
NH[a] White	19,182,480	17.4	27,666,257	22.1	36,012,110	26.9	42,781,474	30.9	44.2	30.2	18.8	31.1	44.2
NH Black	1,083,640	8.3	1,875,860	11.4	2,799,843	14.3	3,949,311	17.7	73.1	49.3	41.1	54.5	73.1
Hispanic	514,340	7.7	1,022,351	9.2	1,910,796	10.5	3,338,885	13.1	98.8	86.9	74.7	86.8	98.8
NH Asian & Other	757,960	26.8	1,660,119	31.4	3,709,662	34.9	5,675,667	42.1	119.0	123.5	53.0	98.5	123.5
Total	21,538,420	16.3	32,224,587	20.4	44,432,411	24.4	55,745,337	28.0	49.6	37.9	25.5	37.7	49.6

Source: U.S. Census Bureau, 1982, 1983, 1992, 1993, 2002, 2003, 2011a; U.S. Bureau of Labor Statistics 2011; Ruggles et al. 2010

[a]NH refers to nonHispanic; values for categories labeled NH are only for the nonHispanic persons in each race category. Hispanic includes Hispanics of all races

Table 8.4 Number and percent of persons 25 years of age and older in the United States by race/ethnicity and occupation, 1980–1990, 1990–2000, 2000–2010, average percent change 1980–2010, and largest decade percent change 1980–2010

	Decade numeric and percent												
	1980		1990		2000		2010		Percent change 1980–2010				
Race/ethnicity	Number	%	Number	%	Number	%	Number	%	1980–1990	1990–2000	2000–2010	Avg.	Largest
Management & professional													
NH[a] White	20,490,500	18.6	28,035,772	22.3	32,952,848	24.6	36,586,206	26.4	36.8	17.5	11.0	21.8	36.8
NH Black	1,320,060	10.2	2,171,045	13.2	3,043,581	15.6	3,882,742	17.4	64.5	40.2	27.6	44.1	64.5
Hispanic	649,920	9.7	1,279,654	11.4	2,237,723	12.3	3,388,169	13.3	96.9	74.9	51.4	74.4	96.9
NH Asian & Other	596,720	21.1	1,218,916	23.1	2,673,776	25.2	3,855,265	28.6	104.3	119.4	44.2	89.3	119.4
Total	23,057,200	17.4	32,705,387	20.6	40,907,928	22.5	47,712,382	23.9	41.8	25.1	16.6	27.8	41.8
Technical, sales, & administrative													
NH[a] White	24,558,340	22.3	30,634,017	24.4	31,394,896	23.5	31,237,117	22.6	24.7	2.5	–0.5	8.9	24.7
NH Black	2,032,980	15.7	3,224,846	19.7	4,082,061	20.9	4,604,191	20.6	58.6	26.6	12.8	32.7	58.6
Hispanic	1,072,320	16.0	2,089,378	18.7	3,247,552	17.8	4,552,593	17.8	94.8	55.4	40.2	63.5	94.8
NH Asian & Other	586,700	20.7	1,249,474	23.6	2,451,054	23.1	3,042,133	22.6	113.0	96.2	24.1	77.8	113.0
Total	28,250,340	21.3	37,197,715	23.5	41,175,563	22.6	43,436,034	21.8	31.7	10.7	5.5	16.0	31.7
Service													
NH[a] White	8,591,340	7.8	10,119,819	8.1	11,147,605	8.3	12,135,720	8.8	17.8	10.2	8.9	12.3	17.8
NH Black	2,311,080	17.8	2,840,407	17.3	3,301,574	16.9	3,992,250	17.9	22.9	16.2	20.9	20.0	22.9
Hispanic	825,600	12.3	1,644,988	14.7	2,885,523	15.8	4,444,094	17.4	99.2	75.4	54.0	76.2	99.2
NH Asian & Other	352,140	12.4	646,632	12.2	1,300,365	12.2	1,716,997	12.8	83.6	101.1	32.0	72.2	101.1
Total	12,080,160	9.1	15,251,846	9.6	18,635,067	10.2	22,289,061	11.2	26.3	22.2	19.6	22.7	26.3

Farming, forestry, & fishing													
NH[a] White	2,432,580	2.2	2,377,341	1.9	2,181,025	1.6	2,094,162	1.5	−2.3	−8.3	−4.0	−4.9	−2.3
NH Black	235,400	1.8	235,927	1.4	220,287	1.1	227,188	1.0	0.2	−6.6	3.1	−1.1	3.1
Hispanic	264,700	3.9	478,292	4.3	798,352	4.4	1,100,258	4.3	80.7	66.9	37.8	61.8	80.7
NH Asian & Other	66,700	2.4	82,979	1.6	117,697	1.1	114,062	0.8	24.4	41.8	−3.1	21.0	41.8
Total	2,999,380	2.3	3,174,539	2.0	3,317,361	1.8	3,535,670	1.8	5.8	4.5	6.6	5.6	6.6
Precision production, craft, and repair													
NH[a] White	10,681,800	9.7	11,224,736	8.9	11,504,876	8.6	10,591,102	7.7	5.1	2.5	−7.9	−0.1	5.1
NH Black	869,000	6.7	1,071,952	6.5	1,317,032	6.7	1,213,100	5.4	23.4	22.9	−7.9	12.8	23.4
Hispanic	696,680	10.4	1,160,948	10.4	2,006,251	11.0	2,765,555	10.8	66.6	72.8	37.8	59.1	72.8
NH Asian & Other	212,960	7.5	355,850	6.7	712,229	6.7	705,805	5.2	67.1	100.1	−0.9	55.4	100.1
Total	12,460,440	9.4	13,813,486	8.7	15,540,388	8.5	15,275,562	7.6	10.9	12.5	−1.7	7.2	12.5
Operatives, fabricators, and laborers													
NH[a] White	12,971,780	11.8	13,040,061	10.4	12,073,388	9.0	11,143,958	8.1	0.5	−7.4	−7.7	−4.9	0.5
NH Black	2,610,580	20.1	2,781,919	17.0	2,871,736	14.7	2,857,217	12.8	6.6	3.2	−0.5	3.1	6.6
Hispanic	1,479,920	22.0	2,160,583	19.3	3,252,783	17.8	3,944,642	15.4	46.0	50.6	21.3	39.3	50.6
NH Asian & Other	368,340	13.0	631,672	11.9	1,119,681	10.5	1,093,966	8.1	71.5	77.3	−2.3	48.8	77.3
Total	17,430,620	13.1	18,614,235	11.7	19,317,588	10.6	19,039,783	9.5	6.8	3.8	−1.4	3.1	6.8
Not in the civilian labor force or unemployed													
NH[a] White	30,494,200	27.6	30,206,896	24.0	32,497,677	24.4	34,561,685	24.9	−0.9	7.6	6.4	4.4	7.6
NH Black	3,596,360	27.7	4,063,654	24.9	4,711,042	24.1	5,558,827	24.9	13.0	15.9	18.0	15.6	18.0
Hispanic	1,723,720	25.7	2,382,903	21.2	3,824,855	20.9	5,356,681	21.0	38.2	60.5	40.0	46.2	60.5
NH Asian & Other	646,480	22.9	1,100,587	20.9	2,254,745	21.2	2,938,199	21.9	70.2	104.9	30.3	68.5	104.9
Total	36,460,760	27.4	37,754,040	23.9	43,288,319	23.8	48,415,392	24.2	3.5	14.7	11.8	10.0	14.7

Source: U.S. Census Bureau, 1982, 1983, 1992, 1993, 2002, 2003, 2011a; U.S. Bureau of Labor Statistics 2011; Ruggles et al. 2010

[a]NH refers to nonHispanic; values for categories labeled NH are only for the nonHispanic persons in each race category. Hispanic includes Hispanics of all races

Table 8.5 Median, mean, per capita, and aggregate income levels (in 2010 dollars) by race/ethnicity in 2010 and projected through 2060 assuming average percent change for the three decades between 1980 and 2010, largest percent change for any decade, and percent change for the 2000–2010 decade

Race/ethnicity	2010	Average percent change		Largest percent change		2000–2010 percent change	
		2030	2060	2030	2060	2030	2060
Median household income							
NH[a] White	$56,466	$58,704	$62,228	$66,761	85,829	$51,062	$43,909
NH Black	35,189	37,243	40,550	45,847	68,182	29,337	22,333
Hispanic	41,543	42,499	43,975	45,579	52,381	36,904	30,898
NH Asian & Other	54,013	57,694	63,690	80,344	145,757	34,060	17,056
Total	51,914	53,030	54,750	58,175	69,011	46,312	39,023
Mean household income							
NH[a] White	76,543	88,686	110,605	101,523	155,079	71,773	65,171
NH Black	47,942	52,875	61,244	63,725	97,656	41,828	34,087
Hispanic	54,456	59,368	67,578	65,370	85,976	49,404	42,692
NH Asian & Other	79,555	94,571	122,571	106,883	166,446	85,204	94,440
Total	70,883	79,661	94,241	91,070	131,016	65,258	58,489
Per capita income							
NH[a] White	32,136	40,205	56,260	45,244	75,582	31,449	30,446
NH Black	18,342	22,788	31,556	27,543	50,681	17,159	15,525
Hispanic	15,638	17,360	20,306	18,578	24,057	15,219	14,611
NH Asian & Other	30,122	42,153	69,781	54,047	129,899	33,285	38,663
Total	27,334	33,177	43,833	38,022	63,914	26,258	24,749
Aggregate income (in $billions)							
NH[a] White	6,325	7,993	10,068	8,995	13,525	6,253	5,448
NH Black	691	1,036	1,745	1,252	2,803	780	859
Hispanic	789	1,365	2,615	1,461	3,098	1,197	1,882
NH Asian & Other	716	1,498	3,994	1,921	7,435	1,183	2,213
Total	8,439	11,893	18,422	13,630	26,861	9,413	10,401

Source: U.S. Census Bureau, 1982, 1983, 1992, 1993, 2002, 2003, 2011a, 2012; U.S. Bureau of Labor Statistics 2011; Ruggles et al. 2010

[a]NH refers to nonHispanic; values for categories labeled NH are only for the nonHispanic persons in each race category. Hispanic includes Hispanics of all races

columns show the values if the percent change from 2000 to 2010 were to prevail for the entire period from 2010 to 2060. The data in this table show that in the absence of factors that provide additional closure in the income gap between racial/ethnic groups the alternative levels of increase will simply lead to larger or smaller values with the same relative differences between racial/ethnic groups. For example, for each of the time periods shown and alternative levels of growth based on historic periods, Hispanic's average household income and nonHispanic Black's average household income stay between 50 and 70% of nonHispanic White incomes. Although different levels of growth will lead to different absolute incomes and the relative buying power of Hispanics and nonHispanic Black households will increase, differences between them and other racial/ethnic groups will not disappear in the absence of change in basic factors, such as education, that lead to increased income closure.

The data in Table 8.6 show the same projection scenarios as shown in the columns in Table 8.5 but indicate the percent change in educational attainment for each racial/ethnic group based on average change in educational attainment for the three decades from 1980 to 2010, for the decade with the largest percent increase, and for the most recent (2000–2010) decade for each race/ethnicity group. The data in this table show that in the absence of an increase in the rate of closure in the relative levels of education for racial and ethnic groups, substantial improvements will not occur in the socioeconomic results associated with higher education. For example, in the base period of 2010, the percent of nonHispanic Black's who had completed a Bachelor's degrees or higher was 17.7% compared to 30.9% for nonHispanic Whites. The rates for nonHispanic Asians and Others were 42.1% and those for Hispanics were 13.1%. Similarly, under the largest percent increase column these percentages were 25.6% for Hispanics and 57.1% for nonHispanic Whites. Hispanic's rates were 44.8% of those for nonHispanic Whites. Such differences clearly suggest that given markets that seek those with the highest skill and educational levels for key positions, substantive improvements in education and critical skills must be obtained by the minority population if it is to improve its socioeconomic resources and related socioeconomic characteristics.

The data in Table 8.7 show similar patterns for occupational differences. For example, examining managerial and professional positions, the results indicate that the percent change in either the 2030 or 2060 periods show Hispanic rates of change that were about 50% of those for nonHispanic Whites. nonHispanic Blacks' rates were 80% of those for nonHispanic Whites. The data in this chapter, while showing that historical patterns of educational, occupational, and income change have promised to lead to better socioeconomic characteristics for nonHispanic Blacks and Hispanics, the change has been limited. What is apparent is that such actions to eliminate differences among racial and ethnic groups cannot lead to socioeconomic equality in the levels of economic growth essential to maintain the socioeconomic base of the future of the United States.

Table 8.6 Educational attainment levels by race/ethnicity for persons 25 years of age and older in 2010 and projected through 2060 assuming average percent change for the three decade between 1980 and 2010, largest percent change for any decade, and percent change for the 2000–2010 decade

		Average percent change		Largest percent change		Percent change 2000–2010	
Race/ethnicity	2010	2030	2060	2030	2060	2030	2060
Less than high school diploma/GED							
NH[a] White	10.0	4.1	1.0	3.1	0.4	4.5	1.2
NH Black	19.0	8.3	2.1	5.5	0.7	8.1	2.0
Hispanic	38.4	28.1	16.1	18.1	4.4	22.5	8.2
NH Asian & Other	14.5	8.4	3.4	2.9	0.2	6.6	1.7
Total	14.9	9.5	5.6	6.2	1.5	8.5	3.3
High school diploma/GED							
NH[a] White	59.1	55.8	45.4	55.9	42.5	56.9	49.3
NH Black	63.3	67.6	64.6	69.3	64.0	67.6	64.3
Hispanic	48.5	54.5	59.3	62.8	70.0	58.6	63.3
NH Asian & Other	43.4	40.0	32.4	44.8	39.3	37.4	25.3
Total	57.1	55.6	50.1	57.8	52.6	56.8	52.1
Bachelor degree							
NH[a] White	19.4	23.1	26.5	21.1	19.8	23.6	28.9
NH Black	11.6	15.2	19.8	15.0	17.8	15.5	20.8
Hispanic	8.9	12.4	18.4	13.2	17.8	14.6	24.7
NH Asian & Other	25.4	31.0	38.3	31.1	35.0	32.6	40.2
Total	17.6	20.8	24.9	20.5	20.9	21.7	28.1
Graduate/professional degree							
NH[a] White	11.5	17.0	27.1	19.9	37.3	15.0	20.6
NH Black	6.1	8.9	13.5	10.2	17.5	8.8	12.9
Hispanic	4.2	5.0	6.2	5.9	7.8	4.3	3.8
NH Asian & Other	16.7	20.6	25.9	21.2	25.5	23.4	32.8
Total	10.4	14.1	19.4	15.5	25.0	13.0	16.5
High school/GED or higher							
NH[a] White	90.0	95.9	99.0	96.9	99.6	95.5	98.8
NH Black	81.0	91.7	97.9	94.5	99.3	91.9	98.0
Hispanic	61.6	71.9	83.9	81.9	95.6	77.5	91.8
NH Asian & Other	85.5	91.6	96.6	97.1	99.8	93.4	98.3
Total	85.1	90.5	94.4	93.8	98.5	91.5	96.7
Bachelor degree or higher							
NH[a] White	30.9	40.1	53.6	41.0	57.1	38.6	49.5
NH Black	17.7	24.1	33.3	25.2	35.3	24.3	33.7
Hispanic	13.1	17.4	24.6	19.1	25.6	18.9	28.5
NH Asian & Other	42.1	51.6	64.2	52.3	60.5	56.0	73.0
Total	28.0	34.9	44.3	36.0	45.9	34.7	44.6

Source: U.S. Census Bureau, 1982, 1983, 1992, 1993, 2002, 2003, 2011a, 2012; U.S. Bureau of Labor Statistics 2011; Ruggles et al. 2010

[a]NH refers to nonHispanic; values for categories labeled NH are only for the nonHispanic persons in each race category. Hispanic includes Hispanics of all races

Table 8.7 Occupation by race/ethnicity for persons 25 years of age and older in 2010 and projected through 2060 assuming average percent change for the three decades between 1980 and 2010, largest percent change for any decade, and percent change for the 2000–2010 decade

		Average percent change		Largest percent change		Percent change 2000–2010	
Race/ethnicity	2010	2030	2060	2030	2060	2030	2060
Management & professional							
NH[a] White	26.4	32.5	42.4	34.4	46.9	30.1	35.4
NH Black	17.4	23.6	34.4	25.5	37.6	21.2	27.1
Hispanic	13.3	15.8	19.5	15.9	19.3	15.3	18.2
NH Asian & Other	28.6	33.6	41.0	31.9	36.7	35.6	45.7
Total	23.9	28.4	34.8	29.6	36.7	26.7	30.8
Technical, sales, & administrative							
NH[a] White	22.6	22.2	20.7	24.4	25.2	20.6	17.5
NH Black	20.6	23.7	26.9	28.1	37.1	19.6	17.4
Hispanic	17.8	18.6	19.0	20.9	24.6	17.6	16.6
NH Asian & Other	22.6	23.4	23.7	23.7	25.0	20.8	17.0
Total	21.8	22.1	21.4	24.1	26.6	19.9	17.2
Service							
NH[a] White	8.8	9.2	9.4	8.5	7.4	9.6	10.7
NH Black	17.9	16.8	14.1	14.6	9.0	19.5	21.3
Hispanic	17.4	21.1	26.9	21.3	26.9	20.7	25.9
NH Asian & Other	12.8	12.4	11.4	11.9	10.6	13.3	13.1
Total	11.2	12.7	15.1	12.0	13.4	13.2	16.6
Farming, forestry, & fishing							
NH[a] White	1.5	1.1	0.7	1.0	0.5	1.3	1.0
NH Black	1.0	0.7	0.3	0.6	0.2	0.8	0.5
Hispanic	4.3	4.4	4.4	4.3	4.1	4.1	3.7
NH Asian & Other	0.8	0.4	0.1	0.4	0.1	0.5	0.2
Total	1.8	1.6	1.6	1.5	1.4	1.7	1.6
Precision production, craft, and repair							
NH[a] White	7.7	6.3	4.6	5.9	3.6	6.0	4.0
NH Black	5.4	4.5	3.2	4.5	2.8	3.4	1.7
Hispanic	10.8	10.7	10.1	10.0	8.2	10.3	9.3
NH Asian & Other	5.2	4.1	2.8	4.9	4.2	3.1	1.3
Total	7.6	6.7	5.7	6.4	4.8	6.2	4.8
Operatives, fabricators, and laborers							
NH[a] White	8.1	6.0	3.8	5.7	3.1	6.3	4.3
NH Black	12.8	8.9	4.7	7.9	3.2	9.5	5.8
Hispanic	15.4	11.7	7.4	10.8	5.9	11.4	7.0
NH Asian & Other	8.1	5.9	3.5	5.9	3.6	4.6	1.8
Total	9.5	7.4	4.9	7.0	4.0	7.5	4.9
Not in the civilian labor force or unemployed							
NH[a] White	24.9	22.7	18.4	20.1	13.3	26.1	27.1

(continued)

Table 8.7 (continued)

Race/ethnicity	2010	Average percent change		Largest percent change		Percent change 2000–2010	
		2030	2060	2030	2060	2030	2060
NH Black	24.9	21.8	16.4	18.8	10.1	26.0	26.2
Hispanic	21.0	17.7	12.7	16.8	11.0	20.6	19.3
NH Asian & Other	21.9	20.2	17.5	21.3	19.8	22.1	20.9
Total	24.2	21.1	16.5	19.4	13.1	24.8	24.1

Source: U.S. Census Bureau, 1982, 1983, 1992, 1993, 2002, 2003, 2011a, 2012; U.S. Bureau of Labor Statistics 2011; Ruggles et al. 2010

[a]NH refers to nonHispanic; values for categories labeled NH are only for the nonHispanic persons in each race category. Hispanic includes Hispanics of all races

8.2.4 Maintaining the Socioeconomic Base of America

The patterns necessary to maintain and improve the United States' socioeconomic status require steps beyond those noted above. They require moving the socioeconomic characteristics of all Americans to the level of those for nonHispanic White Americans. The effects of doing so are shown and discussed in relationship to Table 8.8 and Figs. 8.1, 8.2 and 8.3.

Table 8.8 provides data that show how important closure in socioeconomic resources among racial/ethnic groups is to improving the socioeconomic position of minority populations. Compared to the average rates of change column, the projections assuming closure to nonHispanic White rates lead to a nearly 22 million increase in persons employed in management and professional occupations compared to the use of average rates, a \$20,000 increase in median household income, a \$15,000 increase in per capita income, a nearly \$6 billion increase in aggregate income, a 3.8% decline in poverty, a \$12,000 increase in average household consumer expenditures and a 7.5% increase in the number of persons with a graduate degree. What the data in this table show, when compared to the preceding tables, is that not only change but closure to the levels of nonHispanic Whites is essential to show substantial increases in the socioeconomic conditions of all members of the population and to eliminate the socioeconomic inequality among these groups.

Figures 8.1, 8.2, 8.3 and 8.4 provide a final illustration of what failing to close the socioeconomic differences among racial/ethnic groups through improved education and other factors is likely to mean for households in the United States and for the country as a whole. Figure 8.1 shows a simple comparison of the implications of the continuation of current socioeconomic differences among racial and ethnic groups for households under a set of socioeconomic indicators, assuming the projected rates of change for each factor (in the absence of closure) from 2010 to 2060. Clearly, at a minimum, to maintain current levels of socioeconomic resources for the population overall, the percent increase for each factor from 2010 to 2060 must

Table 8.8 Selected socioeconomic characteristics of the United States population in 2010, projections for 2060 assuming 2010 rates, projections for 2060 assuming the average rates of change by race/ethnicity for the three decades between 1980 and 2010, and projections for 2060 assuming closure of projected minority rates to projected nonHispanic White rates by 2060

		Projected values in 2060:		
Socioeconomic factor	Values and rates in 2010	Assuming 2010 levels	Assuming average rates of change	Assuming closure to nonHispanic White rates by 2060
Employment in management & professional (in thousands)	47,712.4	64,677.8	102,947.5	124,866.1
Employment as operative or laborer (in thousands)	19,039.8	31,754.0	14,431.5	11,125.0
Percent employed in management & professional	23.9	21.9	34.8	42.2215
Percent employed as operative or laborer	9.5	10.7	4.9	3.7617
Median household income	$51,914	$50,933	$54,728	$74,173
Per capita income	$27,334	$24,991	$43,833	$58,101
Mean household income	$70,883	$67,321	$94,241	$111,968
Aggregate income ($billions)	$8,439.0	$10,503.0	$18,421.8	$24,418.1
Population in poverty (in thousands)	40,990.0	66,390.7	62,481.9	46,726.6
Percent in poverty	13.8	16.2	14.9	11.1
Aggregate federal tax revenue ($billions)	$1,854.5	$2,361.7	$3,306.1	$3,928.0
Mean household tax	$15,889	$14,208	$19,889	$23,631
Aggregate consumer expenditures ($billions)	$5,892.0	$7,762.8	$10,866.9	$12,911.0
Mean consumer expenditures	$50,481	$46,701	$65,376	$77,673
Population 25+ with less than high school/GED (in thousands)	29,839.7	58,077.3	16,690.4	3,862.6
Population 25+ with a bachelor's degree (in thousands)	35,173.9	48,055.2	73,562.5	82,821.8
Population 25+ with a graduate/professional degree (in thousands)	20,571.4	27,812.8	57,237.3	79,693.2
Percent with less than high school/GED	14.9	19.6	5.6	1.3
Percent with a bachelor's degree	17.6	16.2	24.9	28.0
Percent with a graduate/professional degree	10.4	9.4	19.4	26.9

All monetary values are in 2010 constant dollars

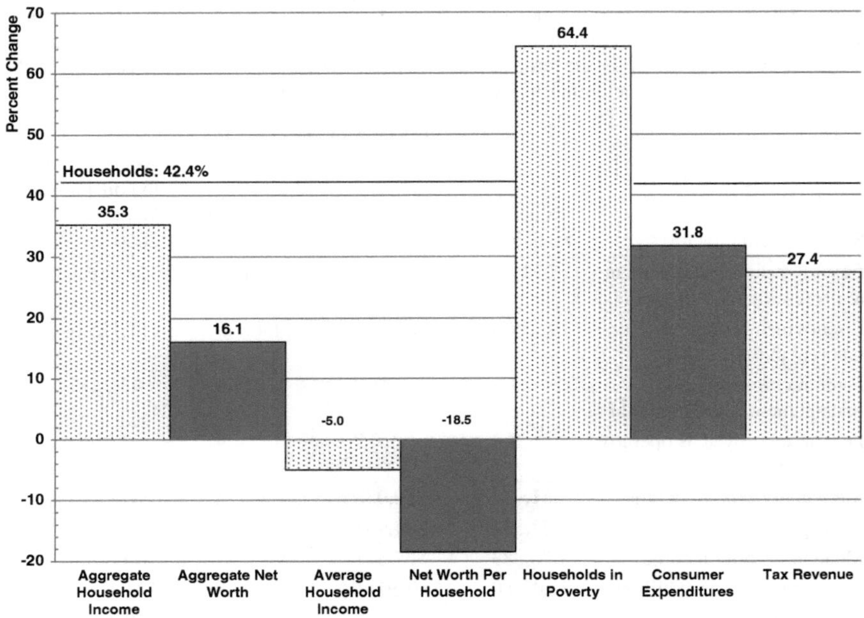

Figure 8.1 Percent change in socioeconomic resources compared to percent change in households, 2010–2060

be equal to the overall rate of household growth (i.e., 42.4%). As the data in this figure indicate, in the absence of closure, only the number of households in poverty will increase faster than the number of households. Aggregate household income, aggregate net worth, average household income, net worth per household, consumer expenditures per household, and tax revenues per household will all fail to keep pace with household growth. Current patterns of economic change if not addressed through increased education and other factors will lead to a poorer and less competitive population and national economy.

The data in Figure 8.2 indicate the effects of various levels of socioeconomic change depending on alternative rates of closure among racial/ethnic groups. These data again show that a continuation of current patterns (i.e., 2000–2010 rates of change) will lead to decreased income and consumer expenditures while both the average of levels of change for the last three decades and especially closure of all racial/ethnic groups to nonHispanic White household levels would lead to substantial increases in socioeconomic resources. Thus a continuation of 2000–2010 rates of change would lead to a $2,343 decline in per capita income, a $3,562 decrease in average household income, and a $3,780 decline in average household consumer expenditures but closure of minority to nonHispanic White levels would lead to large increases in per capita, average household income and average household consumer expenditures. Compared to the levels that would occur if 2010 levels prevailed, each of the three factors shown indicate a minimum of a $12,000 increase in

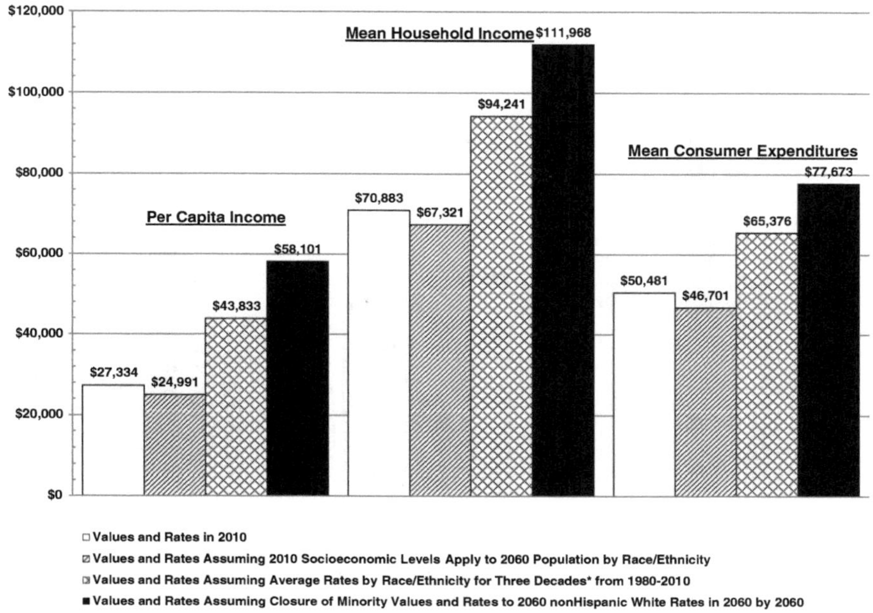

Figure 8.2 Per capita income, mean household income, and mean consumer expenditures per household in 2060 under alternative assumptions of socioeconomic closure between minority and nonHispanic White households

the income and expenditures shown when closure between minority and nonHispanic Whitelevels are compared to averages for the last three decades.

Figure 8.3 shows the same differences as those shown in Figure 8.2 but for employment in management/professional and operative/laborer positions, poverty and educational attainment levels. Again the data indicate that improving the quality of jobs, the income and the education of Americans would have positive impacts not only for the individuals involved but also for the society as a whole. Closure toward nonHispanic White levels would increase the percentage of persons in management/professional employment by nearly 20%, decrease the percentage in operative and laborer jobs by two thirds, decrease poverty levels by 2.7% and increase the percentage of persons with higher levels of education (e.g. a 16.5% increase in persons with graduate or professional degrees). Again this figure indicates that improved socioeconomic growth is important not only for individuals but for the country and its economy as a whole.

Figure 8.4 is similar in form to Figure 8.3 except that it shows values for aggregate income, aggregate consumer expenditures, and aggregate federal tax revenues. As one would expect, given the preceding charts, the data in this figure indicate that all of these factors would increase with closure toward the levels currently maintained by the nonHispanic White population. For example, aggregate income would increase by nearly $16 billion per year, aggregate consumer expenditures by $7

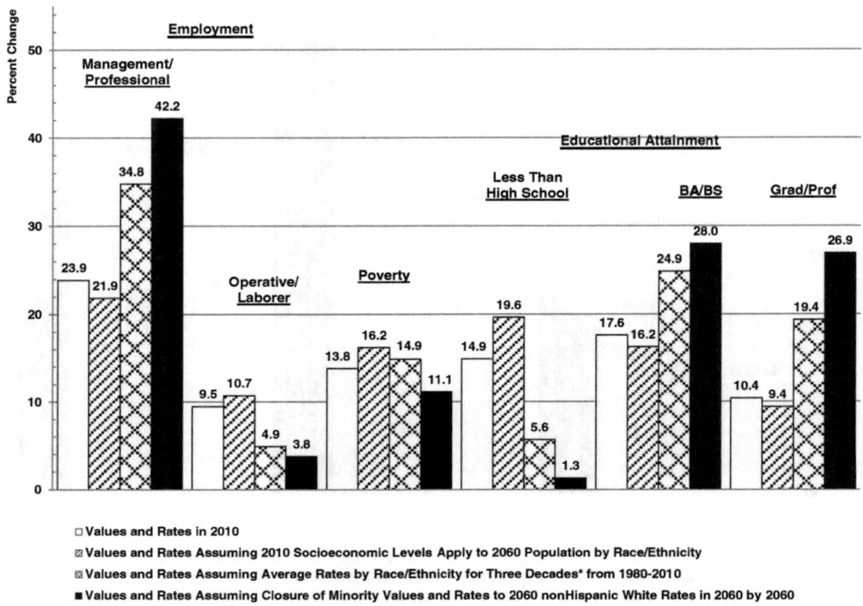

Figure 8.3 Percent persons in the labor force in management/professional and operative/laborer positions, persons in poverty, and levels of educational attainment under alternative assumptions of closure between racial/ethnic groups in the United States by 2060

billion per year and tax revenues by $2 billion more per year. Prosperity for minority households leads to increases in the overall wealth and prosperity for the nation.

8.3 Conclusion

The data in this volume have shown that the United States population, although growing somewhat slower than recent decades, is likely to undergo dramatic change in the coming decades. These changes include substantial growth and extensive change in the racial/ethnic composition and age structure of the population. They have also shown that, due to a variety of historical, discriminatory and other factors, there are substantial differences in the income, education, and other socioeconomic characteristics of nonHispanic White, Hispanic, nonHispanic Black and nonHispanic Asian and Other populations. It has further demonstrated that because the growth in the minority populations of the United States is likely to outpace that of the nonHispanic White population there will be increasing disparity and inequality in the population of the United States, unless the factors responsible for such disparity such as differences in educational attainment, health status and relative

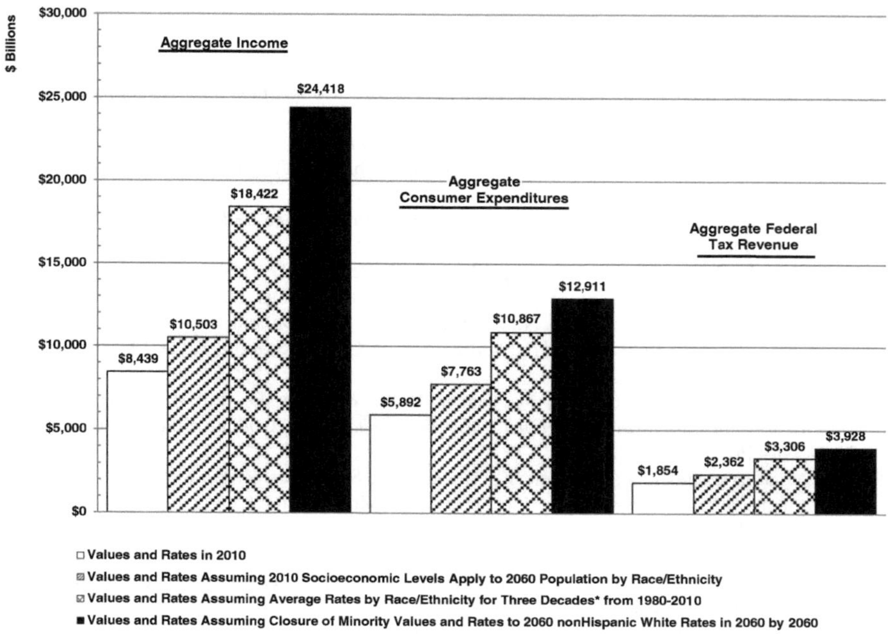

Figure 8.4 Aggregate income, consumer expenditures, and federal tax revenue from households in 2060 (in billions of 2010 constant dollars) under alternative assumptions of socioeconomic closure between minority and nonHispanic White households

economic returns to employment are altered. This volume has delineated the magnitude of such disparity and the data in this chapter have demonstrated that the reduction in this disparity would benefit not only those minority populations whose income and other socioeconomic resources would improve but would also increase the overall wealth of the nation as a whole. It demonstrates that, to a large extent, reducing that disparity through improved education and other factors would improve not only the futures of those who are most disadvantaged but would also improve the overall wealth and health of the entire United States.

Equally important this work shows that improving the economic competitiveness, through increased education, skill acquisition and other factors, is critical for all Americans from all racial/ethnic groups. It is not only good for those with fewer socioeconomic resources but for all Americans because maintaining high socioeconomic levels of resources is the key not only to improving the lives for nonHispanic Blacks and Hispanics and other minority populations, who have often been left behind, but for maintaining the competitiveness of the United States in the world economy. Maintaining that competitiveness and meeting the challenges associated with it is essential to all and is the key to retaining the socioeconomic basis for the "American Dream".

References

Frey, W. H. (2015). *Diversity explosion: How new racial demographics are remaking America*. Washington, DC: Brookings Institution Press.

Mather, M., & Jarosz, B. (2014). *The demography of inequality in the United States*. Washington, DC: Population Reference Bureau. http://www.prb.org/pdf14/united-states-inequality.pdf. Accessed 20 Jan 2015.

Murdock, S. H. (1995). *An America challenged: Population change and the future of the United States*. Boulder: Westview Press.

Murdock, S. H., Hoque, N., Michael, M., White, S., & Pecotte, B. (1997). *The Texas challenge: Population change and the future of Texas*. College Station: Texas A&M University Press.

Murdock, S. H., White, S., Hoque, M. N., Pecotte, B., You, X., & Balkan, J. (2003). *The new Texas challenge: Population change and the future of Texas*. College Station: Texas A&M University Press.

Murdock, S. H., Cline, M. E., Zey, M., Jeanty, P. W., & Perez, D. (2014). *Changing Texas: Implications of addressing or ignoring the Texas challenge*. College Station: Texas A&M University Press.

Ruggles, S. J., Alexander, T., Genadek, K., Goeken, R., Schroeder, R. B., & Sobek, M. (2010). *Integrated public use microdata series: Version 5.0*. Minneapolis: University of Minnesota.

U.S. Bureau of Labor Statistics. (2011). *National consumer price index*. Washington, DC: U.S. Bureau of Labor Statistics.

U.S. Census Bureau. (1982). *1980 census of population and housing, summary file 3*. Washington, DC: U.S. Census Bureau.

U.S. Census Bureau. (1983). *1980 census of population and housing, summary file 4*. Washington, DC: U.S. Census Bureau.

U.S. Census Bureau. (1992). *1990 census of population and housing, summary file 3*. Washington, DC: U.S. Census Bureau.

U.S. Census Bureau. (1993). *1990 census of population and housing, summary file 4*. Washington, DC: U.S. Census Bureau.

U.S. Census Bureau. (2002). *2000 census of population and housing, summary file 3*. Washington, DC: U.S. Census Bureau.

U.S. Census Bureau. (2003). *2000 census of population and housing, summary file 4*. Washington, DC: U.S. Census Bureau.

U.S. Census Bureau. (2011a). *2006–2010 American community survey selected population tables*. Washington, DC: U.S. Census Bureau.

U.S. Census Bureau. (2011b). *2010 census summary file 1*. Washington, DC: U.S. Census Bureau.

U.S. Census Bureau. (2011c). *2010 census summary file 2*. Washington, DC: U.S. Census Bureau.

U.S. Census Bureau. (2012). *2012 national population projections*. Washington, DC: U.S. Census Bureau.

MIX
Papier aus verantwortungsvollen Quellen
Paper from responsible sources
FSC® C105338

If you have any concerns about our products,
you can contact us on
ProductSafety@springernature.com

In case Publisher is established outside the EU,
the EU authorized representative is:
Springer Nature Customer Service Center GmbH
Europaplatz 3, 69115 Heidelberg, Germany

Printed by Libri Plureos GmbH
in Hamburg, Germany